Praise for

"Utterly compelling, heartbreaking, truthful, and yet redemptive, a memoir of the Holocaust, a testimony of irrepressible spirit and an unforgettable family chronicle, written in lucid prose by a truly remarkable woman about her life from Hungary to Auschwitz, Israel to London. I couldn't stop reading it."
—Simon Sebag Montefiore

"Though Lily saw and experienced inhumanity at its lowest ebb, her reaction was not one of bitterness or cynicism, but of hope and compassion. Lily has dedicated her life to sharing her astonishing story so that the world would never again descend into such depths. Yet *Lily's Promise* is only half of the battle. It falls to us to heed her words and to internalize and learn from them. This book calls every reader to action. Lily's message of hope over despair is more necessary today than it has ever been."
—Chief Rabbi Ephraim Mirvis

"We must never forget the horrors of the Holocaust; Lily is an incredible lady and an inspiration to us all."
—Lord Alan Sugar

"*Lily's Promise* is a remarkable account of Lily Ebert's experiences during the Holocaust. The accuracy of dates and facts in her book about her time in the Nazi Concentration and Extermination Camp of Auschwitz-Birkenau contributes to the chorus of voices thanks to which we can get closer to the human experience in a world of utter dehumanization."
—Paweł Sawicki, Auschwitz Memorial Museum

Lily's Promise

Lily's Promise

Holding On to Hope Through
Auschwitz and Beyond—
A Story for All Generations

LILY EBERT *and* DOV FORMAN

HarperOne
An Imprint of HarperCollinsPublishers

HarperCollins books may be purchased for educational, business, or sales promotional use. For information, please email the Special Markets Department at SPsales@harpercollins.com.

Originally published as *Lily's Promise* in the United Kingdom in 2021 by Pan Macmillan.

FIRST HARPERONE EDITION PUBLISHED 2022

Design adapted by Terry McGrath from the original edition designed by Jouve (UK), Milton Keynes

All photos are courtesy of the authors, with the exception of the following:
p. 4 *top* courtesy of the Shulman family
p. 5 *bottom* image taken from film accessed at United States Holocaust Memorial Museum, courtesy of National Archives & Records Administration
p. 6 *top* image taken from film courtesy of the Swiss Federal Archives

Library of Congress Cataloging-in-Publication Data has been applied for.

ISBN 978-0-06-323029-3 (paperback)
ISBN 978-0-06-323027-9 (hardcover)

22 23 24 25 26 LSC 10 9 8 7 6 5 4 3 2 1

In loving memory of my adored mother, Nina, and my little brother and sister, Bela and Berta, all of whom were murdered in the gas chambers of Auschwitz-Birkenau. This book is also dedicated to the many members of my extended family who were killed, and to all those who have no one to remember them.

For the Jewish people, the Holocaust was a personal tragedy. By the end of the Second World War, one-third of European Jewry had perished at the hands of the Nazis. Six million innocent Jewish men, women and children murdered for no reason other than the religion they were born into. A great pillar of smoke covered all of Europe; the shadow of which remains with us still today.

Yet the Holocaust was also a universal human tragedy. It was the greatest crime of man against man, during which humanity showed itself capable of incomparable inhumanity on an incomprehensible scale. Names were replaced by numbers, tattooed on forearms, as a permanent reminder of the depths to which humankind can sink and the evil it can impart on a fellow human being.

The late Chief Rabbi, Lord Sacks, spoke about the profound difference between history and memory. "History," he taught, "is *his* story – an event that happened sometime else to someone else. Memory is *my* story – something that happened to me and is part of who I am. History is information. Memory, by contrast, is about identity… History is about the past as past. Memory is about the past as present."

It is the Holocaust survivors who help us transform history into memory by their ability to humanise the inhumane. It is them and their words that make the past present.

Throughout my life, I consider it a singular privilege to have met so many survivors. As Patron of the Holocaust Memorial Day Trust, I have witnessed, and been greatly moved by, their harrowing testimony. I have drawn personal inspiration from the many Righteous among the Nations, who, like my dear grandmother, Princess Alice of Greece, put their own lives at immense risk to save Jewish men, women and children from certain death. I have seen the impact survivors' words and their sheer presence have had on others, in schools, communities and organisations across our country and around the world.

One such occasion was in 2015 when my wife and I were particularly honoured to light six remembrance candles as part of the National Holocaust Memorial Day Ceremony in London. For the lighting of each candle, we were joined by a survivor who, like many others, had rebuilt their lives in the United Kingdom after the Second World War and contributed enormously to the fabric of our nation. One of the survivors was Lily Ebert B.E.M.

The joint lighting of the candles was a recognition that the responsibility of memory is slowly but surely passing from the survivors to our generation, and to future generations not yet born. It symbolised the need for us to be fearless in confronting falsehoods and resolute in resisting words and acts of violence. It called on us to recommit ourselves to the beliefs of tolerance and respect and the central idea, set out in the Hebrew Bible, of *b'tzelem elokim*, that we are all, irrespective of race, colour, class or creed, created "in the image of God."

These lessons, important then, remain vital now – especially when the events of the Holocaust are sometimes distorted, diminished, or denied, the testimony of victims and witnesses is invaluable and essential. This is what Lily, together with the other Holocaust survivors, understands only too well.

In co-authoring this book with her great grandson, Dov Forman, Lily has lit her own candle, and recognised the urgent necessity of passing both its light and the responsibility of remembrance between the generations. This is a task Dov has shown himself more than capable of carrying forward. Through his engaging and effective use of social media, Dov has demonstrated a determination to share his great grandmother's story with a global audience. In being an enthusiastic partner in this work, Lily is once again showing her passion to use every avenue available to ensure that some good might come from the horrendous losses she suffered and the unspeakable evil she overcame.

Lily's story is as profoundly moving as she is inspirational. It is for these reasons, among others, that I was humbled to be asked to contribute a foreword. She and her story are a beacon of light in the darkness; a symbol of hope amongst the despair.

In the depths of Auschwitz, Lily made herself a promise that if she survived, she would dedicate the rest of her life to ensuring the world knew what happened during the Holocaust. This book, which so powerfully captures her testimony, represents the fulfilment of that promise and the culmination of a lifetime of service to the human conscience. We would all do well to make Lily's history our memory.

DOV

July 3, 2020
North London

"Let's do something, Dov!"

My great-grandmother is restless. Ninety-six years old, Lily's used to spending her days in schools, talking to children about her experiences in Auschwitz, or campaigning at public events. She hates being stuck in her flat alone.

Pandemic lockdown rules have eased at last—at least for the time being. After too many shouted conversations through a window while we stood in the garden, my family can finally spend Sabbath with Lily again, as we always used to.

"Let's do something, Dov!" says Lily.

It's Friday night, and we're gathered in our bubble round the table. We're all so happy to be with each other again, lighting the Shabbat candles together, blessing the bread. Such a special evening. Lily's full of energy.

But I can see how much she misses her old life. She's always thrived on meeting new people. As a living witness, Lily cherishes her role in Holocaust education. It's not easy, but she's determined to make a difference. She knows how much it means to people to hear her story from her own lips, how meeting her face to face can change the way someone sees the past and also the future.

"Don't worry, Safta!" We all call her Safta because that's

what Mum's always called her. It's Hebrew for Grandma. "I'll think of something."

What can I do?

Schools and museums and universities have reopened, but nobody knows when public events might be possible again. It could be years. How many Holocaust survivors will still be alive by then? The Covid crisis has brought home a very painful truth: tough as she is, immortal as she seems, however much I love her, my great-grandma can't live forever.

Lily is amazingly adventurous. She's always curious about new things. A few years ago she sat on a sofa in the middle of Liverpool Street station and invited commuters to sit down and talk to her about the Holocaust. Last year we started a Twitter feed together. I tweeted a few times about Lily's talks for Holocaust Memorial Day in January.

Now I'm thinking more seriously about using social media to introduce Safta and her story to new audiences. She's taught me so much. Everyone who meets her adores her. And if ever there was a time to spread her message of tolerance, it feels like now.

"Maybe we can do another tweet?" I suggest.

"Or another school visit?" she replies eagerly.

Two weeks ago I organized her first Zoom appearance. She shared her testimony with my history teacher and answered his questions carefully. She'd never heard of Zoom before, but took to it like a pro. I was so proud. I contacted a journalist on *Jewish News*. How about a piece on how survivors are now teaching the lessons of the Holocaust online?

"Not as good as in person—I like to see my audience!" she told him. "But my generation's always been used to adapting to new situations. If you have to do it, you do it. It's always good to make the best of what you have in life."

I posted a tweet with the link to her interview. It got sixty-five likes. Not bad, we all thought.

But now what? For the rest of Shabbat I ask her about her story. My mum, Nina, joins in with the questions. Like me, she's always been very interested in our family history. We've both grown up knowing Safta is a survivor, knowing why she always keeps a piece of bread beside her, why wasted food distresses her. We never played with toy guns or fought in her presence. We've heard her speak in public loads of times, yet there are lots of things about her I still don't know.

What exactly happened to Lily and her sisters after Auschwitz? How did she feel when the war ended? Why didn't she go home to Hungary?

"What was it like, Safta?" I ask. "How did you find the strength to keep going?"

"You have to carry on. You always have to carry on."

In the past, Lily made it a rule never to talk about the Holocaust on Shabbat. You're not supposed to think about sad things on this day. I remember being horrified and embarrassed when one of my friends asked to see her tattoo one Saturday after shul. He was in year six, the year above me, and had just started learning about the Holocaust at primary school. He wanted to know more and was full of questions. So for the first time in my life, I saw Lily's tattoo properly myself, as she showed us both. It was a shocking moment, which I'll never forget. And we didn't discuss it again for years.

But recently she seems to have really changed her mind about the kind of conversations we can have on Shabbat. I think we've all suddenly got a new sense of urgency. New stories we've never heard before begin to flow out of Safta. And the more she tells us, the more I want to know.

"What was it like? How did you feel?"

"The truth is, if you weren't there, you can never understand."

But I want to try. To be honest, I've not dared ask *too* many questions before. Every time she talks about the past, she has to relive it. I don't want to cause her pain. But at the same time, I really want to know exactly what happened to her. I want to get everything completely straight in my head. I'm sixteen. Lily's little sister Piri had survived a Nazi concentration camp and slave labor before she turned sixteen.

I've been thinking a lot about Auschwitz already. I'm supposed to be going there on a school trip at the end of the year. What's the chance of that happening now? Lily was planning to travel with us.

Everything's up in the air. Everything's so unpredictable. Life feels a lot more fragile these days.

I don't want these stories to disappear. I want to find a way to hold on to all that Lily's given us, forever.

The next evening, at the end of Shabbat, Mum and I walk Lily back to her flat.

"Why don't you come in?" she says. "I've got some things I want to show you, Dov."

"Hope you can find them, Safta," jokes Mum.

Safta's flat is *so* full of stuff. I don't think she's ever thrown anything away. But only she knows what everything is, and where it lives.

I wait while she rummages in her cabinet. When she turns round, she's beaming.

"Look at this!"

She proudly holds up a football shirt. It's royal blue with yellow stripes. I don't actually recognize the team.

"Wow!" I try to sound interested.

"It's Maccabi, you know. From Tel Aviv. They gave it to me when I went to speak. What year was that? Never mind. Look—it's signed!"

"Amazing!" And then I spot the bright orange cover of a fat little book in the cabinet behind her.

"Hey, Safta, what's that? That album, over there. Can I see it?"

We sit down side by side, and begin to leaf through it. The pages are plastic, like transparent wallets, and each one is stuffed with tiny black-and-white photographs. Some of them are more brown-and-white. Lots have those funny white crinkly borders.

I don't think I've ever seen pictures of Lily's family before, at least not ones from before the war. The first few seem very formal. Except one, slightly blurry: a line of three little children in a garden, solemn and serious and holding hands.

"That's me. That's my brother Imi. That's René. I was the oldest."

"I know, Safta! You're still the oldest!"

Another, a later photo taken not long before they were deported, shows Lily with her brother and all three of her sisters. The girls are dressed alike, except Lily, and they have big bows in their hair. Wait! Shouldn't there be another brother?

Lily looks sad. There's a pause before she replies, and one hand briefly touches the gold pendant she always wears.

"Bela was so serious about his Torah studies. He didn't want to miss *cheder* that day."

Here are her parents, looking both strange and familiar. Her mother's called Nina, like my mother. She's got a shy, slightly crooked smile. And here's her father in a coat and hat. Ahron. Oh, like my great-uncle Roni! There's a white-bearded rabbi in a long coat. And a faded sepia photo of a man with mutton-chop sideburns. Very Victorian.

"My grandfather," Lily told me. "My Engelman grandfather. My mother's father was a rabbi."

"Wow!" I say again. I mean it this time.

Toward the end of the album, time has passed. The three oldest sisters look quite grown-up. "Where are you here?" I ask. "Who are all these other girls?"

"Oh, those are my friends in Switzerland. Hungarian survivors, like us. And that's me with my sisters. That's René. That's Piri."

They all look so similar, especially Lily and Piri.

As I lift the album nearer the light so I can see the pictures more clearly, something flutters out.

"What's this?" I say, picking it up. "A banknote? Is this German?"

"Oh, yes. An American soldier gave it to me after we were liberated. Look, that's his writing."

"You've never shown me this, Safta!" says Mum.

"I didn't think anyone else would be interested," Lily says. "I thought it was only special to me."

I have to turn the note around to read it. The old-fashioned writing goes round the edge, the only space left for the soldier's message: "A start to a new life. Good luck and happiness."

Ten words of hope.

There are some letters along the top that look like Hebrew, but I can't make them out. And at the bottom, the soldier's written "assistant to Chaplain Schacter."

"But who was he?" I asked. "What was his name?"

"Oh, I can't remember now! This was over seventy-five years ago. He was a Jewish soldier. I know that. Jewish American. So kind. We weren't used to kindness."

And suddenly she's silent. She's back in the past, remembering some things, forgetting others.

"Why on earth did he write on a banknote?" I ask.

"He couldn't find any paper, and he wanted to write me a little note. When we were leaving Germany, I suppose. Such a nice man."

"I'll find him for you," I promise. "I'll post it on Twitter. I bet someone out there will be able to track him down."

Lily laughs. The kind of laugh that means, *Don't be silly!*

Mum starts laughing too, and rolling her eyes.

"Just wait. Really. Social media can be incredible," I insist. To be honest, I can't be certain myself if this will work. But you never know. So many terrible things happen on social media. I want to prove that good things can happen too.

"Let's take some pictures now. I'll tweet them in the morning."

Lily holds out her hands—tiny, wrinkled—and I lay the note across them. I take pictures of the back and also the front, clearly showing the soldier's message. And then we photograph another picture of Lily and her sisters, in identical checked dresses—quite eye-catching! They're smiling in the company of some American GIs. Maybe one of those is the man?

"Give me twenty-four hours," I say to Lily. She's still laughing. "I bet you anything I can find him."

And then we go back to looking at the family photographs, and Safta tells me and Mum about her happy life in Hungary before the war, in the little market town of Bonyhád where she grew up.

LILY

1920s

The truth is, I was a born leader. Right from the beginning, all my brothers and sisters looked up to me. There was never any question they wouldn't do as I said. Of course, I was the eldest of the six of us, but I also had that kind of character. I liked being in charge, taking responsibility, and the others were always happy that way too—even Imi, my oldest brother, who was close at my heels, and barely a year younger than me. They knew I knew best. And later, that helped us all.

So I was the first child in the family to sit at the table with the grownups at the Pesach Seder—the feast that begins the Passover holiday. And that evening, all over our small, busy market town in south-western Hungary, other families were also celebrating. In December 1923, when I was born, out of Bonyhád's growing population of nearly 7,000, about one in eight was Jewish. When my great-great-grandparents were growing up there a century earlier, before all faiths had equal rights in Hungary, a third of the town were Jews. Everyone in our long-established community looked forward eagerly to every Yom Tov. We had enjoyed the spiritual guidance of eminent rabbis and respected Talmudic scholars for generations.

That memorable first Seder must have been April 1928. I was four years old and the only child in the household old enough to stay up late. Everything was laid out beautifully—salt water, bitter herbs, roasted egg, horseradish, wine, matzo and other symbolic foods—and the candles were lit. How proud I was to say the first sentence, the *Ma Nishtana*, asking my father the question clearly and loudly, just as I'd practiced: "Why is this night different from all other nights?"

I loved nothing better than being with the grownups. I remember that feeling again when I was about ten, and I had a black coffee for the first time at my auntie's house. Of course, it tasted horribly bitter, but I pretended I liked it. Actually, I just liked the fact that I was drinking it.

Now I'm with the big people, I told myself. And because I acted as if I were grown-up, even when I was really very little, my brothers and sisters respected my judgment just the same.

One Shabbat, when our parents were at shul, we were playing as usual in our enormous garden. It really was huge, with space for everything. In the front were flowers, bright and colorful: chrysanthemums like golden orbs and tall yellow sunflowers. We loved cutting off their flopping heads so we could pick out the stripy seeds, roast them in the range and crack open the kernels one by one, or feed them to our chickens. As you came round the side of the house there was a big lawn where we played endless ball games, catching and throwing and tossing the ball up onto the roof, never quite knowing where it would bounce off next. Then there was the sprawling walnut tree, branches low and easily reached, its bright green fruit always tempting us before the husks split open. We could never resist trying to break them apart to get to the nuts too soon. And always our fingers were left black and stained from our efforts.

Round the back, past the outhouses where wood and coal were stored, you came to the orchard and the vegetable garden. We had apple trees, plums, cherries . . . Every kind of fruit bush you could imagine. Corn-on-the-cob, tomatoes, peppers.

A gardener did a lot of the hard work, but we also took it in turns to help with the watering and the picking. There was always something in the summer to be put away for winter, and something in the winter to be saved for the summer. Cucumbers to pickle. Fruit to bottle or boil up into jam. But, as I said, it was a Saturday, and we were an Orthodox family, and many of our neighbors were also Jewish.

The trouble was that it was also a beautiful summer's day. We were a little bored and hungry, and nobody was around. And the fruit looked just so delicious.

"No picking on Shabbat!" I reminded my siblings.

We all knew the rules. There are thirty-nine different kinds of work which are forbidden on the Sabbath, and reaping is one of them.

I was a good girl really, perhaps ten or eleven years old then. I had responsibilities, and a reputation to keep up. My next sister, René, laughing and lively, was two and a half years younger. After her came Piri, born in 1929, a neat and fastidious child, and very artistic, but much more shy than René. Although René was very outgoing, I was definitely by far the biggest extrovert of us all. Bela, our other brother, was another three years behind Piri—the first birth I remember in the house—and Berta still a babe-in-arms, I think. We were all dressed the same, in our best clothes. We always had nice, neat clothes.

"No picking," I repeated, more slowly, because I'd had an idea. I was sizing up the apple tree, looking at the low branches, looking at Imi, who was growing ever taller, as tall as me already. "But there's nothing to say we can't eat straight from the tree."

And that's exactly what we did. Heads back, hands clasped firmly behind our backs, obedient to the last, we mouthed at the shiny fruit, catching its smooth skin with our teeth. Not picking, though! Not breaking the law. The little ones nibbled at the currant bushes like young goats. They crouched down happily, and we used our lips to slip tart berries straight into hungry mouths.

I was the mastermind. Imi was my henchman. We made a perfect team. He was so good with his hands—like Piri—and had the neatest of fingers. I thought he could do anything. What's more, he would do anything for me. When I had a wobbly tooth and I wanted it gone, Imi pulled it out, with a thread fastened to a door handle and a sharp slam. One day, when he was even younger, I took it into my head that I wanted to play with the pom-poms stitched all around the heavy embroidered tablecloth, a special covering that only came out for guests. I asked him to cut them off for me. Snip! Snip! Snip! Eager to please me, he scissored off every one.

We were both fascinated by small creatures. The two of us would collect crickets and worms and snails and frogs from the garden and watch them for hours on end, trying to work out exactly how they moved, or ate, or made their strange noises.

I loved being with Imi because he always helped me do what I wanted to do; he listened carefully to my ideas and together we put them into practice.

Our parents once bought Berta a beautiful new china doll, which she'd seen in town and fallen in love with. Our youngest sister was bright and bubbly and she could wrap our father round her little finger. We all adored her. The doll was very special and unusual, because when you laid her back, her eyes magically closed. We'd never seen anything like it before!

"How on earth can that be?" I wondered. "Imi, you'll have to help me find out."

"What do you want me to do?"

"Let's smash the head and then we'll be able to see how the eyes work!"

He was a willing accomplice. I expect he was just as curious. But it was no good. Somehow the mechanism also got broken, so we were left with no answers and no doll. Poor Berta! She was very forgiving. Maybe we thought Apu would buy her a replacement? After all, she hadn't had to ask him twice for the big red spotty ball she wanted so much.

Another time I wanted to know how a watch worked, to find out what was happening inside the ticking silver case. Naturally, I asked Imi to take it apart so we could both see. After he'd shown me the cogs and springs of my mother's watch, of course we wanted to check my father's too. I always egged Imi on. How could I be blamed? I hadn't done anything wrong!

In fact, my parents knew exactly who was behind each piece of mischief. Yet somehow I don't remember either of us getting into trouble or being punished.

"*Oh, mein Kind!*" Apu would say to me. He was happier speaking German than Hungarian, and much of his business was in that language. "*Ich hätte nicht gedacht, dass du das tun würdest!*" Oh, my child! I didn't think you'd do that!

And in future, my father and mother—Apu and Anyuka— took better care not to leave their watches unguarded.

They weren't at all happy with me the time they discovered I'd opened the door to a cage full of chickens I'd come across in our garden, and released them into freedom. I felt so sorry for the birds, all cooped up like that, one on top of the other, and they looked so miserable. Yet my parents only actually drew the line twice, as far as I can remember. Quite reasonable of them, really. Imi and I were thwarted in our plan to sell little René. Not that she minded. Even when she was tiny, René would do anything she could to make someone else happy.

And Imi was quite desperate to have his own pet lamb. He simply wouldn't stop talking about the idea, nagging and nagging at our parents. He even went to the trouble of building a pen on the grass for it to live in. Yet no lamb ever arrived.

Apu and Anyuka knew we were adventurous, and perhaps mischievous, but never malicious or cruel. We were generally polite and well behaved at school, and that was what mattered to them. They taught us to be respectful, of course: no child would ever have sat in our father's chair at the head of the dining table, or answered back to him. Conversation between different generations wasn't nearly as free as it is today. We didn't expect to be taken into their confidence, and we never asked personal questions. So to this day I have no idea how my parents met.

Born into a large rabbinical family in 1897, my mother grew up in a summer resort called Szenc, or Senec, near Bratislava, which had been in the old Kingdom of Hungary and then became part of Czechoslovakia, a republic created after the First World War and its treaties. Twelve years older than his wife, my father was born in Bonyhád, like his father, and grandfather, and great-grandfather, and all his many cousins and nephews and nieces. Just like us, both Nina Breznitz and Ahron Engelman grew up in big, close-knit, middle-class Jewish families, Hungarian through and through, comfortably off and secure in every way. Why should that change?

Looking back, I remember only harmony in our home. It was noisy, but peaceful. If Apu and Anyuka ever had cross words with each other, we children certainly didn't hear them. If we little ones had an argument, it was quickly forgotten. It helped that René was naturally such a very kind person, who avoided disagreements at all costs. Whenever Anyuka called for someone to lay the table or tidy up, she'd be the first to run and help. In fact, if anyone ever needed anything, she was always there, ready to do whatever she could.

Every one of us was allowed to be ourselves. Like my father, Piri was quite obsessive about hygiene. She couldn't bear to eat anything that somebody else's hand had touched, for example. But that was fine. Our mother and father were very understanding. So on Friday nights, when Apu recited *kiddush*, the blessing before the Sabbath meal that we say over wine, and then the tall silver goblet was passed around the table for each person in the family to have a sip in order of age, Piri would have her own cup.

Really, I had the best parents any child could dream of: they were kind, calm, loving and very lenient indeed. Despite our escapades, I think they believed we were the cleverest and most beautiful children in the whole wide world. We grew up in a kind of cocoon, so safe and protected from the evils of the world we didn't even know evil existed.

Every morning, Apu would come into the kitchen and have a very hot coffee, and lick the cream from the top of the milk, which we collected each day from the farmer on the edge of town. The baker came past all the houses carrying little butter rolls, called *zemmel*, on his back. That's what we ate for breakfast before we ran out of the house to school.

We weren't the wealthiest family, and there was nothing especially grand about our house, but it was on one of the nicest streets in the town—Perczel Mór, number 32. Our neighborhood was very friendly, and we children wanted for nothing. Really, we had no worries in life at all. And you simply can't imagine what freedom we enjoyed. The wide, tree-lined streets held no dangers: there were few strangers and only one car in the whole town, a taxi service that took people to the station at Szakály-Hőgyész, thirty kilometres away. You could also catch a rather rickety bus. Bonyhád's own small railway station was mostly used by goods trains. Otherwise it was all horses and donkeys, carriages or carts, and sleighs in the long, snowy winters.

Sometimes we played in the attic. The house had only one storey, and in the big roof space we hung up the washing to dry in winter, and kept the Passover china and cutlery. There were also lots of mysterious old papers and letters belonging to my father and grandfather, with interesting stamps on the envelopes, which we liked to take off to stick in our collections. The plaything we loved best indoors was a beautiful, dapple-grey rocking horse, which had real horsehair for its mane and tail, a leather saddle and reins, and proper metal stirrups.

But we were usually outside, playing ball games, skipping or hopscotch, or sliding around on the simple skating rink we made each year by flooding the garden lawn as soon as the weather turned icy in November. Winters were extremely cold, but we enjoyed playing outside in the snow and then coming indoors to toast our frozen fingers by the kitchen range. Soft fur hats and muffs kept us warm when we were sledding.

So many of our friends were our relatives, and our relatives our friends. All year round we ran freely back and forth between each other's houses whenever we liked, sure of there being someone to play with wherever we went, or to make up the numbers for a game. Although she was the quietest, Piri was especially popular. Her friends were constantly dropping by. They loved her because she was so friendly and easy-going and interesting to talk to. Berta, too, had an endless stream of visitors.

One of my own favorite companions was my first cousin Hilda, who was nearly exactly my age and in my class at school too. She was taller and quieter than me, and such a clever girl. Very pretty, she had straight brown hair and brown eyes, a bit like mine. She was the youngest in her family, with three older sisters and a brother. We played together a lot, but, as we got older, most of all we liked to talk.

Bonyhád was a friendly, bustling kind of place, with lots of little shops, a few bigger stores, a couple of small factories, an outdoor swimming pool, two active synagogues and three churches. It was full of Engelmans. Most of the family were in business one way or another, and nobody lived or worked more than ten or twenty minutes' walk away. Two of my uncles, Leo and Sandor, had a big porcelain and china shop at number 4 Horthy Street. Apu's own shop wasn't far from either the house or his brothers' establishment, and we often ran back and forth with messages. My father sold textiles. All the different rolls of material lay stacked on shelves up to the ceiling: warm wools, colorful cottons, fancy silks and satins, practical workwear fabrics, and most of them ordered by post from all over the world, so my father didn't need to travel much himself, and was rarely absent from the family home. But there was so much paperwork! He seemed to be forever writing letters. The shop had several staff, smartly dressed men with wooden metre sticks who measured out the material for the customers with a swish, swish, swish on big tables and cut it with shining scissor blades.

And, of course, we were very well dressed ourselves. My mother had new clothes made for all the family three or four times a year. As the eldest, as well as more privileges and toys, I had more new clothes than the others. But, certainly for shul or for family celebrations, my mother liked us all to dress the same. So whenever I had a new outfit, so did all my sisters. I remember sailor suits were all the rage in Hungary in the early 1930s. In England too, I later learned. So one year all six of us wore identical neat sailor suits, with big square white collars and navy ribbons tied at the front. We looked a fine crew, and we felt like one too.

On the most special days of all—birthdays and Holy Days—I was allowed to wear my golden angel necklace. The pendant was quite simple: a golden disk with a tiny thoughtful cherub hanging from a chain, chin cupped in hand, eyes raised wistfully. A sweet and innocent charm, given to an innocent little girl when she was too young even to remember exactly when or why. I discovered quite recently that my cherub was copied from an Italian painting—one of the much-loved pair of baby angels in Raphael's *Sistine Madonna*. My mother kept my pendant in a little box in her wardrobe. On the days she wanted me to look my best, she would fetch the necklace and fasten it for me. This was a great treat that made me feel loved and special.

I think I had the best parents in all the world.

1930s

The one thing my parents really cared about was education. They wanted us to learn, and did everything to make it easy for us to do so. Luckily, we were all pretty good at school, and picked things up quickly. So I was sent a year early to the Jewish primary school we all attended, boys and girls together, three year groups in one class. At first, we each had our own little blackboard. Later, we got paper to write and draw on.

I remember bursting into tears one day, because some children were given books and I only got sheets of paper.

"But I can read and write too!" I told the teacher when she asked me why I was crying. "Why can't I have a book?"

"Don't worry! Those children are older. Nobody gets a book in their first year," she explained, and I was comforted.

It was more of a struggle at school for Imi at first just because he was left-handed—like Piri—and they forced him to write with his right hand. But he caught up quickly and was bright and hardworking, so in the end he did all his matriculation exams in one year instead of two, at the age of just fifteen or sixteen. Every day after school he would go to the *beit midrash*, the "house of study" beside our fine new synagogue, and learn the Torah. On darker winter evenings, determined to keep learning, Imi would go outside and work by the light of the electric streetlamps: he found the lighting in the house too dim.

I'm shocked now, thinking about some of the things our schoolteachers used to do. Instead of encouraging children who struggled with their learning, they used to humiliate them. If someone couldn't solve a maths problem, the teacher would call in a child from one of the younger classes and get them to answer the question. As I was so good with numbers, I was often brought into the older classes. Still, it was a terrible way to teach a child!

I used to get into trouble at school for one thing only: shouting out the answers. I couldn't help myself. I just wanted to be a good student.

"Lily, you be quiet!" the teacher used to say. (My real name was Livia Engelman, but everyone always called me Lily.)

We had to learn lots of poems by heart, in Hungarian and also in German—we were at ease in both—and I can remember them still. The older you got, the more poems you had to learn. It wasn't very fair, because some children have good memories and others not so good. I was lucky, and found it easy. At home, I'd test the little ones on their verses, and help them learn the lines by heart. As for Imi, he liked poetry so much he used to write his own.

There were plenty of other German speakers in Bonyhád— like the dairy farmer, whose family were Danube Swabians. Like the Jews, Swabians had been encouraged to help build up commerce in the small cities of the new Austro-Hungarian Empire in the nineteenth century. Both communities were valued for hard work and enterprise. The important thing was that we were all Hungarian, whether Catholic, Lutheran, or Jewish. As well as Orthodox Jews like us, there was a separate congregation of Neolog Jews, who were more modern and liberal in their ways, and about half our number. Every single one of us felt Hungarian through and through, without any question.

The Orthodox Jews were certainly much stricter than the Neologs, but few of the men had beards, as some people might expect. Razors are not permitted in Orthodox Judaism, but my father used a terrible smelly chemical stuff called Rasol to get the clean-shaven look.

So we all got along very well. There were even Christian children at our Jewish primary school because their parents thought they'd get a better education there.

I was happiest learning new things, mathematics most of all. But we girls also had to master sewing. I enjoyed embroidery to begin with. Like poetry, it's something you don't forget. So I still know exactly how to do every stitch I learned as a little girl—cross stitch, satin stitch, chain stitch, back stitch, blanket stitch, feather stitch, knots of all kinds. But once I'd mastered each new one, I had no patience for the time it took to finish the whole piece of work, with its patterns of flowers or birds or hearts. I'd rather be working with numbers than a needle.

Beautiful Piri was so much better with her hands than I was. Amazingly artistic, she loved nothing better than to draw or paint. But she was also a perfectionist. She'd never start anything unless she knew she would be able to finish it in exactly the way she wanted.

Although we came back from school for lunch, which was usually potato soup or pasta, we all returned at different times, so we didn't eat together at midday. But still my mother always prepared it for us herself. Looking back, I can't understand why we let her do so much for us. We could easily have got our own food. But that's what she was like, always doing everything for her children, helped by our housekeeper, Burgi, a Christian woman of about my mother's age, who lived with us almost like one of the family. She could do the work we weren't allowed to do on Shabbat, and then go to church on Sunday if she wanted to. There was such a lot of cooking and housework, since everything had to be made from scratch. You couldn't just go and buy pasta, for example—it would have to be made from flour and eggs. But though I was the eldest, and a girl, my mother didn't want me to waste time in the kitchen. She wanted me to study. I wonder whether she knew that I'd never get that chance again. Jewish girls like me rarely went to university, so I suppose the usual next step after school would have been marriage and running my own household and eventually bringing up a family. But we didn't speak of this, even when I was older, and I was never aware of any matchmaking going on behind the scenes. I think Anyuka could see how much I enjoyed school, and using my mind, and she was happy to keep me innocent and shielded from the realities of life for as long as possible. It also meant I could help the younger ones.

We usually did our homework together in the biggest room in the house, where the dining table was, and where we all sat down to dinner every evening at six, after Apu had come back from shul and Imi—and later Bela—had returned from Talmudic school.

There were plenty of books in the house, in both Hungarian and German. Anyuka loved to read too, to herself when she had time and also to us. Her favorite book was a big heavy collection of Shakespeare stories translated into Hungarian. She sat in a chair reading aloud, with all six children sitting at her feet, listening. Every night we read ourselves to sleep, Imi and Bela in one bedroom, the girls taking it in turns to share the other rooms, swapping beds whenever we pleased. Nobody ever had to tell us when to turn out the light. Or maybe the others just followed my example.

They were used to that. If we were playing mummies and daddies, of course I was always the mummy. If we played schools, yes, I was always the teacher. Firm and fair. My word, the law. As I said, harmony reigned in Bonyhád. We had a contented and comfortable life, and, naively perhaps, we took it all for granted.

There was only one big change in my childhood, and that was when the time came for me to go to middle school. My father's family all lived in Bonyhád, but my mother's many siblings were more scattered. One sister, Gisela, lived a hundred miles away in Pápa, an old town the other side of Lake Balaton with a large Jewish population, which had enjoyed the protection of the famous Esterhazy family for several centuries. Gisela was married to David Gunsberger, a man of some standing, since he was the principal of the boys' school in Pápa. But after ten years of marriage, they were still childless.

Who made the suggestion, I cannot say. And I can only imagine how hard it was for my parents to let me go, especially my mother. But Nina had such a full house, and she felt sorry for her lonely sister, so the autumn before I turned thirteen, I was sent away to Pápa, where I started the next stage of my schooling, and lived with my aunt and uncle as their daughter. A very spoiled only daughter, of course! Though I loved the attention, I missed my parents and siblings very much. I didn't let it show, and there was much to distract me, as I made friends quickly and easily in the new town. Who knows how long I might have stayed, if Gisela hadn't finally fallen pregnant?

Loyaush, my baby cousin, was born in the summer. That

meant the party for his *brit*, the circumcision ceremony which took place when he was eight days old, could be held in the garden, and it was a fine celebration, with lots of delicious food. As a girl, I didn't have to concern myself with the details—all that happened out of sight of the women. The Gunsberger home filled up with people. A great crowd, all so happy for my aunt and uncle.

By the time it was Rosh Hashanah, the Jewish New Year, I was home again, and ready to rejoin my friends at a new school. So that was September 1936. Had my place as the head of the children been taken? Certainly not. Imi had no desire to put himself forward. René, Piri, Bela and Berta were also as pleased to have me back as I was to return. Bela, now at school, was turning into quite a serious, studious little boy, and very religious. Berta was still adored and indulged by the whole family, especially by our father. But she preferred to act older than her age rather than let us baby her and always tried to keep up with her big sisters. And so I went back to my old routines, feeling a little more grown-up, and taking on a few more responsibilities. I was always proud to do that.

The girls' high school, where I joined my old friends and cousins, including Hilda, was actually a Catholic school, in Zárda Street, off Vörösmarty Square. The square was the center of town, always so busy on market days, Tuesdays and Thursdays, when peasants from the countryside all around came to sell their produce: geese, chickens, eggs, nuts, fruit, vegetables and cheeses were all piled onto horse-drawn carts or carried on the women's heads in baskets. Our schoolteachers were nuns, but there were plenty of Jewish girls there with us. Although we had to attend school on Saturdays, they respected our religion and we were never made to write anything on Shabbat.

We were certainly never made to feel different. Nobody ever teased me for being Jewish.

As far as I know, Imi's experience at his high school was just the same. I'm not sure we even knew there was such a thing as antisemitism when we were very young. It would have seemed a ridiculous idea.

1939–1941

We never talked about politics at home. I suppose politics was for men, young men most of all. I'm sure my father must have known all about the new laws controlling Jews in Hungary. But he kept that knowledge from his children, maybe even from his wife.

Neither antisemitic violence nor political antisemitism were anything new in Hungary, but both reached new heights after the First World War, and the end of the Austro-Hungarian Empire. The Treaty of Trianon had left Hungary less than a third of its former size. Jews quickly became scapegoats.

A few years before I was born, and long, long before Hitler's rise, legislation introduced quotas in Hungarian universities, cutting the number of Jewish students from 15–20 percent to only 6 percent. The *numerus clausus* (closed number) law of 1920 officially said no more than 6 percent of *any* minority could study, but it was clearly aimed at the Jews, who were at that time by far the most numerous and successful group in Hungary's middle classes. Jewish students were regularly beaten up. As for Jewish women, they had even less chance of an education beyond school. Perhaps the *numerus clausus* law was why, at an early age, Imi decided to become a dentist's apprentice. Or perhaps it was always his vocation, being so quick and clever with his hands and thoughtful about other people.

The Kingdom of Hungary moved ever closer to Nazi Germany, partly because of Regent Miklós Horthy's outspoken antisemitism, partly because an alliance would help win back disputed Hungarian-speaking territories in Czechoslovakia and Romania. After Hitler's takeover of Austria in 1938, Hungary's right-wing, autocratic government passed a series of laws and decrees directly against Jews that stopped us from being equal citizens in our country. By the time war broke out in Europe, a few months before I turned sixteen, and Imi fifteen, Hungary shared a border with Germany.

To be Jewish became a racial matter, not a religious one. If you had more than one Jewish grandparent, then you were a Jew, even if you'd never set foot in a synagogue. Jews were barred from all kinds of professions, including law and medicine, journalism and engineering. Even acting in films or at the theater was no longer possible. They couldn't work in the civil service at all. Most Jews lost the right to vote. The government claimed Hungary was in "the clutches of Jewish bankers and industrialists' and had to be freed. By 1942 further laws would confiscate land and property, and forced Jewish emigration became official policy. Yet Jews continued to proclaim their unswerving loyalty to their fatherland.

These were the Hungarian version of Germany's well-known Nuremberg Laws, yet, as a young girl, I knew nothing about them at all. The two Hungarian fascist parties—the National Socialists and the Arrow Cross—had very little support in our part of the country, Tolna county, west of the River Danube. I didn't know that a quarter of a million Hungarian Jews had lost their income. If the new laws affected my father's business, or that of his brothers, he certainly would not have wanted us children to know. Children were children. Men were men. Not many women could vote.

So, for us, life continued as normal. I remember hearing about the outbreak of war on the radio when I was in the kitchen with Anyuka a few weeks later, not long before Rosh Hashanah. I felt uneasy about the news that Germany had invaded Poland, knowing that something terrible was happening somewhere.

But all that darkness seemed so far away, so removed from our lives. Anyuka was calm and collected as usual, and simply continued kneading the dough. The kitchen was just the same as always—warm and cosy from the gigantic range that was always being heated up for the next meal. Baking was the one kind of cooking we children were allowed to help with, and it was always a treat to lick out the bowl used for the cakes we made every Friday morning: one yeasty milk loaf for breakfast—spiralled with chocolate or poppy seeds or walnuts—and a sponge cake to eat after lunch. These would last until Sunday, or Monday if we were lucky. The whole kitchen—the whole house—filled with their sweet, sweet smell as they baked. The dough for the *challah* also had to be prepared, but this we took to the baker, who plaited each family's loaf and baked it for them, ready for collection later.

For Rosh Hashanah there were all sorts of other foods to get ready too. As usual, instead of plaited *challah* we were making round loaves that week, to symbolize the years going round and round, repeating forever. We'd have carp's head that night, and Apu would say a special blessing, and remind us to be heads and not tails. Leaders, not followers. And there'd be honey cake and sweet fruits for a sweet new year.

"*Boldog új-évet!*" we'd all say to each other. Happy New Year!

And it *was* a sweet new year in 1939, as far as we children were concerned. Nothing had changed. I felt in no danger at all. If my mother wasn't worried, why should I be?

I knew we'd set the table that evening as usual, to look as beautiful as possible for Yom Tov, and that everyone would enjoy the lovely holiday atmosphere in town. Tomorrow, before it was light, Mr. Bácsi, the shamash, or sexton, would be knocking on our door with his wooden hammer, waking us up to go to shul. And I would dress myself and my sisters in our new dresses, and Anyuka would take my necklace from its box.

Within the year, we began to notice some unsettling changes. A new girl suddenly appeared at school. I couldn't put my finger on why this made me uncomfortable. After all, I liked meeting new people, and she was perfectly friendly and settled in quickly. But I must somehow have sensed something secretive and strange about her arrival. She had come without her parents from Czechoslovakia, sent to stay with a family in our town to keep her safe.

My father began to look very sad and serious when he read the newspaper.

"Why are you so sad, Apu?" I asked him.

"The war," he said. "Another world war. And it's not very good for us Jews."

But he never said much more than that. He never wanted to frighten us. And I think he refused to believe anything would happen to our family.

By the autumn of 1940, as well as occupying Poland, Austria and most of Czechoslovakia, Nazi Germany had invaded

Denmark, Norway, the Netherlands, Belgium, Luxembourg
and France. Hungary had annexed Carpathian Ruthenia, a
Nazi puppet republic east of the new Slovak state. It also took
control of Northern Transylvania, which had been part of
Romania. The rest of that country was taken over by a totali-
tarian fascist regime, and in November, soon after Hungary
had entered the Tripartite Pact with Germany, Italy and Japan,
Romania also joined the Axis powers. In April 1941 Hungary
joined a German-led attack on Yugoslavia. Greece also fell.
Two months later Hitler attacked the Soviet Union, quickly
occupying the Ukraine, Moldova, Latvia, Lithuania and Esto-
nia. The systematic massacre of Jewish civilians immediately
followed. Thousands of Jews expelled from Hungary's annexed
Subcarpathian territory were handed over to Nazi German
Einsatzgruppen units—paramilitary death squads. No wonder
Apu didn't want us to know.

In August 1941 it became illegal in Hungary for a Jew to
marry or even have sexual relations with a non-Jew. I had no
idea of this. All the girls of my age expected to marry and have
families. We didn't know who our future husbands might be,
only that they would be Jewish. But there were fewer and fewer
young men to be seen in Bonyhád now. All those of military age
had left the town. Every Jewish man between the age of eighteen and forty-eight was forced to join the *Munkaszolgálat*—
the Labor Service. They became slave laborers for the army,
bearing shovels instead of guns, because the anti-Jewish laws
barred them from regular military service. Sadistically treated
by guards and soldiers in Hungarian and German uniforms,
they worked in mines, built trenches, roads and railways, and
cleared minefields with their bare hands. Some had to dig their
own graves.

In 1941 most of the *Munkaszolgálat* were sent to Ukraine

and Yugoslavia. None of us in Bonyhád had any idea that nine out of ten of these men would not survive.

All I knew was how much I dreaded the day Imi would be old enough for conscription. Surely the war couldn't last that long?

1942

Not long after my eighteenth birthday, in February 1942—the very depths of winter—my father fell ill.

It was quite sudden. I don't remember the exact moment we children realized how bad things were. Apu was never a man to make a fuss. In fact, I could hardly think of a time he had taken to his bed before. Dr. Litzman, who had delivered every one of us in the same room, came and went, but the smile under his little moustache was fleeting. We children moved quietly around the changed house, and, as usual, asked no questions. My mother remained composed, but couldn't completely hide her concern from me.

One evening I went to say goodnight, tiptoeing into my parents' lamplit room. The rooms were always very dark in winter, for it was so cold that we stuffed material into the doubled window casements, filling the gap between the panes of glass to keep out the wind and ice. The heavy curtains were drawn. Coals glowed in the fireplace.

When I sat down beside the bed, I realized how serious his illness was. He must have known he would never recover.

"Lily," he said. "My eldest child. Perhaps you know what I want to say to you."

Perhaps I nodded. Perhaps I wept a little.

"I want you to look after your brothers and sisters. When I am gone, the little ones will need you more than ever, and your mother too."

He could safely trust me to take on this task, I thought. I was proud to lift the responsibility from his poor shoulders. I was already used to spending much of my time watching over the little ones, checking Bela's homework, brushing Berta's hair. All my brothers and sisters still looked up to me. They never doubted me. Still cocooned in ignorance of what was happening in the world outside, I was quick to reassure him.

"Of course, Apu. Always."

Neither of us knew what this promise would come to mean, how long I would carry it in my heart, and how painfully I would feel I had let him down.

That was the last time we spoke together alone. He died a few days later, in the early hours of Friday morning. When we woke, our mother told us the news. The loss was terrible. This would be the first ever Friday night in our lives to pass without us children standing all in a row before him, bending our heads, waiting for the calm blessing of our father.

It was pneumonia. If it had been just a few years later, antibiotics might have saved him. He wasn't an old man—only in his fifties, and younger than all his brothers. And yet, in a way, strange as this sounds, now I feel that he was lucky to die when he did. At least he escaped all the pain that would come so soon. He would never have to know his family's fate.

Someone—I think Imi—went to the synagogue with the sad news, and then, as predictably as a rising sun, the mourning process began.

Though it was the first time death had come to our home, I knew exactly what would happen, because I had seen it so many times before from the other side. Everything is taken care of by the community. The rituals are set in motion, and everyone knows what should happen when. This pattern is so helpful. As a mourner, particularly as a woman, I had nothing to do but let others make decisions, and comfort my mother, and allow myself to be comforted. The burial was delayed a little by Shabbat, but I knew that my father would be laid to rest in the cemetery where all his ancestors had been buried for decades, and his stone set a year later among parents, grandparents and great-grandparents, as well as uncles, aunts and cousins, all sharing his name. This was a cemetery already full of Engelmans. He would be safe there. He lies there now, one of the very last of our community to be buried in Bonyhád.

For seven days the house was full of people—family and friends of all ages, kind and familiar faces we children had known our entire lives. The mirrors were covered, and in the biggest room in the house, where we used to play and work and eat, I sat on a low stool, between the stools of my mother and Imi, while well-wishers lined up to sit with us and offer comfort. This is called sitting *shiva*. Sometimes we were joined on our row of stools by the little ones; sometimes we sat alone. But all day long people came and went, an endless distraction of practical sympathy. They brought food and drink and kind words and above all memories of our beloved father. In one conversation after another we were reminded of every aspect of his life and character: his strength, his kindness, his quiet intelligence. Each day they came, never abandoning us to the agony of the grief inside us. So many people. So many dishes of food. Everyone doing something to help:

cleaning, cooking, clearing up, tending to everything with no questions asked.

And somehow, it works, this very clever system. By the time the visitors had departed and we were alone again, the pain was a little duller. We could find a way to get used to living without our father. And that, for me, marked the very end of the happiest of childhoods.

Anyuka wanted everything to stay the same, at least as far as possible. To begin with, I continued to go to school and study. Daily life got back on its feet, and even began to feel something like normal again, despite the pain of our father's absence. Bela kept studying for his Bar Mitzvah, working harder than ever every evening. Unlike Imi, he would have to read from the Torah without Apu looking proudly on. He also became even more serious about his schoolwork.

One afternoon Dr. Litzman called, bringing his camera with him. Perhaps he hoped to cheer my mother with a family portrait. I don't think it was planned. The four youngest children were home from school, and Bela was about to set off for the *beit midrash*.

He was horrified at the thought of missing his Torah studies for something so frivolous. What would he say to the teacher?

"Oh, stay . . . stay . . . !" begged Berta, as he rushed from the house.

But it was too late. He was gone.

"Never mind," said Dr. Litzman, and he began to check the light and get the rest of us into position. Anyuka looked on, smiling a little, her even white teeth showing through parted lips, just like Berta's and Piri's.

Imi stood behind the high-backed sofa, where nobody ever usually sat. He wore his work suit, complete with white shirt and dark tie. He had the faintest beginnings of a moustache, and looked more like our father every day. By that time I'd left school too, and started to dress differently from my sisters. I looked more grown-up. My collar was edged with lace. René, Piri and Berta were all wearing matching gingham smocks that day, with cloth-covered buttons and sharply pressed white collars, and ribbons tied in huge bows in their hair. I had learned to roll my dark hair nice and high on top of my head, in that bouffant film-star style so popular in the 1940s. Half up, half down, it framed my face very fashionably. I'd brush it out thoroughly, morning and night, to keep it shiny.

Dr Litzman looked through the lens and made gestures with his hands.

"In a little, left a little, that's right . . . lower . . ."

I sat with Berta on the sofa, bolt upright, head straight and serious like Imi's, trying to set an example. Behind us, on either side of Imi, René and Piri leaned on the back of the sofa, each propped up by an elbow as instructed.

"Charming. Look at the camera . . . And smile!"

A blinding flash. I knew I had kept my eyes quite steady. René's attention had wandered, though. And only Berta and Piri, their heads tilted toward each other, had remembered to smile.

"One by one, now?" suggested Dr. Litzman.

Suddenly on her own for once, Berta turned shy and wistful, unable to meet the camera's gaze. That wasn't like her. But I think we had all become more serious since our father's death.

And then it was over, and the girls rushed out to see their friends, and Imi set off for shul, and I went back to my household chores with Anyuka. The house was quiet again for a few hours.

How bitterly I now regret our carelessness that day in letting Bela go. How could we have known that this would be the last ever photograph taken of us children all together? Bela's absence still hurts so much, whenever I look at this picture.

March 19–May 15, 1944

The truth is, nobody was prepared for what happened. Relatively speaking, you could say we lived in cloud cuckoo land. We heard some rumors, perhaps, but we didn't believe them. How can you believe the unbelievable? How can you imagine the unimaginable? The war years kept slowly passing, and still we felt perfectly safe in Bonyhád. Hungary was Germany's ally. We were Hungarians. Anyway, surely it would all be over soon? The fighting couldn't go on forever. Surely Hitler was in retreat? On the Eastern Front, the Red Army had been advancing steadily for months.

So when news came of Germany's occupation of Hungary, we really were taken by surprise. The German army took over Budapest on March 19, 1944. It was shocking how incredibly fast German forces seemed to appear in Bonyhád itself, soldiers in boots with revolvers, taking over the town hall.

Within a few weeks we felt our freedom slipping away.

It started with a curfew. We couldn't leave our house between six in the evening and seven the next morning. We couldn't leave Bonyhád at all. All Jewish shops had to be marked with a big yellow Star of David, and above this, the sign *Juden Geschaft*, Jewish Business. Radios and cameras were confiscated.

The orders came from Budapest, from the Minister of the Interior, and local Bonyhád officials and leaders of the Jewish communities had to carry them out. Some families had already been thinking ahead, giving a few possessions to their Christian friends for safekeeping until the crisis passed, or in case everything else was taken away. Sometimes these were valuables, sometimes life's necessities, like linens or stores of goose fat. Neighbors who'd lived side by side in harmony for decades were happy to help at first. But soon even these items were hunted down and seized. A special unit of sadistic gendarmerie was sent from the capital to find the "hidden treasures" of Bonyhád's Jews, helped by members of the Volksbund, a new pro-Nazi organization for Hungary's ethnic Germans. They knocked on doors without warning, carried out barbaric interrogations, and took away money, jewels, bicycles, clothing, typewriters and telephones.

These were not people who could be disobeyed. Not once did I consider breaking the curfew. None of us did.

Two days later we were sewing yellow stars onto our clothing. We couldn't leave the house without one. My brother and sisters started to hear the word *yidlach* at school. Yids. Some of the boys began to pick fights with Jewish children.

Our congregation leaders were forced to list every Jew in Bonyhád. All Jewish organizations were banned. German officers came to live in people's homes. It's a measure of how confused and helpless we felt that I can no longer remember the exact order of events. We were completely stunned at how quickly our lives were changing.

Imi must have known before the rest of us how serious things were. He had already had to stop work. The dentist's house was raided, one of many such invasions, and the license for his hunting gun revoked. He sent anything of value left to him to a highly respected friend—even some bits of gold for filling his patients' teeth. Imi decided to disguise our Shabbat candlesticks, dipping them in some chemical he knew would turn them black and hiding them in the cellar. He couldn't stand the thought of losing those.

On April 22 there was another surprise inspection. This time the gendarmerie were on the hunt for "foreign Jews." The Hungarian gendarmerie. They began rounding up Jews from the countryside.

When the order came to leave our house for the ghetto, we had maybe an hour's notice. When uniformed men with guns order you out of your house, you have no choice but to obey. There was fear, of course, but not much panic, because we understood so little of what was happening.

They lied to us. So many lies. We believed them because we wanted to believe them. We couldn't contemplate not believing them. We thought we were going for a few days, a few weeks at most. We had no idea we'd never come back. So we took what came to hand, whatever we thought would be useful for the next few days: bedding, and cooking things. Some food. Perhaps Berta grabbed a favorite doll, or her hair ribbons. Bela probably took schoolbooks and prayer books. My own instincts, like my mother's, were all practical. What might we need to keep ourselves alive? Salt, flour, candles, soap, blankets, pillows . . . what else? We were too rushed to think. Burgi couldn't help us now. Anyone who wasn't Jewish could no longer work in a Jewish household. So she lost her home too. We never saw her again.

In those days, few people went on family holidays. If we ever left Bonyhád, it was only for summer day trips with my mother—never my father—or visits to relatives in other towns. Then we older children would take the train with a trusted friend or cousin who was already travelling that way, and could look after us. So we didn't have lots of suitcases. When we were ordered to the ghetto, we could take only what we could carry, awkwardly bundled in our arms. Well, it wasn't far, we thought . . . hardly even two streets away.

Again, my oldest brother thought ahead. It was Imi who ran to our mother's bedroom and rescued a few pieces of jewelry—not because they had great value, but because he knew we loved them. Some sparkling stud earrings of Anyuka's, a couple of rings and my own golden cherub necklace. Not much at all. Small things, easily pocketed.

Such a short walk, into such a great change. The lower ghetto, which was for observant Orthodox Jews like our family, was created in the poor, run-down quarter right next to our synagogue. Over 700 friends and family and neighbors, all weighed down with whatever we could carry, converged in the one narrow street where we were now forced to live. Here the houses were much smaller and more cramped than our own, and all joined together. At either end of the street was a wooden barrier or fence, with a door-like entrance built into it, easily guarded. We would be allowed out just twice a week, for one hour, to go to the market. There was another ghetto, not far away, for the Neolog congregation, set up in their communal buildings, called the "upper ghetto." And then there also were Jews brought in from the small villages and hamlets all around Bonyhád, from quite some distance away. Everyone was rounded up, but for what purpose, we had no idea. It was a Monday, May 15, almost exactly eight weeks after Adolf Eichmann's arrival in Budapest. That name meant nothing to me then.

We soon realized we were moving into somebody else's home. It was horrible to be forced to become invaders ourselves, but everyone was in the same situation by then, all of us crammed into a few buildings, with no privacy, no space to call our own. Each Jewish family was allocated a room—ours was on the ground floor. Of course, there weren't enough beds for everyone, so we laid out bedding on the floorboards for René and Piri and Berta and we tried to make the best of things. I suppose I must have shared one of the beds with my mother while Imi and Bela took the other. It was very cramped, but at least we were all together. At least we were still a family. We were like prisoners, unable to leave the ghetto, but we were trapped with the people we loved best in the world. That was the most important thing.

It was clear to me that as long as Anyuka and Imi and I kept our heads, the others would be not be afraid. And they were OK. They trusted us. Berta may have been the baby of our family, but she was nearly twelve years old by then, and I don't remember a single tear or complaint from her.

Imi certainly kept his head. I don't know when or where he packed them, but he'd had the good sense to bring a few tools with him. As soon as we were safely in our own quarters, and the door was shut behind us, he looked at all our feet and then asked Anyuka to give him one of her shoes. Was she surprised by this strange request? I don't remember, but I remember the shoes quite clearly. Neat and narrow, they were made of dark brown leather. Quite plain lace-ups, with little eyelets. Practical and elegant at once. But nothing remarkable. No frills. Shoes just like hundreds of women wore in 1944, which went well with everything. And they had a good-sized heel—sturdy and high at once, stacked and square—perhaps two or three centimeters high. Don't forget, shoes were made to last then. When the soles and heels began to wear, they could simply be resoled, reheeled.

We all watched, transfixed, as Imi carefully prised off the

hard layer of leather on the heel of our mother's shoe, making sure to keep the little metal tacks good and straight. Then he chiseled away at the next layer to make a tiny hiding place. And then he took her earrings, her rings, and also my golden angel pendant, and pushed them inside, so they were completely out of sight. They fitted perfectly. No need for any extra stuffing. No rattling.

Although Imi didn't want to draw attention by making too much noise, he managed to hammer the old heel cover back in place, and once Anyuka had walked around a little, stamping her feet more than usual, he was sure they'd be secure. There. That was something. Nobody could possibly find them now. My own necklace was not particularly valuable. I don't think Imi ever intended this kindness as an insurance policy. Something in the bank. He simply knew I loved the pendant, and that I wouldn't want it to fall into the hands of any stranger. So he saved it for me. Always thoughtful.

And then we finished unpacking the few things we'd been able to bring, and went to investigate the tiny kitchen, which all the families in that house now had to share, and find out what washing facilities there might be.

It helped that we had our old friends and relations all around us, so we could support each other. Our rabbi was there. A Ghetto Council had been appointed by the authorities, drawn from our community leaders. Everyone quickly agreed that the children's education should not be interrupted, and it was better for them to have something to do, and be able to play together. As it was summer and there was space outside, classes began right away in the open air. That was a good distraction.

And some people had thought to bring sewing machines, or perhaps they were already in the ghetto's few houses. With such bad times ahead, everyone needed a skill, it was agreed. Who

knew how any one of us might make a living in the future? So
they made sure that all of us girls could use a sewing machine,
and knew how to thread the top spool through all the hooks
and eyelets down to the hammering needle, and how to fill the
bobbins and replace them in cases like silver bullets, and hook
up the bobbin thread from underneath the silver plate. We
quickly learned how to guide the material through, and control
the speed, and keep pins safely between our lips.

But the truth is, I couldn't think ahead beyond the next few
hours, the next day at most. I had to help Anyuka make sure
everyone had enough food and water, and that the food could
be prepared, and we could sleep and wash. I don't think we
really wanted to look beyond that. Although the authorities allowed us to shop only at set hours, after the rest of the population had got what they needed, we didn't go hungry, because
on market days the stallholders kept back what they knew they
could later sell to us, and brought it to the ghetto.

Years later, I heard a few stories of both horror and hope
about those days in the Bonyhád ghetto. About the jeweler,
Mr. Fulop Eibenschutz, an old man who found the gathering
tension and uncertainty so unbearable that he killed himself.
About postcards to relatives thrown over the fence, which sym-
pathetic passers-by then picked up and posted. About some local Gypsies who took pity on us, and threw freshly baked bread
over the barrier. But by that time I was gone. For Imi and I
spent only a short time in the ghetto before we were both sent
away again.

May 16–June 28, 1944

Our names were on different lists. Imi and twenty-one other teenage boys were handed over to a local paramilitary commander. I suppose we were glad then that they thought Bela was too young to go. We had no idea where the older boys were taken.

I was sent with a bigger group, nearly all women, to a farm called Juhe-Manor, a hot walk from the town. All the labor shortages caused by the war were to be filled by Jews. Other young women were sent to a different farm. I was one of the younger girls in our group, along with my old school friends Berta Herman, Olga Pollak, Edit Berkovits and Hilda Banda. Hilda's little sister Frida was also sent, and she and Livia and Tibor Liechner were closer to René's age—not yet eighteen—but at least the Liechner children had their parents with them. That was the important thing, we all agreed: for families to stick together. The Engels and the Bricks were allowed to bring a child each too, a girl and a boy who were only about twelve—Berta's age. Older women were sent along, not for field work but to cook for us.

And so we found ourselves sleeping the next night in a barn, on straw. Fortunately, we had brought blankets with us.

Our job was weeding, clearing the hard earth around new stems of maize that grew in great fields that seemed to stretch forever. Well, we had a garden ourselves at home. We even grew corn-on-the-cob every summer. I knew how to weed. It was still early in the year, so the plants were fresh and green and not that high yet.

But the sun was baking, and we weren't used to hard physical labor of that kind, let alone working all day long in such heat, with so little water. For twelve hours I dug, a repetitive movement that needed the strength of my entire body: foot on fork, drive it in under the weeds, pull back the shaft, bend down, shake out the earth from the weeds' roots, throw them onto the pile. And then the weeds had to be collected and added to a bigger pile. Within a few hours, my soft hands were blistered. Barely used to cooking or washing up, they were accustomed to turning the pages of a book, not turning over soil. By the end of the day they were rough and bleeding, and my back was aching. It didn't help to be so small.

We were all so tired we could hardly fail to sleep that night. In the morning the work started all over again, and by then our limbs were stiff as well as aching. So this was what our lives would be, we thought. The work was hard, and there was a great deal of it, but it wouldn't kill us. We'd survive, we thought.

Nobody was sent to guard us. Yet none of us tried to run away. What was the point? Where would we have gone? And, tired and anxious though we were, wondering how the rest of our families were faring in the ghetto, or worrying about fathers and brothers far away, who knew where, we weren't truly afraid. Not yet. One week turned into two, two into three. By the time the sixth week came, we were beginning to lose track.

One day, well before the work was actually finished, we were ordered to put down our tools and return to the ghetto. All I could think about was how much I wanted to see my mother and sisters and Bela again. I hoped to find out, if I could, how

Imi was managing, and if anybody knew where he was. Maybe he was back, and I could see him again? I think we had all been worrying most of all about our mothers, coping alone with only younger children, babies and old people. We were eager to get back to Bonyhád. We felt happy to be going home. Somehow, we still suspected nothing.

Together again. We were so pleased to see each other. René hugged me and Piri didn't say much about what had happened while I was away, and so I didn't ask questions. I could see for myself how difficult it had been. People commented on how lovely and kind Berta had been through all these terrible weeks, which made me very proud of my little sister. What a gorgeous girl she is, they said. So much ahead of her in life. Bela had quietly kept on with his studies, and never complained. Our whole family just wanted to make things as easy as possible for our mother.

I'd hoped that perhaps Imi would also have been told to return, but there was no sign or news of him or the other young men. The ghetto had been reduced to women, infants and the elderly.

I was still washing off the dust and dirt of the field when the order came to pack up again. This time we were only told to prepare a few belongings: just two sets of underwear and a little food. Of course, we wanted to take more, but they told us not to worry and that we wouldn't need much.

And, of course, we trusted them. Maybe it was because our instructions were relayed by people we'd always known—the Jewish officials in the ghetto. Rumors quickly spread from building to building, room to room, but nobody knew anything for certain. We wouldn't be gone for long. They would make us work somewhere else. We had no radios, no newspapers, no way at all of knowing that in small towns and villages all over Hungary our fellow Jews had already been rounded up and their makeshift ghettos emptied. We expected a journey somewhere, but about our destination we had no clue. We must trust in God, we told ourselves. We will trust in God.

Word that we'd soon be leaving must have spread quickly around the town, because at one point there was a terrible commotion. On the other side of the fence, a young woman called Chava was weeping and wailing with all her heart.

"Forgive me, forgive me, *Mame*," she implored.

She had come to say goodbye to her sisters and her mother, who were inside the ghetto. Chava hadn't seen her mother since falling in love with and marrying a Christian man. At that point her very religious mother had dutifully renounced her, mourning her as if dead, even sitting *shiva* as was then the custom.

"I forgive you," she told her daughter now.

June 28–July 3, 1944

That night we were herded into our synagogue, with nowhere to lie down but the tiled floor. We hardly slept. With every move we faced new humiliations, and the situation seemed a little worse. It was as if we were being slowly hardened. In the morning we were moved on again. This time we were trooped off to the town's sports field, a big open space not far from the goods station.

Piri was bursting for the lavatory, but here there were no facilities at all. Just a tap. She held on for as long as she could – we all tried to—but there was clearly no choice but to go in the open air, in full view of all the community. The shame of it. She felt it more than most, as she cared so much about cleanliness, and she was by far the shyest of the six of us, and only fifteen. She didn't complain, but I knew how hard she found this.

But we were all in the same boat. And we were still together. For two days and two nights they kept us waiting on that field, sleeping out under the stars with no protection, never knowing what might happen next. The nights were warm so we didn't need much. We managed, the six of us, and tried to keep our spirits up, but it was much harder for others, who could carry even less than we could—mothers with young babies, very old people, the sick. Everyone did what they could to help them. Some people from the town, a trio of car mechanics, took pity on us and brought us warm food, defying the new rules that forbade contact between Jews and non-Jews.

The second day was Friday. Anyuka insisted we girls wash our hair. Our thick dark wavy hair that she was so proud of, and which probably earned us the title, "the beautiful Engelman girls." We had exactly the same color hair, all four of us. She could see no reason to let standards slip. Maybe she realized it was something to do. We could persuade ourselves there was something still normal about our lives if we needed to wash our hair before the Sabbath. It helped us not to panic. She helped us not to panic.

It took ages, queuing for the tap, taking it in turns to bend our heads and shiver under the cold water, helping each other, combing out and drying our hair under the sun, working loose every tangle. The sun sets very late in June. The day was very long. We had no candlesticks, but Anyuka had hidden our Shabbat candles in our small bundles. Just before nightfall, Anyuka kneeled with us on the parched grass, trying to get our pair of candles to stand up straight.

Lighting each wick, she swept her hands before her to welcome in the Sabbath and covered her eyes.

"*Baruch ata Hashem Elokeinu, Melekh ha'olam, asher kid'shanu b'mitzvotav v'tzivanu l'hadlik ner shel Shabbat,*" she said, as she did every Friday night. Blessed are You, Lord our God, King of the universe, Who has sanctified us with His commandments and commanded us to light the Shabbat candles.

When I looked up, I saw perhaps a hundred other pairs of flames flickering in the darkness, lighting up the faces of a hundred other mothers and their children for the last time.

"Don't worry," they told us as we left Bonyhád. "You'll all be together. It's only temporary. You'll be back."

How gullible we were. How easily fooled.

We carried what we could. Always a little less.

Our first train journey was only forty kilometres, but it took all night. The carriages had wooden benches. The train stopped in darkness, without warning or explanation, and we waited at some small station, or somewhere in between, for hours and hours, listening to each other's breathing, trying not to ask questions nobody could answer.

They let us out at Pécs. From the station we were marched straight to the Lakics army barracks. It was a kind of transit camp, already heaving with thousands of people, Jews rounded up from across Tolna county and Baranya county. People like us, who made us see ourselves as we were—wretched and ever more degraded, sleeping on straw in filthy stables, like animals instead of human beings. The whole experience was so bewildering. What could be the purpose of bringing us all here? We tried to reassure each other and ourselves. There must be another work camp ahead. That was the only reason we could imagine for moving us on again.

And again the Nazis deceived us. It was how their whole plan operated. To some extent, perhaps, they also deceived those who willingly carried out the orders. So, when the guards told us that the young people would work and the old people would stay at home and look after the children, we believed their lies. We couldn't think of any alternative explanation. Three-quarters or more of the Jews in Hungary had already been exterminated. But we knew nothing of this. And anyway, when you are caring for youngsters who need to be fed and washed and rocked to sleep, and people who are ill, or weak with age, and there is not an able-bodied man among you, it's hard to think beyond the next few hours. Or perhaps we were too accustomed to being told what to do by men.

It must have been the same all over Hungary. The hardest part to understand, the thing most painful to think about, is the fact that the German authorities could never have done this without Hungarian help. There weren't nearly enough German soldiers to control so many thousands of people, all over the country. Hungarians, not Germans, gave us our orders in Bonyhád and in Pécs.

How could they? How could our own people suddenly turn against us? Not everyone, of course. The mayor of Szekszárd had bravely refused to allow a ghetto in his town. But that simply meant that the hundred or so Jews of Szekszárd were sent twenty kilometres away to join us in the ghetto of Bonyhád. And then on to Pécs. He couldn't save them.

There was no escape from here. Perhaps a young man might have tried, but everyone in the camp was putting all their strength into helping someone else, someone who was finding the situation even harder. Mothers looked after little ones. Young girls looked after mothers. It was hot. We were thirsty and hungry. Minute by minute and hour by hour, we tried to work out the next small step and then the next. We simply didn't see the danger we were in.

Now we had no control over what we ate. We had to queue for soup from an outdoor kitchen they'd set up in the courtyard. Privacy was at an end. But the worst thing was the latrines. The only place you could relieve yourself was in communal outdoor pit latrines, completely exposed, no separation between women, men and children, and people waiting around at all times. Can you imagine how distressing that was for Piri? Such a mass of people everywhere that I was constantly frightened of losing my sisters and my mother and Bela. We never did anything alone.

All we could do was wait.

Time passes so slowly when you don't exactly know what you're waiting for.

Three days. Three nights. Surviving somehow, because we were still a family there, all six of us still together.

July 5–9, 1944

And now I must pause, and think. Words can barely describe what happened next. But words are all I have.

Even while I was living through this time, I could not comprehend it, so how can I convey the experience to somebody who was not there? I try to go back in my head, to understand how our hearts kept beating, how our lungs kept breathing, how we did this, how we did that, the mechanics of our moments, how this could possibly have happened. I know it did, because I can't forget it.

I realize that at this point we simply went numb. I felt, yet I could not feel. I thought, yet I could not think. In the face of such brutality, nothing about me worked as it should. The idea that one human being could do this to another overwhelms me.

With every change in our situation, the pretense slipped a little further. It became less and less worth hiding what lay ahead. Its inevitability. Or maybe the cruelty was deliberate, designed to start the process of dehumanization. Now we were shuffling, in huge numbers, toward the freight yard at Pécs station. Men with guns kept us moving forward. Uniforms and boots kept us quiet. Hungarian policemen forced us on. We could see right away that these were not trains as we knew them, with seats and windows and compartments. Here we were faced with goods wagons, windowless, dark, high, with sliding doors and padlocks. We had to help each other into them. How could we fit so many inside?

Our wagon was already crammed with people. We were pushed in from behind, yet there was nowhere to go, because as you moved forward you were crushed into the bodies of the women and children forced inside before you, and some were falling, and it's hard to step onto a living body, and anyway we couldn't breathe. There was no air to breathe. Just bodies, fearful, horrified, unwashed bodies, pressed relentlessly into a space that could not contain them. And sensing, perhaps, the bodies that had been there before ours, given the hot stench that already filled the wagon. You couldn't turn and flee. There was nowhere to go. It was obvious what would happen if you tried. And why would we leave each other? Where would we go? We had to stay together. The six of us. At least we weren't with strangers. All around us still were our friends and our cousins from Bonyhád, though not everyone. I couldn't see Hilda. You couldn't keep track of all your friends. In all our little groups, we wanted to keep together, every mother, young or old, desperate to keep hold of their daughters, their sons, their babies, their aging parents and even their grandparents.

Pushing. More pushing. How many more people could possibly be shoved inside a space so small? We nearly fainted. And then the doors were shut and maybe locked—I can't say now. We were all so tightly packed inside that at first we could only stand, trapped, overwhelmed by the worst smell in the world, except for one. Human excrement, sweat and terror and vomit, fresh and stale at once. You had to fight for each breath. I had never felt such panic. I held on tightly to René's and Piri's hands. The train began to move.

Each wagon had two buckets, one for water, one to use as a toilet. How they stayed upright, I cannot imagine, though I was there. How we ever reached them, and bore the humiliation of using them or not using them, I don't know. How we shared out what little water and food we had. How anyone could swallow anything in such a fetid atmosphere. All these details escape me now. I believe that when a situation is so unbearable, your mind doesn't function as it should. When there is no logic, no explanation, you really cannot properly think or feel. You become a kind of zombie.

I also believe that there are some things my mind no longer wants to recall. There's so much I do remember, every detail so clear, even after so many decades. Yet when I think back to those days and nights on the transport, when the nightmare truly began, and I ask myself questions about how we managed, how we breathed, what we did for those days and nights, my mind is blank. I have no better understanding than you of how any of it was possible.

We were all close, pressed together, but my mother kept Berta closest of all to her, always protecting her. Bela—thirteen and only just Bar Mitzvah'd—felt he was a young man now, not a child, not a boy. He didn't feel he needed protection himself, but to protect others. I was cramped beside René and Piri, who was even more distressed by the foulness all around than the rest of us. There was no space to lie down, sometimes not to sit. You just had to sleep as best you could wherever and however you found yourself. It was impossible to shut out the world with sleep for long at a time. There was no chance at all of washing. The filth was unimaginable.

July was always the hottest month of the year in Hungary, but the summer of 1944 was the hottest we had ever known. It would not be so hot again in Europe that century. The temperature rose and rose. The stink grew worse and worse. Every jolt made the overflowing bucket spill, until muck spread everywhere. Intolerable, and yet we had no choice. We had to tolerate it. A kind of stupefaction set in.

Once every day the train stopped, sometimes for hours. The truck door would open, to reveal uniformed men standing outside, machine guns pointed toward us, so that nobody could escape, and nobody could get any sense of where we were or what was happening. The buckets were emptied, or filled again, and the dead were dragged out.

Of course, people died. The heat was suffocating. There was so little to drink. Dry lips. Dry throats. People were sickening and ill before the journey started. Later I was told that every train had an empty wagon at the back, to hold the dead. Every Jewish body had to be accounted for. We were locked in with corpses, a few more each day. These must have been the first dead bodies I had ever seen, other than my father's, but his was covered, out of respect. Yet I remember little of them now. Even though I must have known these people, I could not tell you their names. Unbelievably, it was not even a shock to see them perish: by then the situation was so utterly inhuman that everyone wanted to die. You were beyond caring. So numb that something which should have been shocking meant nothing. I think we already envied the dead. How could dying be worse than living, on this journey?

At some point we must have crossed the border into occupied Poland. At some point the Hungarian guards must have left and Germans taken over. At some point we must have understood that we were no longer in Hungary, but still we didn't know what this meant.

People didn't speak much. Babies cried, on and on. That was the worst. Mothers had nothing to give them. Bela kept track of the days. We left on Wednesday. On Thursday we were still living and together. On Friday we were alive, and I suppose the sun set through that high barred opening, our single source of air, which you could not call a window. We only knew that the darkness became more intense, and so it must be Sabbath. On Saturday we grew weaker still. I imagine that we prayed, but whether we prayed alone or together, I can't say.

Anyuka gave nothing away about her own fears or expectations. But she must have had some kind of premonition, some idea. Because on the last full day we spent on the transport, on Shabbat, she suddenly said to me, "Lily, maybe we should change shoes."

She was already untying her laces. My own shoes were not very different from hers, but I didn't ask any questions. It was hard for us both to move without pressing against others. I quickly unlaced my own and passed them over to her. Warm from my body. The warmth of my mother's body was still in her shoes. Of course, I knew she meant me to take charge of her rings, her earrings and my necklace. I remembered that my brother Imi had hidden our jewelry in the heel. But right at that moment I was in too much shock from the journey to think very hard about the significance of the exchange.

I think a lot about this moment now. Why then? If she hadn't somehow suspected that her risk was greater than mine, why would she have asked me to change shoes like that? What might she have known but would never have told us? Perhaps far more than we ever imagined.

That's all I can remember. I saw no other sign of her premonitions. As selfless as ever, she tried to shield us to the very last. A family habit.

The next morning it was July 9, and Anyuka brought out a tiny bit of food she still had in her pocket—a carrot perhaps, or a dried-up crust of bread she'd still been saving. But Bela shook his head.

"I can't eat today, Anyuka. I must fast today. You know that."

As I said, my little brother had become a very religious young man. Perhaps this was even the first fast day since his Bar Mitzvah. Certainly he took his obligations very seriously. This was the seventeenth day of the Jewish month of Tammuz, though the day itself had fallen on Shabbat, so Bela had properly postponed his fast till Sunday. This is the day that marks the beginning of *Bein haMetzarim*, Between the Straits. It's a mourning period to commemorate the breaching of the walls of Jerusalem, which led to the Roman destruction of the Second Temple. It also marks the moment Moses broke the Tablets bearing the Ten Commandments, and ensured that in future people would need to search for godliness.

"Please eat, Bela," said Anyuka quietly. No family wanted to draw attention to what little food they had managed to hide. And we had no idea how much longer the journey might last, or what we would be forced to do when we arrived. "Please. You've had so little. You need to eat. We don't know when we'll be able to eat again. God will forgive you."

However much she pressed him, he refused.

"It's just till nightfall," he insisted. "I'll eat then."

July 9, 1944

The truth is that if they had told us exactly where we were going, we would never have believed it. Even up to the very last moment when the door of the goods wagon opened for the last time, we could not contemplate the idea that we could be taken anywhere other than to work. There are some things the human mind cannot take in.

You cannot fear the worst if you cannot imagine it.

The train suddenly slowed and stopped. For a moment I was able to peer out through the little so-called window to see what was happening. But I could not understand what I saw. An enormous colorless place, so many buildings, and huge fences, and you could see things moving but you couldn't tell what they were. They didn't seem human. Figures without hair, moving rocks. It looked to me like a madhouse.

And before I could take that in the doors slid open and the sunlight came in, and our eyes were shocked by the sudden change. It was a beautiful summer's afternoon and the sky was so blue and bright. Sheer relief. They were going to let us out. Fresh air. This nightmare was ending. Just for a moment we were happy. We thought that any minute we would be able to stretch our legs. We were finally leaving this stinking truck.

The people outside, hard-looking men in striped trousers and shirts, instantly began shouting and hurrying us out.

"*Geh raus! Geh raus! Schnell! Schnell!*" Get out! Get out! Quick! Quick!

After five days so cramped and squalid, it was hard to move our limbs. We were aching, hungry, half-asleep, dirty beyond belief, feeling half-crazed ourselves. We stumbled out, trying to take with us our precious bundles, the few things we had managed to save from Pécs.

"No! Leave everything here," these strange people told us. "We will bring them later. Don't worry about your things. We'll take care of them."

People who had collapsed were dragged out. There were soldiers standing there too, watching everything, making us move faster to get in line, controlling the men who controlled us, keeping us all moving steadily forward. And thousands of people all stumbling off the train, every one as disoriented as we were, arriving at a huge and alien place like nothing we'd ever seen before, with the strangest smell hanging in the air, utterly foul, and all those people in the distance who barely looked like people at all.

Everything seemed to move so fast that we didn't realize what had happened until it was over.

"Hurry! Hurry!"

We were all pushed forward, and the elderly men and older boys were separated from the women and children until we were divided in two vast parallel columns, five people wide. Everything had to be done quickly. Everything was perfectly organized. The striped men did the work. They knew what they had to do. The German officers made sure of it. Their dogs prowled around them.

Suddenly it was our turn to stand in front of a different kind of man. I see him even today, yet his face is a blank. His boots shone like mirrors. He wore white gloves, and a peaked hat, and held a baton in his hand. A military-style uniform. Very elegant.

With one glance at you, this man gestured with his stick to the right or to the left. What this meant, we had no idea.

My mother and Bela and Berta were sent left. It took no time at all.

I was sent right. René and Piri too.

So fast we couldn't exchange a single word.

That was it. Over.

I assumed it meant simply that Anyuka and the little ones and all the other mothers with babies and young children and the old people with them—most of the people on the train, it seemed—they wouldn't have to work. We who had been separated out, the young and strong, would no doubt be put to some task. We would see the others afterward, at the end of the day, I thought. We weren't worried about that. There was no panic. If somebody had told us what was about to happen, we'd have thought them mad. We didn't have the faintest idea where we were. We couldn't have imagined such a place could even exist in the world.

"That's impossible. It can't be true," we'd have said.

Our first cousins were with me and René and Piri: there was Hilda, thankfully, and her big sisters Magda and Jolan and Boriska. Their brother—the second-youngest in their family— had already been taken to be *Munkaszolgálat*, like Imi. And a few of the girls I'd been working alongside in the cornfield were with us still. So at this point everybody in our group was known to us.

I grabbed my sisters' hands, on either side of me, as tightly as I could. More of the men in striped clothes who had ordered us off the train—prisoners who were also guards, it seemed—now marched us away to a big open space they called a *Lager* and then into a large room inside some kind of barracks, to prepare to shower, they told us.

"Undress! Leave everything outside! *Schnell!*"

I remember folding all my clothes nicely, as I was ordered, and making sure my sisters did the same. We left them in a neat pile. And then we had to stand completely naked and in full view of strangers—strange men—for the first time in our lives. As children we had bathed together, but now we were young women. I hadn't seen even my own sisters unclothed like this before. Piri was so young, just a girl, hardly a woman at all yet, barely accustomed to her own body's changes. We couldn't look at one another.

But the humiliation grew worse. They lined us up in front of a man with clippers, and he cut off all our beautiful hair, so thick and long, washed so carefully by our mother before our journey. They shaved our pubic hair. Hair that nobody had ever even seen before. For some these assaults were too much to bear. A girl ahead of us in the line was driven insane, there and then. She lost all control. She couldn't take the shame and fear and horror. They took her away.

The showers were cold, no soap, no privacy, and all of us stood there together under the pipes. But we were so dirty from the journey that even just water was a relief.

Everything continued to happen very quickly. It was still so hot that it hardly mattered that there were no towels to dry ourselves when we were ordered out again.

Our own clothes were all gone. Only the shoes we had arrived in remained. My mother's shoes, safely waiting for me. I didn't even think then about what they still contained, what this meant for me. I didn't realize until much later how lucky we had been, how extraordinarily unusual it was for any prisoner to get their own shoes back. I suppose they had brought Hungary's Jews here in such huge numbers in the past few weeks that eventually their supply of wooden clogs was exhausted.

I didn't have time to think. We were immediately marched in line past a table piled high with other clothes. Other people's clothes. As you passed, somebody threw something at you at random—a dress, a skirt, a blouse. It didn't matter what size you were—and my sisters and I were all quite small, all much the same height—you just had to put it on. What did they care? My hands closed on a long grey skirt, far too big for me. Bigger women quickly pulled on dresses far too small. Everyone's clothes were so peculiar. No underwear. I looked at my sisters. They looked at me. No hair. Strange garments. We simply didn't recognize each other. And we just could not take in our situation.

Then it was back out into the *Lager*, and now the sky seemed darker, greyer. A pall hung over everything, blocking out the sun. The foul smell that had choked us on our arrival, the most sickening and overwhelming smell I had ever experienced, was getting stronger and stronger. Not far away was a tall chimney, smoking furiously, with flames emerging red and bright.

"What kind of factory is that?" I asked one of the women prisoners who had arrived before us. "What are they making here? What's this horrible smell?"

"They're burning your families there," she told us. "Your parents, your sisters, your brothers. They're burning them."

The guards had told us when we went for our showers that we would see our families again when we came out. So how could we take such a monstrous idea seriously? The people here were so strange.

"You must be crazy," I said. "What kind of story is this? That's impossible. It can't be true."

We simply could not believe the other prisoners. We couldn't even imagine why anyone would say such a thing. It was impossible to comprehend. Hadn't we just been standing with our families, only a few hours earlier? With newborn babies, children still small enough to rest on your hip, or gather in your arms, little innocent creatures barely old enough to walk? Who could think of burning another human being who had never done anything to hurt another creature? A child? Why were these women telling us these awful stories?

"Don't worry," I reassured Piri. "Of course Berta and Bela are fine. They're just with Anyuka in another place. We'll probably see them tomorrow, like they told us before."

At this point we were handed some dark brown lumps they called bread. We turned it over in our hands. It was hard. Almost black. It had a funny sour smell. My sisters and I were very hungry by then, but not yet hungry enough to eat that.

"Give it to us! Give it to us!" begged those other women, the prisoners who had arrived before us, who had been there just a little longer. And we were happy to. We gave away our bread so freely that first day, unable to believe that anyone could contemplate eating something that barely passed for food.

That was our first evening.

For days already we'd had no sleep. And now there was nowhere to lie down except for the bare stony ground of the *Lager*, the big open space between each barracks building. Just stones, and powdery grey soil. The whole place was grey. All night long we lay there, huddled together, René and Piri on either side of me, staying as close as we could, not for warmth but for safety. I knew that as long as we were in this place, I could not take my eyes off my sisters. I had to look after them, as I had promised. I was the one thing they could trust now, the only point of stability. They would do anything and everything

I said, without question. They trusted me completely. I had to live up to their faith in me.

Floodlights ensured that no part of that vast area went unwatched, day or night. It never really got dark. And so you could always see the watchtowers and barbed wire and the concrete posts and the electric fences on all sides. The noise never stopped either: guard dogs barking, men shouting, feet marching, gates clanging, people crying out and sobbing, everything so loud and harsh. And other noises too, terrifying sounds that were impossible to identify.

What I Didn't Know

There was so much we didn't believe or understand that first day. It was impossible to understand. Nothing made sense. We were told so many lies. Knowledge came slowly, if it came at all. Some facts I didn't learn for years.

We spent the night on the ground outside the barracks because Birkenau was already full. The way they made room for those new arrivals who'd been granted life only for as long as they could work was to kill their predecessors. Human beings were no more than numbers here. This is what the Nazis did. They always replaced people. To make room for us, they destroyed others, gassing them to death, then burning their corpses.

Even before Germany's invasion of Hungary, they had begun to make the camps at Auschwitz still bigger, and the transports more brutally efficient. To an existing concentration camp, they added a death camp. By May, the new extension was finished: a railway track with a ramp beside it in the very heart of Birkenau. The train line now ran almost a kilometre and a half from the freight station at Oświęcim as far as the gas chambers. It stopped between two of the four crematoria. No time was ever wasted.

I didn't know that trains like the one we suffered in had been arriving for more than two months already from all parts of Hungary, including the newly annexed territories, bearing

400,000 or more Jews before us. That all my mother's family, who lived scattered in the small towns in the south-west of the country, including my aunt Gisela and my uncle David, with whom I'd lived so happily in Pápa the year I turned fourteen, and my six-year-old cousin Loyaush, who had arrived so late in their lives, and also every other one of Anyuka's nine brothers and sisters, and their half-siblings, and nearly all their children too, and their cousins, nearly all the people I had grown up loving and knowing and visiting, and other relations I'd never met, had already been transported here before Bonyhád ghetto was emptied. I didn't know that I would never see any of them again.

I didn't know then that our transport, that stinking train from Pécs, was one of the very last to enter Auschwitz carrying Hungarian Jews. That on July 7, while we were slowly travelling toward occupied Poland, Miklós Horthy, Hungary's ruler, finally ordered a halt to the deportations. That by then, only Budapest was left to be emptied.

I didn't know we had arrived in hell, to be greeted by the Angel of Death. The man who decided so casually whether we would live or die was Josef Mengele, the most notorious of all the doctors who worked at the camp. These doctors stood on the platform called the Ramp, and made the first of the many, many selections my sisters and I would endure. This is what shocks me. It was doctors, trained physicians, highly educated and cultured men, who could have used their education and experience and knowledge to save people's lives but instead made the decision whether any one of us would walk straight into a gas chamber and die the moment we arrived, and be burned. Sixteen of us in every twenty. Or if we would instead become slave laborers, face the ordeal of multiple selections, and die more slowly from starvation, thirst, exhaustion, disease, overwork, suicide, violence, cold. Or, in rare cases, like my own, live to tell their story.

I didn't know that the stench was burning flesh and bones.

And really it *was* a factory. An extermination factory, in which they always wanted to be ever more efficient, to kill more people in less time.

July 10, 1944

A whistle blast shocked us awake in the middle of the night.

"*Schnell! Schnell!*" Quick! Quick! Always that word.

Day after day, it would be the same. The sun would not rise for some hours, but this was how our mornings always started. *Appell*: roll call.

We learned what it meant to stand in columns in the place they called the *Appellplatz*, row after row, each five prisoners across. I always tried to stand between René and Piri. It was not rational, I know, but I felt that this somehow gave me a better chance of doing something if they tried to take one of my sisters. I needed to be close to both of them, and they to me. We had become numbers now. Every day, sometimes several times a day, SS officers came to count us. We could stand for hours, all morning, all day it seemed, waiting for something to happen, someone to be found, trying not to move. You had to keep completely still. Even corpses were put out for roll call. Anyone who had died in the night was carried to the *Appellplatz* and lined up with the living. However ill you were, you had to go out. The only thing they cared about was adding up the numbers. Nobody could escape.

When they were satisfied, we were given "breakfast." Just an unrecognizable black liquid to drink. They called it coffee but it tasted nothing like it. It had a strange smell, like a chemical. No nourishment, and nothing to sweeten its sour and acrid flavor. There were rumors that it contained a sedative called bromide, to end rebellion and menstruation at once. But starvation and extreme stress had the same effect. One container for five people to share: the first person could drink and then they passed it back to the next, and the next, and then the next.

This was a particular horror for Piri, so obsessive about hygiene. Remember, if somebody even touched her glass, she would not drink from it again without first washing it. We had grown up in a family where food accidentally dropped on the floor was thrown away as a matter of course. And here you didn't have so much as a cup to call your own. There was no knowing whose lips had been on it before yours. A strange, forced intimacy.

And then we were sent to the barracks where we would sleep that night. They didn't tell us that the occupants before us were already dead. It was a place where they used to keep horses. There had been space for about fifty animals. Now they crammed in five or six hundred women and closed the door. Lines of three-tiered bunks were all the barracks contained, layers of wooden boards, really: planks covered with straw, and one thin louse-ridden blanket to cover seven or eight bodies or more.

The open latrines were another daily ordeal, for all of us. I never let Piri or René go there alone. Thousands of prisoners had to make do with fifty or sixty holes, cement pits in a triple line, with no seats, no partitions, no doors, no paper and often no water. You could never be alone. You were always rushed and jostled. You couldn't use them except at set times, at their command. And so many women were suffering from upset stomachs, in pain, unable to control themselves. There was hardly any way to wash—just a bit of cold water, and always so many people around the tap that you couldn't get near it without a long wait. Even so, we resorted to drinking this water, secretly, though it tasted foul, as if contaminated. Otherwise the so-called coffee was all we were allowed to drink all through the day.

How can you believe yourself to be a human being in such conditions, when you are forced to live worse than a beast? But that was their intention. To render us subhuman.

We had not yet been assigned work. On that first day, we were trapped with hundreds of others in this stinking dark windowless cavern with nothing to do but keep hold of each other's hands.

Until lunchtime came.

Again, one big plate for five people. They called this soup. You could not tell what it was made from, and again it smelled revolting. Piri could not stomach it at all at first. None of us could eat to begin with, not just because of the food but because of the way we had to eat it, from one big dish, like animals, without even a spoon between us. Not knowing what we were eating. Not knowing what meat there might be inside.

The afternoon brought another whistle blast, another roll call. Standing in the heat to be counted for a few hours. Roll call was at least twice a day, always. When they had counted us once, they would count us again. If they didn't reach the same number twice, they would count us again. If someone had died since that morning, we prisoners would have to carry her corpse to the *Appellplatz* to be counted, as before.

And then our final meal of the day: a loaf of black bread, to be divided into five, with a smear of margarine or sometimes a spoon of something like jam, made of swede or some other root. That chunk of bread had to last until the following evening. We soon learned to save it, to eke it out. Later, I needed the precious bread ration for another purpose altogether.

At that time I think the barracks had never been more overcrowded. We crammed together on the wooden bunks as tightly as sardines in a tin, nose to tail, tail to nose. When one person turned in the night, everyone had to shift. One twitch or kick was felt by all. Every sigh or groan or sob was heard by all. Every breath you took someone else had just exhaled. I slept with René and Piri on either side of me, and cousins nearby. We were on the top layer of the three that first night, nearest the roof, where there was most space above you, and nobody could fall on you. I made sure that we always kept that advantage.

At some point on that first day, or perhaps it was even the second day, a woman came by—a prisoner-functionary with privileges perhaps? At the beginning I didn't know who anyone was, or what they could or couldn't do. She told us that she was going to the camp where they kept the families, where all the old people and the children now lived.

"Do you want to send a message? You can write to them."

Of course I did. I remember actually writing a letter to my mother. Believing she would read it. Wearing my mother's shoes on my feet, I wrote her words of reassurance.

Dear Anyuka, We are OK and I hope you are too. I'm with my sisters and I'm looking after them and we'll see you soon . . .

Something like that.

They must have given us paper and pencil. I don't know why anyone would do something so cruel. If it was some kind of joke. Or perhaps they thought to be so deceived would keep us docile or sane or simply alive for a little longer. It's inexplicable.

What did they even do with such letters?

———

I couldn't tell you exactly when I knew for certain that I would never ever see my mother again. That Bela and Berta were lost to us forever. That they would never grow up. I never spoke of it with René or Piri. It was a slow and painful realization. The pain was physical. And it was unspeakable.

July 1944

When I try to remember what I felt and thought through all this time, when I try to describe my inner experiences to anyone who wasn't there, I cannot find words. I can tell you what happened. I can't recall the sensations. I think this was what was so terrible: to be so utterly stripped of your emotions, so dehumanized, you could no longer feel. As if your own body didn't belong to you. Your own mind, even. People could survive only by not feeling anything.

So we became those people we had seen when we first arrived, spending our days wandering aimlessly from place to place. Wandering as far and as often as we could. Not thinking. Not planning. Not hoping. Not looking back. Not looking forward. Completely numb. We became automata.

I always walked with René and Piri. I didn't let them out of my sight, not for a moment. And this gave them a sense of security. It gave me a sense of purpose. This was my nature and that was their nature. As the eldest at home, I was always in charge. They listened to me. There was no discussion about what we should do, ever. Whatever I said, that was it. And so even here, if I said it would be OK, they thought it probably would be OK.

Our understanding of what was happening around us came slowly. At least we understood German: some young women from other parts of Hungary spoke neither German nor Yiddish and so they were even more bewildered than we were. I tried to help them. The Jews in striped clothes who always told us what to do, who were always hurrying us to eat faster, empty our bodies faster, wash faster, tidy our bunks faster, line up faster, the people who punished us, shouted at us, controlled our every moment, these we called the kapos. They were prisoners too, prisoner-functionaries, or *Funktionshäftlinge*, but they were also our guards, with complete power over the rest of us, day and night. They told us when to go out, come in, go to the lavatory. The Nazis always gave their dirty work to someone else. Sometimes the kapos were even more brutal than the German officers.

Every barracks had its own *Funktionshäftlinge*. A few were Hungarians, but most were Czech or Polish girls who had already been there for a couple of years, surviving by proving their brutality to others. The *Lagerältester*—the camp leader— was at the top of the kapos. In each block there was also a *Blockältester*. The female SS overseers, who were called *Aufseherinnen*, told the *Blockältester* what to do, and the *Blockältester* told us, so together they kept order. As a kapo you got more food, some privacy, maybe cigarettes and other privileges, and your job was to force others to work or to do the things the SS wanted them to do. The prisoner-functionaries organized everything. That was the system.

They could not be humans, because they weren't allowed to be . . . a human being could not survive in that role. It is true that if a kapo showed any leniency, they lost all they had gained. To become an ordinary prisoner again—that was a fate to avoid. But I think the people the Nazis chose to be kapos were usually not very nice people to begin with. They had a way of finding the nastiest individuals for these jobs, people already experienced in brutality.

This was a place where every value you had learned to live by was overturned. I had been brought up to believe that the most important thing in life was to try to be kind and fair and honest. Always. That's how it should be. Here, everything changed. The nastiest people were now at the top—people who could kill, who were cruel, who cared for nobody except themselves. And all the nice people in the world, people who in their former lives were highly respected and admired—teachers, professors, lawyers—these people were nothing. They were nobodies. Only numbers. Seeing such cruelty with your own eyes, punishment so harsh for the smallest thing . . . slowly you began to believe anything could happen.

So you learned to stay on the right side of the kapos as well as the SS guards. Best not to be noticed. Best not to meet their eyes. I tried to stay invisible. Every prisoner lived their life on a knife-edge, all the time, night and day. At any second, everything could change.

Never more so than during the selections. And these too could happen at any time.

Again we had to stand in fives. But this time it was not for counting, but to be chosen.

The overseer would suddenly order the selection, the kapos would get us in line, and when we were ready, the German officers would appear, one, two, sometimes three men, in uniform. Sometimes the Angel of Death himself. Sometimes others. And then they would begin to walk among us, inspecting every prisoner one by one, looking for something, but we never knew exactly what.

"You come," they would say.

"You come."

"You come."

"You come."

And those women would not be seen again. At first we were not sure what was actually happening. People who had been there longer explained what they knew, and it became clear to us too. Sometimes they chose the weakest, frailest prisoners. Then we understood they were selecting for the crematorium. Sometimes they chose the strongest. Then you knew they were looking for people for work. But you never knew what kind of work. To work was a privilege. The moment you were given a job to do, you knew that, for that day at the very least, you had a chance of staying alive.

One day they came for my sister René.

"You come," they said, and she went.

It happened so quickly. We were like machines by then. It didn't cross her mind to do anything else.

And so she started to go. René was already leaving our line.

No! I instantly took her hand. I didn't know what I was doing. I wasn't thinking. Her reflex was to obey, mine was to protect. I had no plan. I just grabbed her and pulled her back by instinct alone. I could not lose another sister. I couldn't let her go.

I suppose the SS guard simply expected her to follow, as everyone nearly always did. He didn't look round. He kept going as if she were behind him, and soon enough the next girl was there in her place. I suppose they didn't look at our faces as we didn't look at theirs. They were accustomed to obedience at the selections. He never knew, never noticed our defiance.

And for another day we were alive. There is no question that she had been selected for the crematorium. No question at all.

And yet it was all so quick, so unnoticeable, over so quickly, I even wondered that evening whether perhaps René hadn't actually realized what had happened. This thought was comforting. Of course, I wouldn't tell her. I didn't want her to know. I certainly didn't want Piri to know.

We didn't speak of such things.

Especially in those early weeks, when we were still with our old friends and cousins, and we had nothing yet to do, when we did speak, our conversations were nearly always on one theme. I think you can guess what this was.

When you are hungry, you think only of eating. It is on your mind incessantly. It is the one thing you cannot block out of your thoughts. So our conversations revolved around food. What would we eat when we got out of here?

We cooked in our heads. We gave each other recipes. How we made chicken *paprikash* differently from each other—with which herbs and spices, what vegetables, how much salt, boiled or roasted or stewed. How we made a salad nicely. What way we sliced an egg. One food above all others was on our minds and tongues: bread. Not even special bread, for Shabbat, or sweet breads. Just normal, ordinary bread, which we all knew how to make. Even Piri, who had hardly learned to cook, had seen how bread was made. We all used to make bread at home before the war. We talked about different kinds of bread, when and how we made it and what was special about our own bread.

The truth is that, even at home, before the war, bread was always precious to us. It's what allows a person to survive. And my mother had always taught us to be very careful when we were eating bread at table. We always had to treat it with respect.

"Never let a single crumb fall to the floor," she told us.

My sisters and brothers and I knew it was a very bad thing to tread on bread—a Jewish tradition, I believe. We would never throw bread away. I've never thrown a piece of bread away. I can't throw any food away.

Perhaps bread was also a way we could talk about home and family. It stood for something we could hardly bear to remember. How could I talk about Anyuka, or Bela or Berta? One moment they had been with me, and I was still enveloped in my mother's love, that feeling of protection so strong it made me feel invincible. The next moment she was taken away, with no chance to say goodbye. I never saw her again. And however much I tried, I could never remember what her very last words to me had been.

Between July and August 1944

So the roll calls continued. Whatever the weather, they would let us stand for hours and hours. We were like ants to them. They could step on us with as little feeling. They knew exactly how to rob us of our humanity, until we felt ourselves that we were utterly worthless. The humiliations never stopped.

I remember watching a girl of about Piri's age who was there with her mother, but her mother was weakening fast and could barely stand. Her daughter encouraged her to sit down to rest, but a kapo noticed. Immediately they were punished. Both were forced to kneel. For so long that the mother fainted. She was taken away. I am quite sure they never saw each other again.

One boiling hot day when we had already stood for hours like statues, always in lines of five, a sudden thunderstorm exploded above us. It poured with rain. On and on. And still we had to stand there, immobile. Utterly drenched, in the only clothes we had. Never complaining. Never saying a word.

And when we were finally allowed back into the barracks, hundreds of shivering unwashed people, the only way our clothes could dry was from the heat of our bodies. All that moisture slowly evaporating created an unbearable stench. The blockhouse filled with the foul-smelling steam. I remember the stink of all our wet and sweaty clothes to this day, and I can feel it now as I remember it.

People got ill just from the roll call.

"Be careful," a woman warned me one day, quietly, out of my sisters' hearing.

"What is it?" I asked. She looked so worried. The longer you had been there, the more you knew. What now?

"Your sister, Piri. She's not your twin?"

"No, no . . . I'm nearly six years older than her."

"But you look so alike. They could mistake you."

Still I didn't understand. Perhaps she didn't either, entirely, not then. But one thing clear to anyone who had been there for any length of time was that twins were more likely to disappear.

"They will take you if you're not careful."

Josef Mengele, the Angel of Death, was constantly on the hunt for twins, for his experiments. He was known to call for twins to step forward on the Ramp, when transports first arrived. It was hard to know what to do with this information, scant as it was. We could hardly alter our appearances. Though worryingly, Piri was becoming even thinner than I was.

So the selections continued. When we heard the summons, we would pinch our cheeks, as hard as we could, trying to get a bit of color, trying to look a little healthier. When Mengele himself appeared, we were so frightened we couldn't look up. Lines and lines of girls with bowed heads. In my mind now there was always the extra worry that he'd see the likeness between Piri and me.

The earliest surviving photograph of Lily and her siblings in the garden of the Engelman family home in Bonyhád. Lily is in the middle, Imi on the left and René on the right.

Lily's youngest sister, Berta, 1943, aged about eleven.

The last photo of the children together in 1943. (*Left to right*) Piri, Berta, Imi, Lily, René. Bela is missing.

Lily's mother, Nina (*top*),
and father, Ahron (*middle*).

(*Left*) Ahron's grave
in Bonyhád.

René, Lily and Piri wearing their matching dresses in Germany
in spring 1945 after their liberation by US soldiers.

Private Hyman Schulman was the assistant to Rabbi Herschel Schacter, who was one of the first Americans to enter Buchenwald concentration camp, and who organized Lily's evacuation to Switzerland after her liberation.

(*Below*) The message on a banknote that Schulman gave to Lily in 1945, and which she showed to Dov in July 2020—kicking off the events that would ultimately lead to this book.

Lily's identity card (in German and English) which was stamped and signed by the mayor of Schönberg on May 4, 1945.

(*Below*) At Weimar railway station on June 19, 1945, waiting to board the train to Switzerland and begin a new life. Lily is third from the right; the checked collar of her dress is visible.

Lily, Margot, René and Piri at Neuchâtel train station
after finally arriving into Switzerland.

The girls at the Agudah home at the Hotel Alpina in Engelberg, Switzerland.
Lily (*middle*), René (*left*) and Piri (*right*) are in the front row.

Lily's Swiss I.D. document, May 1946, in which she wears the gold cherub pendant.

The Department of Health document marking Lily's arrival in June 1946 in Haifa, Israel, which was then under British control as Mandatory Palestine.

Lily and Shmuel's wedding in 1948. Lily's wedding dress was shared between brides and René (*bottom, left*) and Piri (*bottom, right*) would both later wear it at their own weddings.

Different people were taken away all the time. And you rarely saw them again. When it was clear they were looking for more workers, everyone hoped it was for the cooking, and that they would be chosen. Prisoners made the food in the kitchens, and one way or another, anyone in a kitchen *Kommando* could get more food. And you could swap food for anything else you needed.

But they always chose the big strong girls for those jobs. You needed strength to heave the huge cooking pots, and stir such quantities of soup. We three were too tiny. Somehow our size didn't make me more fearful. My biggest fear of all was that only one of us would be taken, and not all three. I told myself that if I could manage to stay alive, my sisters would too, because I would always be there to look out for them.

One by one our cousins and friends from Bonyhád disappeared. Hilda was quickly sent to a different block. So although we had been on the same transport, I only saw her a few times in Auschwitz. Then we were separated. I thought I might never see her again, but then one day I suddenly spotted her through the electrified fence that separated the different sectors, which we also called Lagers.

"Hilda!"

We only managed to speak for a few moments. We couldn't plan to meet again, as neither of us knew what would happen to us from one minute to the next. But we kept looking out for each other.

One other time—I think it was in September—we saw each other. Just once. Just a glimpse . . . A moment of recognition and connection. And then never again.

People listened out for news of their families all the time.

Some Czech cousins from my mother's family—cousins of cousins, really—heard from someone else that we were there, quite soon after our arrival. One of them, a slightly older woman we'd never met before, came to find us to give us presents. They'd taken the Jews from her country earlier, and she'd managed to survive some time in Auschwitz already. That meant this cousin now had it just a little bit easier. She knew everyone and everything and how it all worked, officially and unofficially, and so she was able to get hold of a few more things. She came to give all three of us big handkerchiefs to tie around our heads.

You cannot imagine how special it was to have such a present in such a place. We hated our shaven heads more than anything. We felt naked with no hair. Everyone was desperate to find some kind of covering—something to make you look less strange, less inhuman, and also to protect you from the hot sun. If your dress was too long, you could use some of that. Some other sisters we knew shared out one dress—a sleeve for one sister to make a scarf, another sleeve for another.

And here was a real headscarf that was just mine, something different, something pretty. It showed there was somebody else in the world, not so far away, who cared about me, even if they didn't really know me. What a difference those scarves made. I have mine still: dark blue cotton, with a pattern of little pale sprigs of flowers. It was my very own. Someone had given it to me. I thought about that a lot.

Flowers in Auschwitz, where not even grass could grow. If there had been grass there, we would have eaten it.

Selection. Again. And again. And again.

And then at last, after some weeks, it was our turn. The

officer looked at us and paused. Numb, exhausted, we waited. And then he said the words. Three times.

"You come."

"You come."

"You come."

We were experienced enough now to tell from the type of people chosen just before us that this was definitely a selection for work, not death. What a relief it was for us all to be picked together this time. We followed the officer, all three of us, and he took us to another part of the camp altogether.

This new place was huge, much bigger than the area we'd come to on our arrival, or the place we'd then been moved into, Sector BIII. We called that the "C" Lager. Now we were to live in the "B" Lager, officially Sector BIIe.

It didn't look very different. The latrines were just as bad. It stank like the other place. It was dark and noisy and airless and full of the stench of unwashed bodies, vomit, stale urine and diarrhea. Nobody's stomach could work properly on what they gave us to eat, and when you have no control over when you can empty your bowels, your guts suffer terribly. There were just as many lice. Perhaps sometimes there were not so many girls to one bunk. Sometimes more. Again I got my girls an upper bunk. Not much, but it was something I could do for them. And I showed them I was not afraid, and this lessened their fear.

And now it was not just my sisters I wanted to protect. I had quickly adopted Margot, a young Hungarian girl who came from a village not so far from Bonyhád. Suddenly she had found herself entirely alone in this nightmare world. And that was the hardest thing of all: to be alone.

So I took her under my wing too, and we went everywhere together, all four of us. She was open and easy-going, and we all got along very well. Even though she hadn't come from a religious home, she wanted to stay with us and do what we did. Margot always came to me before she did anything, always wanted to know what I thought. She really became like a third sister to me.

I soon heard rumors about why this area was now empty. Before we came there this had been the Gypsy Family Camp, we learned. The Nazis wanted to destroy Roma and Sinti people as they wanted to destroy the Jews, completely and utterly. By the time we arrived, not many were left in Auschwitz-Birkenau. The night before we came there, I heard the last had been killed—more than 4,000 gassed and burned. Other girls told me much later they heard screams and cries that night. I remember nothing. I had learned to block out the noises all around us, the constant uproar, to separate myself from everything except my sisters and Margot. It was as though I could no longer hear.

At the new Lager, they asked us what we could do. They needed people to do all kinds of different things. Some girls could sing or dance. Some knew how to make shoes or pastries, or were skilled at metalwork. Some resorted to invention. But we knew by then how dangerous it was to lie. Though I never saw it happen myself, I had heard rumors of people who had volunteered their skills, claiming to be able to do this or that. Everyone wanted to save themselves. That much was clear . . . If you could do something, if you could give them anything at all, you had more chance of living. But if you pretended you could do a particular kind of work, and they discovered you were lying, then you were in trouble. Then they killed you.

What could we three all do? We could sew.

Some weeks in August 1944

They took us to a big room full of tables and sewing machines: the *Nästube*. There were other tailoring sections in the camp, but I didn't know that then. Nobody ever told us anything. It was one of the ways they controlled us. No information meant no power.

Our *Nästube* was a place for mending things, as well as making them from scratch. We could sit as we worked, so it was less exhausting than many jobs, and we could be together. I could still watch over René and Piri. Luckily Margot was sent to the sewing room with us. And we were all good at this kind of work, fast and efficient, though Piri was neatest of all. We spent most of our days handling men's uniforms that had come in for repair, sewing on buttons that had fallen off, mending tears in tunics, patching holes in breeches, pinning and cutting, pushing the stiff, thick fabric under a hammering needle or restitching a shirt's split seam. You could see easily what you had to do and you could do it without thinking. Sometimes we made new clothes, military and civilian.

There was always more to do, so we didn't have the fear of work running out. The room was hot, and very noisy with all the machines running . . . but the whole camp was such a noisy place all the time that the racket in the *Nästube* didn't bother us. We were together still. The supervisor kept us under close scrutiny. She was a young German woman—not a Jew. She wasn't evil, but she wasn't nice either. She always made sure we knew that she was superior to us.

Sometimes, especially when I could see that René or Piri was in a particularly bad way, I could use the time when we were working to talk, and to try to cheer them up a little. I could quietly take them home, if only in our heads.

"Do you remember Shavuot, last year?" I had been working in the field for this festival in May, while the others were in the ghetto. We had not been able to celebrate the holiday at all there.

"Oh yes, all the wild flowers," said Piri. "We picked so many."

"In the poppy field? You made such gorgeous arrangements, Piri. The house never looked so lovely," René said, almost stopping her work.

"Keep sewing," I whispered.

"Why did we never think of gathering cornflowers before last year, Lily? They looked so pretty with the white daisies."

"I suppose we always had so many flowers in the garden. But last year was like a competition, with Hilda and the others."

We had all gone to the fields together, with our friends and cousins. Shavuot—the Festival of Weeks—commemorates the day God gave the Torah to the Israelite nation, when Mount Sinai suddenly blossomed in anticipation, so each year we fill our homes and shul with greenery. We all wanted our houses to look lovely. Piri, of course, was so talented at making decorations, with flowers and fruits, ribbons and paper. She could make anything look beautiful.

"And that was the first time Bela stayed up all night."

Did we say that out loud? Or did we just think it? Remembering home was always bittersweet. I couldn't help but think of Imi too. Where was he now? Could he have any idea what had happened to us? I never stopped holding on to the hope that being in the Labor Service, not at Auschwitz, might give Imi a better chance of survival. With Piri and René, I only spoke about the good times.

When we left the *Nästube* each day, the supervisor usually checked our hands, to make sure we had taken nothing. Not every time, but often enough for us to know how careful we had to be. Needles were so precious, and also thread: with these you could repair whatever worn-out garment you had, or use a part of one thing to make another. If you had a needle and thread, you even had a chance of making underwear from another part of clothing. Any scrap of material, any piece of cloth you could get your hands on was useful for something. To be caught stealing anything was too great a risk to be worth the gain. There were so many punishments, from having your head shaved to sudden death, and you saw them happening all around, all the time, with so little warning.

There were plenty of things in the workshop that I longed to take, but at this point I didn't dare. I was already hiding my cherub necklace and my mother's earrings and rings under the heel of my foot. I never talked to anyone, not even my sisters, of the hidden treasure I walked around with every day, but I thought of it often, and of course they knew about it. At night many of us made pillows of our shoes—not for comfort, but to be sure they wouldn't be stolen as we slept. So there was nothing especially strange about the fact that I never let mine out of my sight or clutches. Knowing the jewelry was there meant so much to me. It gave me a kind of strength in the face of utter helplessness. Keeping it hidden was more than dangerous enough.

Once we'd been moved to the work block, the torture of roll calls eased a little. We endured less time standing in the sun or the rain, waiting, doing nothing, because they wanted us to get on with the work. It was always best to stay on the right side of anyone with power over you. There were dangers in being too good or too bad. You didn't want to be too eager, in case they picked you to be a *Funktionshäftling*, but disobedience meant death. I had quickly realized how useful it would be to all of us if the *Blockältester* liked me and found me helpful. And here it was a girl from my town, Babi Salomon. I'd grown up with her! How had she ended up with this job? Nobody knew. Some decisions seemed completely inexplicable.

Usually nobody liked the block elders, because they were bossy and told us what to do all the time. But whenever I could, I tidied the beds for Babi—just arranging the straw and blankets ready for any inspection, because even though we had no bedding the straw had to be nicely laid out—and I did other small jobs to help her keep the blockhouse orderly. Like that I kept her happy. If I saw something needed doing, I did it without being asked. I didn't ask her for special favors, but sometimes Babi gave me extra food, which I shared with the others. Piri in particular was growing ever frailer. I knew that not just girls but grown men could waste away to nothing with so little food. How can you live when you no longer have strength to move? It seemed there came a moment when it was too late to turn back nature. Bodies give up. We saw it happen every day.

I could not let it be too late for Piri. When they put something in the soup that turned it to glue, and made her retch too much to eat, I gave her my bread.

They must have decided we were trustworthy, because after a while, from time to time, I was ordered to work not in the sewing room, but in one of the huge storehouses they called Kanada—the *Effektenlager*. Why Kanada? Canada was for German Jews a land of hope and plenty, the place where emigrant relatives went to make better lives for themselves, and then they sent back glorious presents for those less fortunate, the left-behind.

Another world within a world. We all left our bundles of belongings on the Ramp on the day we arrived. We folded our clothes so neatly before we went into the showers. Our parents' corpses were searched for valuables before their removal to the crematorium. And every single item stolen from us was brought here to be sorted, saved, then sent on. In room after room, hundreds of prisoners labored. I never worked there very long myself. I was never in the privileged Kanada Kommando, and I never had to pick through a bag packed by someone else, some innocent unknown person imagining a completely different kind of future from the one that actually faced them. I was just sent for a few days here or there, perhaps to cover for sickness or punishments.

Warehouse after warehouse. Vast piles of clothing. Too much to comprehend. Whether rich or poor when they left their homes, people often arrived at Auschwitz in their best clothes, though they would usually be filthy after days on packed trains. Mothers wanted their daughters to look nice . . . just in case. In case of what, nobody knew. But isn't it natural to imagine that if you look just a little better than the next person, something better might happen to you?

And if you have time and can take something small and precious and hide it away before you are transported . . . Of course, you would do that too. Not money, which can become worthless overnight. Something that has value anywhere you might end up. Something that could be sold. Or just something you love because of the person who gave it to you. What Imi had done for me and for my mother, other families had done for their parents and sisters and brothers and grandparents.

One of our jobs in the sewing room was to look for hidden valuables in clothes sent over from Kanada. The Germans knew that women hid jewelry in the shoulder pads of their dresses. That was the style then. It was a very distinctive silhouette. So they told us to unpick and remove these pads from the dresses, unstitch each one, and look inside. They sent any gold or jewels that we found to Germany to be sold. And that was how they made the Jews pay for their own death camps.

By now we were in the habit of simply doing what we were told. We rarely thought beyond the moment we were in. I certainly couldn't consider who these dresses might once have belonged to, just as I couldn't think about what was happening in other parts of the camp. When you are utterly preoccupied with your own survival, and with that of those you love who are in front of your eyes, there's no time to wonder what others are going through, out of sight and earshot, even when they're in the same camp. Most days I had little time for any thoughts at all beyond those few questions which never stopped running through my head: What will happen today? Will they take us away? Will they kill us? What will happen now? How can I save my sisters? What can I do to keep us invisible? But this day was a little different. It stands out in my memory.

The four of us were working alongside each other, as usual, this time searching for gold, jewels, earrings, brooches instead of mending soldier's tunics. René, Piri, Margot and me. In fact, now we were five. I had quickly made friends with another girl in the sewing room. Henchi was a Chassidic girl from Kisvárda, so her family was more religious than ours. She also had a sister, whose name was Rivka. Henchi was a nickname—her full name was Lili Hensia Deitsch—and she was kind and open-hearted, always very straightforward and outspoken, like me. We immediately got on very well with each other. It made such a difference to make friends you could depend on, and each know there was someone else looking out for you.

As ever, the room was hot and noisy. I had unpicked pad after pad already. The same routine. Over and over again. I felt the foam cushion carefully, looked for tell-tale holes, checked the seams, turned each pocket of material inside out, put it to one side. And suddenly I found something. A dress with a diamond sewn in. A diamond! A beautiful one too, perhaps.

But not to me. More than anything at that moment, I was struck not by its worth, but its worthlessness. In my new world this diamond had no value whatsoever. Could a diamond ease my hunger? Could it even get me food? The sight of this sparkling jewel, the image of luxury, wealth and beauty, simply made me see my own wretched state more clearly: a dirty, shorn girl in a filthy, ragged skirt she'd worn for weeks, every seam of her clothing and every crevice of her body crawling with lice. The diamond meant nothing at all to me. It was just a little stone. I could have thrown it away without a second thought.

I put the dress in the checked pile. I gave the diamond to the supervisor.

Still I never talked of my own hidden treasure, the precious necklace I walked around with every day, but I thought of it often. That had a different value. It connected me with Imi, with my parents, with my past. In the face of utter helplessness, it gave me a little hope. I never saw it, but I knew it was there. And simply walking in my mother's shoes made me feel a little stronger.

Late August 1944. Maybe.

I was in the sewing room when I first noticed how sore my throat was. When I tried to swallow, it felt as though everything was closing up, and I wanted to choke. I said nothing to anyone, and hoped it would soon pass.

The room grew hotter and hotter, in waves. *It's summer*, I told myself, and bent my head over an officer's tunic. Of course it was hot. And the *Nästube* was so very airless. But my fingertips couldn't help but creep up my neck. The space under my jaw felt as swollen and lumpy to the touch as it did inside. My tongue felt strange. I began to struggle to hold my head up—my mind seemed turned to soup. I couldn't think straight.

I forced myself to keep sewing. Focus on the knot. Focus on cutting the thread. Focus on . . . It was hard to thread a needle.

René noticed sooner than I'd hoped.

"What's wrong, Lily?" she asked.

"Nothing's wrong," I told her quickly. "I'm just tired."

We were all tired, always. Hunger is so exhausting. She accepted that.

By the end of the day my throat was more painful than it had ever been before. I could get no water. Perhaps it wouldn't have helped. That night, there was no hiding my illness from my sisters. I could hardly bear the touch of their skin against mine. René didn't need to feel my forehead. She was pressed against my burning limbs.

"What are we going to do?" she whispered.

"It will be OK," I told her. It had to be OK. I couldn't leave them.

"Should you see a doctor?"

"No!"

There was a medical block in the camp, we all knew, a kind of hospital or infirmary. But not the kind of hospital where people got better. Why would they care here if you got better? Nobody really seemed to know quite what happened there. You wouldn't want to find out. My instinct was to stay away from there at all costs.

By the morning my throat and tonsils were so painful I wanted to cry out. But instead I had to stand in roll call, trying not to collapse with the effort. Evening roll call was still worse. I may even have refused food by then. I can barely remember the next days and nights.

Now René and Piri and Margot were helping me. Almost overnight I had changed from a strong, all-knowing oldest sister to a frail girl who could barely stand. I needed help to get safely in and out of our high sleeping place. I couldn't use the latrines without assistance, or wash myself. But still they tried to make me eat, made sure I was upright at every roll call, that I sat and seemed to work in the sewing room. If they realized you were sick, they killed you. Perhaps my sisters did my work for me? I really have no idea. I simply do not know how we all got through those frightening weeks, when I felt too weak even to sit, and not for a moment could I lie down and rest.

Infectious diseases spread so quickly round the camp. Most of us had dysentery. Typhus came and went, spread by lice and fleas on rats and humans. Contaminated water spread other sicknesses. Another prisoner must have seen how red my cheeks were, or noticed the strange, fine bumpy rash that crept over my body. It was scarlet fever, she told me. Perhaps it was already doing the rounds.

Eventually, my fever lessened and my throat felt calmer. I could swallow again. I could even stomach food. And then I noticed the palms of my hands. For weeks after that my fingers and toes kept peeling, shedding fragments of skin like dried glue.

What a miracle it was that my sisters and Margot didn't catch the illness from me. We were constantly together, always so close.

While I was recovering from my fever, Piri was getting weaker. She never complained or cried, because she didn't want to make us anxious about her. Soon she was so weak that it was my turn to hold her up in roll call. We had to change positions, so that René and I could keep our little sister upright between us. She was so much the youngest of the three of us, not even fifteen yet, and always the thinnest too. Perhaps she didn't have the same reserves of strength inside when we arrived. She was also the most upset and horrified by the way we had to live there, and the food we had to eat. There were times we had to force her to eat anything at all.

René was so selfless that she claimed one day not to be hungry.

"You take a piece of my bread, Piri, and you can have some too, Lily. Go on. I really don't want it today."

Of course, this couldn't have been true. This was a place where hunger was so intense that you saw mothers stealing their own daughters' bread to eat. When a person died, someone else would instantly take their food ration. It didn't seem like stealing. It could be no use to them any more. If one prisoner didn't take it, another soon would. And here was René, always trying to have a little bit less herself, so that her sisters could have a few crumbs more.

Here we saw every value our parents had carefully taught us overturned. Wrong became right. Right became wrong.

One wrong in particular.

Could death be better than life?

Temptation enclosed us. Electric fences surrounded every part of the camp. All you had to do to finish your misery was run at the nearest fence. We imagined it would be over so quickly. If you had nobody else left to live for, if you knew you were utterly alone in the world, why stay in it? We looked at the fences, and we heard their deathly whine, and inside, secretly, we all wondered. Although, thankfully, I never actually saw another girl take this final step, we heard stories about this, often. Someone would vanish. She has "touched the wire," they said. And then one day I heard that my cousin Magda, Hilda's sister, had killed herself on the fence. In one way, we were desperately sorry and sad to hear this. In another way, we felt jealous. It meant the end of Magda's suffering. Who wouldn't envy that?

In Judaism the prohibition on taking your own life is very strong. But how often I thought about it. Yes, secretly, we all thought about it, all the time. We lived with death. If the very worst happened, I was ready.

Again, I never talked of this to my sisters. As my parents had always protected me, as they had looked after me, I wanted to do the same for my sisters. Anyway, the truth is that I could never have abandoned them like that or in any other way. Never. I could never forget my promise to my father. Then or now. So I kept them alive, and they kept me alive.

And that's what made the difference to all of us. If you could help someone else when they were at their lowest, if you saw somebody else in danger and you did whatever you could for them, this kept you alive too. It meant you hadn't been defeated. If you gave up your humanity, the Nazis had won. Now I know that the worst situation can change in a split second. You can't control that change. It may be good or bad. But as long as you haven't given up, as long as you still have life, you have a chance of continuing to live.

The truth is, the world can turn upside down in less than an instant, and you may not even understand what has happened.

All these years later I still can't stop myself from returning to one such moment. That second when my mother and Bela and Berta were snatched from us, without warning. Over and over again I ask myself, what could I have done that I didn't do? What shouldn't I have done that I did do? Was there actually a way I might have kept that promise?

August or September 1944

Physically, we started to shut down quickly. Not one of the three of us ever had a period in Auschwitz. I think we were too thin even by the time we arrived. Or perhaps it was shock. We ceased to see our bodies. We could never look at our own faces or our clipped scalps. But you could not avoid seeing other people's. It made me remember that moment when we first arrived and looked at those people without hair, and wondered who they could be. And in the end, we were all just the same. And that was a terrible feeling.

Hunger took over everything. We all thought about food, all the time. That was the only thing you could depend on—if you were alive, you would feel that pain of emptiness. We took it for granted. The feeling of hunger would lessen, a little bit, perhaps, when you ate your ration, but it never went away. Hunger was the norm. It was a hunger so intense I cannot describe it. I could never make you understand.

And eventually I found there was another way to get a little more food. If you were careful, and if you were lucky, it could be done.

All the food for the kitchens was dumped in the *Lager* just outside the cooking block, for the cooks to pick up and bring inside to turn into the gruel-like soup they fed us. You could be sure that two things were in that soup, because you saw them arriving: potatoes and onions. If you could get away at exactly the right time, if you kept your eyes peeled and your wits sharp, you might be able to slip in after the vegetables had been thrown down but before the broad-armed cooks came out to get them.

For several days I kept an eye on the kitchen. I'm sure I wasn't the only one. But it was all a matter of timing. One day, just before going to the sewing room, I was lucky. I was so busy checking the coast was clear—that the lorry had driven off, that the door hadn't opened, that no guards with dogs were passing—I almost forgot about the watchtowers which kept the whole camp under surveillance from above.

Whole potatoes. Whole onions. Two great piles. Nobody would miss one or two.

I darted in, and darted back again.

Unbelievable luck. Instead of machine-gun fire, silence. Or at least only the usual hellish racket. The guard high above me must have been looking another way. I could have been shot on sight. Sometimes they killed. Sometimes they maimed. They seemed to take pleasure in wounding any captive they caught in a misdemeanor—or even just in the wrong place, at the wrong time—as if by drawing out the punishment, keeping someone longer in pain, they might deter others better.

I couldn't wait to show René and Piri and Margot. So little to share between four mouths—just a couple of hard onions, and no way to cook them. But it was food. Where to put it? The only place I could keep them safe and out of sight was in my armpit, under my dress. I was lucky to have a blouse with sleeves that were big and loose. Nobody noticed the awkwardness of how I held my arms.

Our eyes spurted tears as we ate them, secretly, in hiding. We didn't care. It was food.

"Let me try next time," said René.

"Let me," begged Piri.

But I shook my head.

"Too dangerous," I said. "You mustn't think about it."

The idea of putting my sisters in such danger. In a million years I wouldn't have let them try.

After that I did my best to get extra food whenever I could. It didn't happen very often. And sometimes my efforts backfired. Once, when we ate stolen raw potatoes, they had a terrible effect on our struggling stomachs. Maybe they were green. Maybe we just couldn't cope any longer, but the pain and diarrhea put me off stealing potatoes forever.

It wasn't just the nutrition in the stolen food that made me feel a little stronger. It was defiance. With your soul fed by a small act of resistance, even if it made no difference to anyone else, you imagined you could live for just a tiny bit longer.

Everything we wore became more ragged every week, but the biggest problem I had was under my feet. My mother's shoes had not been new when we left and they were not made for so much work, or walking all the time on stony ground. First the laces broke. I tied them together as best I could. In the sewing room I could quietly repair the stitching as it came loose. But when the heels began to wear, there was little I could do. I checked them secretly, more and more alarmed, until one evening when I took them off I knew I could not safely walk another step in them. The bottom of the shoe was almost completely broken. My secret was falling out of its hiding space.

I didn't have much time to think. René and Piri were looking at me with horror in their eyes.

"Don't worry!" I said. "I have a plan. I won't let anyone take them."

As long as I sounded sure of myself, they would be sure of me. This was how it was, always. I worked out how to survive, and then I told them what to do. And they had faith in me.

Was it then, or much later, that I noticed the mark on my cherub pendant made by Imi's nail and hammer? You can see it still, if you know where to look.

There was one place I knew my necklace would be safe. What was more precious than jewels in Auschwitz-Birkenau? What did every captive guard as closely as their lives? Their piece of bread. We watched over every crumb. In the habit of making each day's portion last as long as possible, we nibbled it only when absolutely necessary. You didn't want to finish one piece until you could be absolutely sure there would be another.

So I always kept a small piece of bread on me, tucked into my armpit somehow, to keep it safe. And after my shoes had worn out, that bread contained my necklace—my golden angel charm—and the earrings, and my mother's rings. René and Piri were the only people who knew this. Each evening, I'd find a quiet moment, push the jewelry inside the new hunk, and at last I would eat the old. It was a daily ritual.

My shoes—Anyuka's shoes—were now almost too worn out to wear, but I kept repairing them as best I could. I wanted to keep walking in my mother's shoes. I certainly didn't want to have to wear clogs. Ill fitting, crudely carved from solid wood, the clogs wore out your feet in a day. Every chisel mark and splinter rubbed against bare skin. No socks to protect you. You were soon limping. Blisters and sores could quickly become infected, oozing with pus. Then you were walking on your wounds. And clogs stopped you going anywhere fast. They stopped you going anywhere quietly. They weren't meant as shoes, but as hobbles. I was desperate to keep my shoes. I patched the soles with material. I helped Piri and René fix their shoes too.

We had arrived in summer, in suffocating heat. We couldn't measure time passing by falling leaves, or harvests. But we could tell the days were getting shorter, and we began to shiver in the icy chill of the pre-dawn roll calls, and the colder evenings. Without a kapo's privileges, with so little to eat, how long could a girl survive in this place? Four months? Five? No more than six, surely. But I don't think we were capable of making such a calculation. We couldn't think about winter coming because we had to focus all our efforts on surviving the next hour.

September 17–26, 1944

Thousands experienced what I experienced, yet everyone remembers something different. If you asked Piri what happened at a particular time, she will tell you nothing at all. I have memories so intense that I can never forget them, and others that escape me. I'll never chase them down. I can only tell you what it was like for me. What my own circumstances and my own mind and my own body and my age have allowed me to remember.

When the Hungarians arrived in Auschwitz, it meant one good thing for those Jews already captive, at least those who were still strong enough to survive the next rounds of selection: they could celebrate the Holy Days once more, and know they were saying the right prayers on the right days. For Polish and Czech Jews, without watches, without calendars, it had been impossible to keep track. At last they had a way of finding out when *Yamim Tovim* should be, because the newcomers had not yet lost track of the festivals.

The women's camp depended on the men for word in turn. And somehow, it always came. There were a few places where the fences were close enough to shout or call. Sometimes a man came to the women's barracks to do a job, to mend something. There were enough brave people to pass the messages on, or prisoners moving from one part of this vast complex to another. For many, Auschwitz meant the end of faith. And there were Jews among us, condemned because they were Jews, who barely thought of themselves as Jewish. But there were others like us who arrived with faith and whose faith stayed strong, no matter what. It was how we kept our parents alive inside us. It was what they would have expected of us.

On the very eve of Rosh Hashanah, when we barely knew what day it was, word came that it was New Year. No candles. No rabbi. No call to prayer. Anything to do with our religion was strictly outlawed. How our lives had changed since we last baked bread and cakes and honeyed things, and wished each other a sweet new year. We could no longer remember the taste of honey. This year we would not hear a shofar—the ram's horn blown in synagogue on Rosh Hashanah—and could hardly hope we ever would again.

The truth is, the Germans knew the High Holy Days better than we did. Those most important days of all in the Jewish calendar, the period around Rosh Hashanah and then Yom Kippur, were like weapons for them, when they tried to break us further. They tried to use our holiest days to prove to us that God did not choose who would stay alive and who would die. They chose. Our fate was in their hands, not God's. That meant selections. More and more of them.

This was the most relentless time for selections we had ever experienced. It never got any easier to bear, because the fear never changed: if I was taken, my sisters could not survive. If one of them were taken, I could not survive. The only way we could sustain hope and life was to stay together. And over that, we had no control at all.

On the eve of Yom Kippur, there was yet another selection.

We were not taken. Once again, the boys had sent us word that the Day of Atonement was coming. Somehow they even managed to smuggle extra food to the women the day before, to give us a little more strength to fast when night fell.

God forgives our wrongs on Yom Kippur. That is our belief, and that's why it's one of the most important days of the entire year. God forgives our wrongs and we must forgive our fellow human beings the wrongs they do against us. This was a very hard day for us in Auschwitz. We had spent so many months thinking only of the present moment, the next minute, the next hour. We had refused to let ourselves think ahead in time, to imagine the future. To keep going, we rarely allowed ourselves to look back.

That day it was impossible not to. The whole of the past year unfolded in my mind.

A year earlier, on Yom Kippur, we had all been together in Bonyhád. As usual, we had spent most of the day at the synagogue, our lovely shul, women and girls upstairs in our nicest dresses, looking down from the gallery at all our friends and families, our brothers, uncles and cousins, fasting and praying. We could see Imi and Bela down below. Bela—Benzion was his Hebrew name—was twelve years old, his Bar Mitzvah soon approaching. Imi was now far away, and could not know he'd never see his little brother again. And all I had left were my two sisters. So much had been taken.

The Yom Kippur we spent in Auschwitz, we knew we had to pray. And though we imagined we could never get hold of the correct *machzor*, the special High Holy Day prayer books, or even a *siddur*, the little books containing our daily prayers, somehow we all got a portion. I believe somebody must have smuggled out one or two of the hundreds and thousands of prayer books that had arrived with all the transports and ended up in heaps with other abandoned belongings. Then some parts of these had been smuggled into the women's section.

Not enough to go round, of course. Not nearly enough. But the flimsy pages were torn out, so they could be better hidden. Quietly, secretly, lovingly, every one of these was shared out, so that nobody in our barracks had to pass Yom Kippur without a prayer between their fingers. Maybe not the right prayer. But a prayer, nonetheless. And when we had read our own, we swapped, exchanging page for page, so that we could spend as much time as possible in prayer, even as we continued to work.

Not everyone fasted that day, of course. After all, we had been fasting every day for months already. And to go from even that little portion of food to nothing at all, that was a very dangerous thing to do. But all three of us were determined that no food or drink would pass our lips till after sunset.

A Polish man came into our section to do some repairs and I saw him eating. I was shocked. Worst of all—to my shame forever after—I could not stop myself from expressing my shock.

"Don't you know what day it is?" I asked him.

"Hungarian, you must be new here," he said to me. "If you had been here for as long as I have, you too would eat."

And that annoyed me at the time. But now, when I think back to that day, as I do on every Yom Kippur since, I feel terrible. How I wish I could apologize to him.

But that was also the day on which I made an important decision.

I had survived. So far. All that time I had survived, and so many had not, and I thought there must be some reason for this. My life could not have been preserved for nothing. My mother and my little sister and my brother could not have died for nothing. So, on Yom Kippur 1944, I made myself a promise.

If I ever came out of that place, I was determined to do

something that would change everything. I had to make sure that nothing like this could ever happen again to anybody. So I promised myself I would tell the world what had happened. Not just to me, but to all the people who could not tell their stories. And on the day I made that promise, I thought the world would listen. I thought I could do it single-handedly. Perhaps I was a little optimistic. A little naive. But I really believed it.

October 1944

Sukkot came—the Feast of Tabernacles—and we had no way to mark it. I remembered the paper chains and cut-outs we used to make each year. The *succah*—the shelter made of wood and fabric—which Imi and our father and a few friends would always build in the garden. The stuffed cabbage rolls we used to eat—*holishkes*, two together, like the two scrolls of the Torah.

The selections continued. Still we tried to be unnoticeable. Never to stand out in any way. Always to stick together as we stood supporting each other in our lines of five, day after day.

But something was changing in the war. We felt it in the atmosphere. Maybe the guards betrayed their fear somehow, and we felt it too. The sense of danger was growing stronger.

And then, for the second time, we heard the words.

"You come."

"You come."

"You come."

All three of us. We followed the officer. Walking as quickly as we could manage, and trying to look as strong as we could. As always, I held my sisters' hands. We had no possessions to gather up. I had last night's hunk of bread tucked into my armpit, my pendant safely hidden inside. We had no idea where we were going.

Our line was led back toward the area where we had first arrived, toward the Ramp and the railway track. We saw again the smoking chimney of the crematorium. And other buildings whose purpose we didn't know. This was "A" Lager.

Here we were assigned to Block 10. It looked exactly like the others we had slept in. The same windowless, wooden walls. The same rows of bunks, three layers high, but even more cramped than before. The same fetid air. The same filthy latrine blocks at the back. But I will never forget it because I associate "A" Lager, Block 10, with the number that has been written on my arm ever since. This is a place I have always imagined as literally etched into my identity.

Because not long after we were brought there, we found ourselves waiting in line for something new. This time we were made to stand in three lines. We quickly realized why. At the front of the line three women with pots of ink and pen holders, but instead of nibs, their pens had needles.

Left arm. When it came to our turn, we had to roll up our sleeves and present our left forearms.

Three tattooists were at work. They engraved our numbers onto our arms. I had been standing between my two sisters, as usual, so my number is also in the middle.

A-10572.

That was mine. René was A-10571. Piri A-10573.

Never people. Always numbers.

But the strange thing was that our tattoos gave us hope.

In July, when our transport arrived, they were killing so many of us, so quickly, they didn't even bother marking us with tattoos. And since then, more and more had been taken, or died in other ways. The fact that we were being marked now could only mean that we were worth saving for a little longer, because we were still strong enough to be useful. So the small amount of physical pain didn't bother us. As long as they could use us, we had a chance of staying alive.

But for what? For some days, this remained unclear. With nothing to keep us busy, we were back to wandering, and wondering. During that time, I was once sent to fetch something from the barracks, when I heard the noise of an approaching train. I was quite far away, but close enough to see the goods wagons pull in at the Ramp. I watched mothers and children stumbling out, just as we had done four months earlier. It was an unbearable sight, yet I couldn't tear my eyes away. This time I knew what awaited these beautiful children. That was a terrible thing to see. It's one of the things I can never forget.

Now I realize that those mothers must also have known their fate. This was one of the last transports to come from Theresienstadt, or Terezin, the ghetto north of Prague used by the SS to deceive the world. Only a few months earlier it had been dressed up to prepare for an inspection visit by the International Red Cross, who noticed nothing wrong. By the end of October, most of Theresienstadt's residents had been deported to be murdered in Auschwitz.

Hate was in the air. I watched as they tore small children and babies from their mother's arms. They knew the cruelest thing you could do was separate a mother from her child. They didn't care about the screaming, the desperate screaming. Imagine: to be a mother, and have your precious child snatched from you, the thing that is dearer to you than life, and to be able to do nothing. And then, before your eyes, they throw your baby against a wall. You are witness to your own child's murder. I saw that happen. I cannot imagine a worse pain.

———

Within a few days we returned to the same platform, the same empty goods wagons. They told us nothing about where we were going. They never communicated with us because in their eyes we were not human beings. This time we carried nothing with us at all. And the trucks were filled only with young people, only the strongest girls, about 500 of us. There were no old people left now. This time we were able to sit on the floor of the wagons more easily, for they were not so crowded. We were given only a little water, but it was cooler. Under my armpit, I clenched my precious bread and thought of Imi, and hoped the journey would not be so long that I would be forced to eat my bread.

The train took us away from Auschwitz through the countryside to Germany itself, although I discovered this only much later. At some point, I remember, the engine slowed, and I peered out through the wooden slats to try to get some sense of where we were. And to my amazement, there was a world outside. A very ordinary, normal-looking world, where nothing had changed at all, it seemed.

A young woman with a white pram was walking by. There was a baby in it. They were just walking along. As if it were an unremarkable day. It shocked me horribly. While we were going through hell, somewhere else in the world, not far away, other people had carried on living their normal lives? They had gone on getting married and having babies? They changed nappies, went shopping, cooked, ate, drank, slept, talked, worked? As if nothing was wrong at all? As if nothing had happened?

It was impossible to take this in. Even today I find it hard to understand, to put these two things together: a freight truck full of starving, vermin-infested girls in wretched clothes passing through a village where babies were born and mothers sang to them.

And then we arrived. It was clearly another prison camp, with low barracks surrounded by barbed wire, and two watchtowers. Always watchtowers. The SS officers shouted at us to line up, as usual. We were counted, as usual. But this time, a new order came:

"Hold out your hand."

Every one of us had to hold out our right hands for inspection as they passed. What could that mean?

Inside the barracks that was to be our new accommodation we found the same lines of bunks, three-layered, just as we had been used to, but these were narrower than before. How would we fit? Then we discovered that here every woman had her own bed to sleep in. We each had a straw-filled pillow and our own blanket. No more sleeping head to toe.

Not only that, but we also got our own bowl, made of white china. And a spoon that was entirely ours! Just the idea of not having to eat from a communal pot like a pack of dogs seemed incredible.

"How fantastic it is here!" Piri exclaimed.

"Come and see," called René. "Look down here. You won't believe it."

In the basement there were toilets in cubicles with actual doors. Six or seven of them. We could have privacy at last. And running water. There were showers. We could wash. Not every day, it turned out. No soap or towels, but still, what luxury! It seemed like a five-star hotel to us.

We were joining several thousand prisoners who were already working there. In fact, we soon discovered, as before, we were replacing others. Most of the women here were Polish, and the majority were political prisoners, sent from Ravensbrück a month earlier. Before us there had again been the so-called "Gypsy" women, Sinti and Roma prisoners originally from Belgium, Germany, Yugoslavia, France, Poland

and Czechoslovakia. And hundreds of other Hungarian Jews, who'd been working there for about five weeks already.

We introduced ourselves to our new companions. "This isn't so bad," we said, full of relief.

"Not bad?" they replied. "Wait until the work begins."

"Why? What is this place?" we asked, dread descending.

October 29, 1944

Of course, the relative luxury had deluded us.

We had arrived in Altenburg. Not at the little German town, lying forty kilometres south of Leipzig, but at the vast work camp they'd built some distance from normal human habitation, so that ordinary Germans could pretend it didn't exist. Auschwitz-Birkenau was a complex: a concentration camp that also became an extermination camp. But there were over 1,000 other smaller slave-labor camps in the new German empire, like this one at Altenburg, which was a subcamp of Buchenwald.

We were now imprisoned in an *Arbeitslager*. Hundreds were set up near German-owned factories to keep them supplied with forced labor. Earlier in the war the policy had been annihilation through work. Now nearly all the Jews and Roma and Sinti in Europe had been killed, and the supply of slaves, which once seemed limitless, was running out. There could be no more transports. If companies wanted the work to be done, they had to keep the slave workers alive for a little longer than before.

The Altenburg camp supplied the workforce to keep a munitions factory running. The factory was owned by HASAG—Hugo Schneider Aktiengesellschaft Metallwarenfabrik—one of the biggest arms manufacturers in Germany, and a company that had enormous contracts with the Third Reich. Demand for labor had skyrocketed since the war, and able-bodied German men were fighting at the front, so HASAG's profits depended on forced labor. HASAG liked to use women slaves because the SS charged less for us than for men. And women seemed to take longer to die. Better value all round. When workers sickened—for example, from tuberculosis, or contamination from explosives—they could be sent back to Ravensbrück or Auschwitz and replaced with fresher supplies.

Twenty-four hours a day, seven days a week, the factory kept producing infantry ammunition: bazookas and grenades and cartridges and machine-gun bullets. Shifts ran from six in the morning to six in the evening, six in the evening to six in the morning. When they had looked at our hands, they were checking to see what kind of work we had been doing already, and which section we should now work in. There was little automation. They needed the strongest girls to do the heaviest manual work. The most dangerous work, of mixing and packing explosives, was done by Jews, Roma and Sinti women.

Before we started work they disinfected us, making us strip naked and taking away our clothes. For several hours we stood around in the cold wrapped in blankets until our garments were returned. The same old skirt. Still no underwear. No socks or stockings. But no lice either now, at least for a while. We kept our worn-out shoes, so I had somewhere to hide my bread while I had no clothes. We would have to walk some way from the barracks to the factory site, perhaps fifteen or thirty minutes. It would soon be November and winter was well on its way. To our amazement, they actually gave us coats to wear, with pockets. But to be sure we wouldn't run away, they cut out a square in the back of every coat and replaced it with a different fabric. We wouldn't get far without being turned in. We were marked women.

Carefully guarded on our daily walk by SS women and their dogs, we never approached the factory through the grand entrance, with its square brick columns and deceptive sign: *Haus der Gefolschaft*. Loyalty Hall. Behind this building was a complex of smaller structures, each manufacturing a different kind of weapon, each full of people, noise and machinery. We entered these from round the back. Invisible.

At first my sisters and I were put in a weaker group.

"Over here. Sit down."

Together. That was all that mattered. We'd never seen weapons at close quarters before. Now, working in a line at a table, our job was to inspect bullet after bullet, to make sure they had all been made to the necessary standard. We had to put each one into a machine like a meat grinder, and if the bullet didn't fit, that was a reject. If the measurements weren't perfect, it would jam in the firing device. So that wasn't difficult work, perhaps, just sorting for quality control. And at first we felt quite relieved at our assignment. One thing we knew for certain: we were working. And as long as we were working, we were relatively safe, because they needed us.

But doing exactly the same thing for hours on end was unbearably monotonous. One week of nights followed one week of days. Day shifts were not quite so bad, though you had to be up at 5 a.m. for roll call, and to use the washrooms. You actually had a half-hour break for lunch. Always soup.

The night shifts were much harder than we could ever have imagined. We had arrived at Altenburg weak already, and the conditions there kept weakening us further. As each night wore on, you felt your eyelids droop with tedium and exhaustion, and your whole body wanted to sleep. We had to help each other stay awake. A nudge here. A poke there. Twelve long hours, with no food, except what you might have saved from the previous day.

Then back to the barracks, and straight away another roll call. We stood to be counted in lines of five, swaying with fatigue, and anyone who tried to sit down was beaten. Then we had a chance to wash, and then they gave us our bread ration for the day—just a few hundred grams, even less perhaps than we'd got in Auschwitz. Some margarine. Sometimes a little jam-like substance. And I would have to find a quiet moment to transfer my necklace and other jewelry. Easier now that we had toilets with doors. And somehow by then I had managed to get hold of a needle and thread, and we had also been given different clothes. So I cut a piece from my old grey Auschwitz skirt to make a tiny bag for the rings and earrings and necklace to keep them safely together.

And only then could we crawl into our bunks and try to sleep. But not for long. Because at lunchtime they'd wake us for our soup—they gave us tickets so we couldn't come back for a second bowl—and you couldn't risk sleeping through that. Always so much noise. And before long we were lining up for another roll call, and marching back to the factory in our patched coats and broken shoes or painful clogs. And the weather grew ever colder.

Margot, Henchi and Henchi's sister Rivka were all still with us, fortunately, but I can hardly remember having time to exchange a word with them when we were in Altenburg together. If you were on a day shift and someone else was on a night shift, you barely ever saw them. And although it was much, much smaller than Auschwitz, there were still several thousand women in the camp.

The best thing about my new job? It finally gave me what

I had been longing for: a chance to resist. To be a saboteur. When the trays of bullets were full, you had to take them to the storeroom: one big heavy tray for the good bullets and another for the bad ones. Each tray had fifty holes. There was a bullet in each hole. From time to time, if I knew nobody could see me, if nobody else was there, then I would quickly swap a few bullets round, good from one, bad from another.

And then I could imagine, in weeks to come, a soldier trying to load a bullet and unable to fire. In a way it was stupid. A mistake. It could hardly have made much difference to the outcome of the war, and if I'd been caught, the price would have been extremely high. I didn't mention it to anyone, ever. I didn't even tell René or Piri what I was doing. I didn't want them involved and I certainly didn't want them to try anything so dangerous.

But I needed to do it myself. I needed to feel I had done something. And it gave me strength and courage to think that, in that act of disruption, I could have saved a life or two. Perhaps I could have had some small impact for someone, somewhere. They might be living instead of dead. This meant a lot to me. Even if I was deluding myself, the hope helped keep me alive.

After three weeks or so, in late November 1944, a group of Germans came by our table toward the end of a very long night, and stared at us. It was a Friday night, if I remember rightly.

"What do they want?" René whispered, and I shook my head. I was still in the habit of avoiding attention. Whenever they looked at you, your heart beat faster. What if they had noticed my feeble efforts at sabotage? Piri was pale with fear.

She was still by far the weakest of us. I worried about her all the time.

The men looked at us, and talked among themselves, and then they went away again.

We relaxed a little. But soon they were back, still deep in discussion. Still we didn't know what they wanted. They kept looking at me. I tried to hide my uneasiness from my sisters.

Eventually, one said to me:

"You come with us!"

I had no choice. I followed the men to another part of the factory, into an area far noisier and busier. This was a different part of the production line altogether, right at the beginning of the process. It seemed they were looking for new workers to operate the equipment at the back of the factory that actually cut the steel. My heart sank right away. It really wasn't mechanized or automated at all. Yes, there were machines, but you still had to use all your strength to make these work. First the steel had to be cut in one way. Then in another. From having had it easy at the final stage of production, working in quality control, I was suddenly faced with the second hardest job of all: slicing the edges of the bullet cases to a particular width.

On the first night I worked there, it took all my strength to produce seven small bullet cases. I found it so difficult: the blades in the machine kept going blunt, or slipping out of place. But when I looked around, I realized that the bigger, stronger girls operating the same machines were managing to turn out forty or fifty bullet cases in a single shift. How could I possibly survive in this job? And what would happen to me if I failed?

Two other prisoners, a Polish man and a French man, both Jews I think, had the task of inserting the blades into the machinery in such a way that made them strong enough to cut with. They were called masters. The cutting work was so tough that the blades quickly had to be replaced. Precision was vital. Every case had to be cut to exactly the same shape and size.

I watched the *Meisters* at their work and I thought hard. This was surely something I could do. I had noticed that the supervisors here were not as harsh and brutal as they had been in Auschwitz. I suppose it made better sense to be a little kinder so that they could get more work out of us. All the more now, when supplies of slaves were dwindling.

I decided to go and put my case before the German foreman as quickly as possible. I didn't want to wait to get into trouble.

"Excuse me, sir," I said to him. I was direct. I was straight-forward. I had a nice smile. And I spoke perfect German. "I'm not very good at this new job. You can see that I'll never produce as much as you want me to."

He waited, eyebrows raised.

"But I'm quick and I'm fast at other things. I speak good German. I'm good with numbers. I would be much better at administration. Or, if you want, I could do that job, over there, monitoring the blades and replacing them."

I waited. Holding my breath. I would never have dared to speak to any German in Auschwitz in that way. It would have been madness. But here, it proved a risk worth taking. The foreman could see right away that there was no point in keeping me trying and failing at this impossible task. And luckily for me, he was a reasonable man.

"OK. Fair enough. Show me what you can do."

And that was how I was promoted. I became a *Meister* myself, and I was also given paperwork to do.

I began to understand how their systems worked. How they set people against each other to get more work out of us. In my new job, I got to know those few big girls who were so strong and efficient. Luckily, I've never been afraid to speak my mind.

And small as I am, people do seem to listen to me. I took these girls aside one day, when we couldn't be overheard.

"Listen, you really have to slow down," I said. "Can't you see what's happening?"

"Slow down?" one replied. "And miss out on the extra food they give us? You must be joking!"

"Yes, I know. And I know why they do that. But the trouble is that the quicker you work, the harder it is for the rest of us who are not so strong."

I don't think this girl had considered this before. When you're so hungry, all you think about is how to get more food.

"If you can do so much in one shift, then they think it's possible for everyone," I continued. "They demand the same from each girl here. You're just making it harder for us all."

Would she be angry? Upset? I wasn't sure. But I could see how the others were struggling. I had to say something.

She thought it over. And she slowed down.

You have to do your best to survive. Of course. But it's hard to survive alone. Your best chance of life comes from working together.

November 1944–April 1945

All the time we grew weaker, and less able to withstand our wretched situation. We helped each other fashion makeshift footwear using our blankets, and any other scraps we could get our hands on or barter for. We newcomers had formed as friendly a group as we could, given how hard we worked, and many of the girls looked to me as their leader. As I said, Margot was with us still, and another family had come with us to Altenburg, five sisters who had stuck together just as we had. Very sadly, one had fallen ill and was taken away—to the infirmary. They were able to visit her after liberation in an Allied Forces hospital in Germany, but she passed away shortly after their visit. So we all looked out for one another.

We were so tired. But still we thought it better than Auschwitz because we no longer lived with quite so much uncertainty. At least you knew in Altenburg what was likely to happen in the next hour, or the next day. Survival felt more possible. There was no gas chamber there. No selections.

And there was even some kindness to be found. One day, instead of working on the factory floor as usual, we were sent to clean another building. A middle-aged German man was put in charge of us while we worked. I didn't know who he was or what he was doing there, or even what he knew about us. But he must have felt sorry for me. I was on my hands and knees scrubbing away when he came over and told me to stop.

"You don't have to work today. Just go and sit down inside—there's a chair there."

I was frightened. What if they came back and caught me?

"Don't worry. If I see anyone coming, I'll call you and warn you. And I'll tell them you've been working."

Before I left he gave me two presents: a sugar cube and a tiny mirror. It was the first time I had seen myself since leaving the ghetto.

It was hard to persuade myself that I was looking at the face of Lily Engelman. My hair had grown back quite a bit by then, I remember. And I had a scarf to cover it, so I didn't look as awful as before. But by then I was really beyond caring. Now I think it would have been better not to have set eyes on that mirror. What good could it do to see yourself, looking so changed, when what mattered was the next meal?

Though it was easy to lose track of the days and nights, we continued to measure the passing of time by the change in temperature. The cold became ever more biting, entering our very bones. Our coats were thin, and our feet and legs cruelly exposed. The walk between camp and factory became slower and more painful as we tramped through ice and snow. Our feet and ears and fingers throbbed and ached, turning from white to blue. Even when we were inside and could warm up, we suffered from swelling and itching. The skin blistered painfully, and turned red. I couldn't cover my calves at all, and one area became very badly affected by frostbite. A patch of blisters turned to black scabs. My flesh was dying, and it would never fully recover. In cold weather, I still feel the pain of that scar even today.

My twenty-first birthday came and went and I didn't notice. For months we thought of nothing except how to get through the night. We had only one question: When will morning come?

But as the days became longer again, we realized that the course of the war really was changing. Beyond the racket of the factory, and the noises of hundreds of people living together in barracks, we heard other sounds: the roar and scream of bombing raids. Explosions shattered the nights. Anti-aircraft guns rattled. As these noises grew ever louder, drew ever closer, it became ever more difficult to sleep, by day or by night. It wasn't so bad when you were working, and sent to the bunker in the middle of a shift. But to be woken from sleep, and have to get up after such exhausting days, was very hard. And no sooner had you got back to bed and dropped off than you were jolted awake. Or roused by another girl's fearful cry. And then all you could do was lie there and listen and wonder and hope.

From February, Leipzig came under heavy attack. I discovered only later that we were listening to the Allies bombing the city, the oil refinery, the airfields. All of the enemy's industry, civilians and troops—and refugees—being destroyed together. Chemnitz was raided too. We were also right beneath the Allied flight path to Dresden, a hundred kilometres east of Altenburg. No wonder we got no rest. We had little idea of where the front line lay. We just heard the sirens repeatedly, and night after night we kept having to leave the factory and go to the bunkers and then come back again, back to work.

Between shifts, walking between camp and factory, in any free time we had, we actually began to talk about the future.

"They're getting closer! That was the loudest yet."

"Do you think the Allies will bomb the factory?"

"It's possible."

"Don't talk like that."

"If they want to destroy Germany, they have to destroy its munitions."

"But what about us?"

"Does anyone even know we are here? Does anyone know what's happening to us?"

"Does anyone care?"

"The war must be coming to an end. One of the overseers told me. Hitler is nearly *kaputt*."

"How can we get away from here?"

"I can't believe the Germans will let us survive now."

"Surely they will kill us rather than hand us over to the Americans or the Russians?"

"Shhh."

We had no real news from the outside world at all.

Were we more afraid than before? Not exactly. Although the end of the war had really begun to seem a possibility, and we could not stop thinking about this, at the same time, we simply could not work out how it might end for us. We were enemies of the Reich. Why would they let us live? Surely Germany would do anything it could to prevent us from surviving the war and from telling our stories?

It was a Thursday in April, and we went to work like every other day. My sisters and I were on a day shift. But after a few hours the lights went out, the factory doors suddenly flew open, and the order came:

"Put down your work! *Zählappell!*"

Roll call? Now? We were counted and marched hastily back to the barracks.

There they told us that the camp was to be evacuated.

"The Americans are too close. We're leaving right away. *Mach schnell!*" Make it quick!

We were miserably ill prepared. We had no time at all. One girl who had been waiting for her dress to dry had to set off wearing only her slip and a blanket. The gates were unlocked and out we marched.

The sudden release was extraordinary. Our spirits lifted. It was enough at that moment simply to know we were leaving. Did that mean our lives might still be preserved? That there was some purpose in letting us live? When you are expecting any moment to be executed, and suddenly you are on the move, it feels like freedom.

I grabbed Piri's hand on one side, and René's on the other.

April 12, 1945

More than 2,000 women and girls, on the march to an unknown destination. The entire camp emptied. The SS kept us closely guarded and told us nothing, except to keep moving. Whispers came again: we were being taken somewhere to be killed. We didn't know that for months already columns of walking corpses had been driven from place to place across the shrinking Reich.

In the third week of January, as Soviet forces advanced relentlessly across occupied Poland, the SS had cleared out of Auschwitz-Birkenau and its subcamps. Destroying evidence, abandoning those too weak to move, they evacuated the remaining 56,000 prisoners—supposedly the healthiest ones—and sent them to distant camps deep in the heart of German territory. Up to a quarter of these men, women and children were killed in this process, if not in massacres and summary executions then by exposure, exhaustion or starvation. After the war these terrible journeys became known as the "death marches."

We had no food. No water. Our footwear was quite useless by then. We might as well have had none. I'd been patching and mending and binding our feet in rags for months already, trying to keep our shoes wearable. Some girls who still had the remains of wooden clogs threw them away and went barefoot.

It was impossible otherwise to keep up the pace. It soon became clear that there would be no mercy. Weak and enfeebled though we were, if anyone lagged behind for a moment, they were shot.

I gripped my sisters' hands more tightly. Looked out for our little group as best I could.

"Help me, Margot," I called.

Piri could not walk fast enough. She could hardly walk at all. Her face was pale, and her eyes kept closing. The only way to keep her going was to march her between us, supporting her as best we could, as if she were a rag doll.

It was very frightening. We sensed the end of our ordeal must be near, but to survive even another few days felt impossible.

At some point, quite quickly I think, the mass of people must have divided. When I looked back and ahead we seemed to be a much smaller number. I learned only recently that a bigger group kept walking south, toward the Ore Mountains. Fifteen hundred women. None ever heard of again.

We began to pass through villages and small towns. It was so strange to see people who actually lived in houses. Again, that sense that the whole world had changed and yet here, for these families, life seemed almost normal. People came out of their houses and they looked at us. We looked at them. Nobody did anything to help. Nobody gave us food. Nobody gave us water. We just stared at each other, as though we were from two different planets.

Spring had come early and fast. The sky was bright blue. The sun beat down on us. We could barely carry our own debilitated bodies. How heavy our thin coats seemed now. Many girls cast theirs aside, to use what strength they had for marching. We had brought with us our bowls and spoons. But we were never given food, or water. We never stopped. We had so little energy. And it was torture to carry an empty bowl. We threw these away too. But in my pocket, in its little bag, I still had my jewelry.

The need to sleep was overwhelming. We nearly fell asleep walking. All we wanted to do was to sleep. Sleep. Sleep. Sleep. Our bodies begged for mercy. Our minds resisted.

"Try to keep marching," I told the others. "We have to keep going. We have to. It can't be far now."

Wherever we were going. . . . Yet we were still alive. We had to stay alive.

"Lily," René said to me at last, quiet and breathless. "Maybe we should disappear? Maybe the Germans won't notice, and we could just disappear?"

We hardly had time to think. To march or to run away? I tried to work it out. And all the time we had to keep going, keep going. March. March. Don't sleep. Don't sleep.

Could we just disappear?

Was there anywhere near the road we could hide?

Would anyone help us if we did?

I couldn't think straight. All I could do was move one foot in front of the other. Keep hold of my sisters. Make sure we were together.

Disappear? In the end, I was too frightened. One person could make themselves vanish, perhaps, but two, or three, or four? Or six? For how long? Who could we leave behind?

And always I thought of my promise to my father. Piri could hardly walk. How could she run away?

"Lily?" René was still waiting for an answer.

I couldn't let her doubt me.

"It's too risky," I replied. "If they see us, then we'll be shot for certain. No. We can't."

She nodded. Her faith in me was unshaken.

———

They kept us marching till nightfall. We reached a great barn, on the edge of a farm. Lots of outbuildings. Straw on the ground. It smelled of horses. Manure. No food. No water. We collapsed into straw. We were instantly asleep, almost unconscious.

Not for long. Hours before it was light, we were woken. And then we were on the move again.

That day was a Friday. We marched all morning, all afternoon. That night we slept again on straw in farm buildings. And we were woken by the scream of planes. Bombs were falling hard, not far away at all. Yet this didn't scare us in the least. We felt relief. *These are our people*, we told ourselves. *They're on our side*. It didn't even occur to us that Allied bombs could kill us just as surely as German ones. We simply didn't think of that.

The next day was the same. Marching, marching, marching. No thinking. No eating. Half sleeping. Never letting go of my sisters. Never knowing where the Germans were taking us, or why. The sky so blue. Then full of planes. And noise. We could see American planes overhead now. We even waved at them. We were so empty. So exhausted. On. And on. And on. And on. All the time, people dying on the road. If somebody sat down for a second, they were executed on the spot. But we had got so far. We had survived so much. We had to keep going. We had to. I couldn't let my sisters down now. I refused to let them stop.

And then that afternoon, as we were coming into a village or town, four loud bombs exploded very close to us. The ground shook. Sirens screeched. And Margot suddenly gasped: "They've gone!"

We looked around. Our guards had vanished. Just as we had hoped to do ourselves, they had melted away and we hadn't seen them go. We didn't dare believe it. We stumbled to a halt, expecting any moment to hear gunshots, cries of pain. But there was nothing. We were entirely alone. What had happened?

Within moments, coming out of the clouds of dust and noise and confusion, military tanks appeared, each one covered with US soldiers. Helmets. Uniforms. Jeeps, with American flags.

That was one of the happiest days of our lives. We were free. By this time only a few hundred of us remained together.

We stood and stared at the men. And they stared at us, just as bewildered. They couldn't stop staring at us. They didn't have the faintest idea what had happened to us.

We were unrecognizable as human beings, let alone young girls. Emaciated creatures, filthy, hollow-eyed, half-crazed with relief and disbelief. Headscarves. Ragged clothes. Hands like claws. Bare feet. Our skin stretched over the bones of our faces, and even when we smiled, it was probably hard to distinguish from a grimace. We must have looked like pitiful ghouls to these well-fed young men, so strong and fit, and yet also far from home. From the expressions on their faces, you would think they had driven into a column of ghosts.

And we had no way to communicate. We spoke no English. The Americans spoke no German. But we could see they all wanted to help us, to give us everything they could. Utter joy. Utter confusion. I didn't know if I wanted food or sleep more. I just wanted everything to stop.

Our liberation took place at Pfaffroda, in Saxony, a village barely five kilometres from the Czech border. The American soldiers who rescued us didn't know who we were or where we'd come from. They did their best for us. But they were used to fighting, to killing people, not taking care of them. They weren't social workers. Nobody could understand what people like us might need because people like us were unheard of. Unthinkable. The outside world still knew almost nothing about the camps.

The cry went up.

"Food! Food! Give us food!"

Out of kindness they gave us what they had. Soda and candy and chocolate. And heavy food, like corned beef. But what did they know about frail bodies, whose systems were shutting down with starvation? What did we know?

For the next few days they put us up in the village, wherever they could find a space. The soldiers organized everything, placing small groups of women either with German families or in abandoned houses whose occupants had fled from the Allied advance. We were assigned an empty property. How strange it was to be taken to a house, a real home, with rooms and furniture, wallpaper and windows. Everything in its place, except for its owners, who must have left in a hurry, and taken little.

We found it hard to eat. Our stomachs had forgotten what to do with food, we thought. Once we'd been billeted, the soldiers gave us easy things to eat, like porridge. Fortunately, we took it very slowly, and my sisters and I had never been big eaters anyway. A few days later we began to hear of deaths among our surviving friends from the factory. Later still we heard of many others who had died a few hours or days after liberation, poisoned by the food they had been deprived of for so long.

There weren't enough beds for everyone, so they put pillows and blankets on the floor for some of us. That night we lay down in safety at last. Yet we somehow couldn't find the release of rest. We listened to each other breathing, in the dark. The rhythms of our bodies refused to settle. I simply couldn't believe we were here. We were alive. All three of us. For us, the war was over. When something so extraordinary happens, whether good or bad, it's impossible to take in. Our minds were so active—humming, it seemed, with shock and amazement and happiness—that they would not let our bodies sleep.

"Are you awake, Lily?" whispered Piri.

I couldn't pretend.

"Yes."

"Can you hear something?"

I froze, and listened. Some faint knockings perhaps, and muffled conversation. The noise of footsteps on the ceiling above. Was there a room there? An attic? I didn't remember stairs in the house.

"Yes, I hear it."

"What do you think it is?"

Now we were definitely all wide awake. All terrified. Straining our ears in a silence that was not quite silent enough. Piri gripped my hand.

"I thought this place was empty. Do you think we're safe here?"

"Yes. Shh. Try to sleep. Of course the Americans wouldn't put us somewhere that wasn't safe. Go to sleep." .

In the morning we learned the truth. At first light, more strange noises roused us, and from the window we glimpsed the figures of several men, running from the house as fast as they could. In the roof right above where we were sheltering, German soldiers had been hiding all night from the Americans. It was their boots and voices that we'd heard. And though we were afraid, the truth was, they must have been even more afraid than us.

But by the time we realized this, they were gone. And we were safe.

Mid-April to early May 1945

The shock was even greater when, a few days later, the soldiers took us to a small town called Schönberg, less than an hour's walk from Pfaffroda. We were placed in another temporary home, which had more space for us, this time in the care of an aristocratic German family. Two other Hungarian friends from Altenburg were in our group, one called Adèle and another girl, whose name I no longer remember. Other girls went to other families. I don't suppose the German hosts had any more choice about this than we did.

The Americans brought us to a particularly grand house, where we were greeted politely by a mother, a father and a grandfather. Perhaps they had grown-up children somewhere? We arrived with no belongings, nothing but the ragged camp dresses we still wore, filthy and alive with lice. Suddenly we were the guests of strangers, who only weeks before had been our enemies. We were to live with them almost as if we were family.

Everything in their home was so beautiful it felt utterly unreal. We slept in real beds, with well-filled mattresses, crisp white sheets, warm soft blankets. There were paintings on the walls, curtains at the windows and carpets on the floors. Towels. But this wealthy German family only followed the orders to feed and house us. They didn't lend us fresh clothes or offer to wash our squalid garments.

That first meal was unforgettable. We couldn't believe the sight of the dining table, with its candlesticks and linen tablecloth laid with gleaming silver, fine china plates, sparkling glassware, napkins. Servants to cook and wait on us. A short time before, these women working for them had been this family's domestic slaves. And we had been lining up for a ration of thin soup from a huge pot. Now we had all been liberated, but it was a peculiar kind of freedom.

Adapting to "normal" life was very hard. We had to learn how to use knives and forks again. We had to remember that nobody would steal our food. What an unfamiliar and uncomfortable sensation it was to be able to eat your fill. We couldn't eat everything. It had been a long time since we'd been able to keep kosher, but here at last we could try, so we mostly ate vegetables. Yet we simply could not break the habit of saving a little bit of bread from every meal. We always needed to keep some bread safe. To tell the truth, I still do.

Every evening we sat down to supper with this family, and I did my best to behave as a well-brought-up guest should. All five of us girls spoke German, fortunately, and we tried our hardest to make polite conversation. But our hosts—and they were perfect hosts—still seemed like our enemies, and the fact that they were so civilized made us almost more uneasy. How could we change how we felt overnight? I remember how upsetting it was, after all that we had just been through, to see how they had been living all this time, in such luxury, and realize how little their lives had changed.

Oh, the strain of those mealtimes. The family gave so little away. All the questions you wanted to ask that had to be held inside. They never asked us anything. They claimed they knew nothing. But how could that have been true?

And we weren't the only ones eating their delicious food

with them now, so nicely served. During the war, when their usual farmhands were away at the front, this wealthy family had used slave labor to take care of their land, cows and horses, as well as their house. Their slaves were Russians or Poles, I believe. Political prisoners or prisoners-of-war. Now the German family had to treat these men and women, who had been second-class citizens to them for so long, like the human beings they were.

And the young men were excited by our arrival. Girls! And foreigners, just like them! At least they assumed an affinity. They tried to flirt, and did their best to get our attention. There was something scary about the way they looked at us. We could tell what they wanted, and it made us very ill at ease. But fortunately the German father was very strict.

"Absolutely not!" he told them. "You must keep away from the girls at all times."

And for that we were grateful.

We needed everything and we had nothing. No clothes, no belongings and no money either. The Americans took a group of us to explore a small hilltop town nearby called Waldenburg, to try to find some decent clothes. It had been the scene of a huge battle just a few days after our liberation. Now the town was a ruin. Like the German soldiers, many shopkeepers had fled. There was rubble everywhere. Shops and factories lay abandoned, with doors wide open, and sometimes windows smashed.

"Help yourselves," the soldiers told us. It didn't feel right, but we had no choice.

So we looked for shoes and underwear and hairbrushes. We weren't picky. And we found some material, a bright checked cotton in green and white—a cheerful, diamond pattern. When we got back we kept ourselves busy sewing matching dresses. One each. We wore nothing else for weeks. Anyuka would have been proud to see us, all dressed alike again. Buttons down the front. And pockets, so we always had somewhere to put a piece of bread. And my jewelry.

Now we looked a bit smarter at that grand table, although the conversation never got any easier.

Our hair grew longer and thicker and shinier. We could wash it properly at last. Our curls returned. Our bodies began to fill out a little.

It was fun getting to know the Americans when they came to visit us, and trying to speak a little English. We learned to smile and laugh. There was also some squabbling over the cigarettes and pieces of chocolate they handed out. They arranged Shabbat evenings. We could be Jewish again, freely, together. One afternoon, when it was time for the soldiers to go back to their camp, we stood in front of their jeep in our new green dresses. And we posed and joked and smiled, and one of them took photographs.

On May 4 they took us to the Town Hall, and we were given new identity papers. I have mine still. I gave my official name—Livia Engelman—and Ungaru, Bonyhád, as my place of birth.

"Date of birth?"

"Nineteen twenty-three," I said. "December the 29th."

Now I was no longer a nobody, or a number. In my hand I held a piece of paper. Stamped and signed by the mayor of Schönberg. It was typed out in German and English, although the translated words and spellings were a little strange. I could be identified.

"Miss Livia Engelman . . . was because being a Jew deported from Ungaru [Hungary] to Germany and interned in the concentration camp Auschwitz Altenburg. On the 13.4.1945 she was brought by the 'SS' to Pfaffroda and relased here by the amerikan troops. All identifikation proofs and dokuments were taken away at the concentration camp. All the authorities are kindly asked to give the utmost help."

Three days later, on May 7, Germany surrendered, unconditionally. But I have no memory of this. Did anyone even tell us?

May–June 1945

Our strange and aimless routine was soon unsettled again. Within a month, more American soldiers arrived in Schönberg. Different ones. Men from the Third Army's VIII Corps. Two days before we were freed from our death march, they had liberated Buchenwald. Now they were looking for Jews from all Buchenwald's many subcamps, and they'd heard we were here. They wanted to help us, but came with worrying news.

"The Russians are coming," they told us. "They will be the occupying force here soon. Best to get away quickly and come with us. You'll be safer in the American zone."

And they soon returned with a huge truck to take us away.

The Russians had liberated Auschwitz after we left, stumbling on the camp by chance in late January, horrified at what they found. Now they were coming to occupy the territory around Leipzig. Although they were their allies, the Jewish Americans didn't want to leave us in Soviet hands. Perhaps because we were girls. Or maybe because we were Jews. I can't say.

We were so used to being told what to do and when to do it that we didn't hesitate. And despite the luxury and comfort, we could hardly make a home with our defeated enemies. Welcoming the chance to move on, we piled happily on board the lorry. It had a big open back, with a sort of wooden fence around it, like a giant crate, and we stood up and held on tight, and lurched and probably screamed with every bump in the road. There were a lot of bumps, because we were moving through what had very recently been a war zone. The signs of destruction were everywhere. That was another shock. We were completely ignorant about what was happening in the rest of the world. News travelled so slowly. We didn't even know that Hitler had killed himself.

But where to put so many young people, such vulnerable creatures? Where could we all be safely housed, even temporarily, while we regained our strength? Nobody wanted us. We had no parents to claim us. Nobody knew where any of our family was.

We drove west for several hours, though forests, valleys and ruined villages, toward Weimar. Only when we found ourselves driving through the main gates of Buchenwald did we understand our destination. *Jedem das Seine* it says on the gates. Each to their own. We were back in a concentration camp. A *Konzentrationslager* (KZ). Buchenwald was one of the first and the largest to be built in Germany, and all types of prisoners were sent there, to die from overwork and starvation: Jews, Polish people, Slavic people, people with mental and physical disabilities, political prisoners and people alleged to be in resistance movements, Roma and Sinti people, Freemasons, homosexuals, criminals, prisoners-of-war, and people of banned faiths such as Jehovah's Witnesses and the Bahá'i. Nearly a quarter of a million prisoners from thirty or more countries. There were no Nazis there—only refugees, like us—and we entered Buchenwald freely. They called us "displaced persons." For the time being, the American troops were running the camp, and there was a rabbi there—Rabbi Schacter—to look after us.

The sight of the barracks and blockhouses and the empty *Appellplatz* was very hard to take. But luckily—perhaps because I was in charge of our little group, or because the barracks were still occupied by many of Buchenwald's former prisoners, who had nowhere else to go either—we were allocated a room in one of the houses the SS guards had lived in. So my sisters and I slept in proper beds where Germans had lived before us. We never had to sleep on a three-layered bunk again. We couldn't even see the barracks from the window as these buildings were set apart from the prisoners' camp, where so many had been killed. We couldn't see the chimney stacks of the Buchenwald crematorium.

We thought we could bear it. We told ourselves we were lucky. And yet when it came to our first meal, when they brought us soup in exactly the same enormous communal containers they'd used in Auschwitz-Birkenau, the horror returned. It was a terrible feeling. All three of us felt overwhelmed with images and memories we couldn't control. We hated being there. And yet we had no choice.

"Look," I told Piri. "This soup is very different. It smells very good. And you can eat as much as you like."

I was already concerned about our next step, although I didn't talk about this with René, Piri or Margot. I wanted them to leave the worrying to me. I had begun to grasp how bad our situation was. There were thousands here, like us, with no parents left alive and nowhere to go. Some did not even have a state that would recognize them. This crowded camp could only be another temporary stopping place.

Some girls had left Germany as soon as they could after our liberation. They just wanted to get home as quickly as possible. But I couldn't bear the thought of going back to Bonyhád and knowing that Apu and Anyuka and Bela and Berta wouldn't be there. I had little hope that Imi could have survived. I couldn't imagine returning to our empty house, and finding out what the Nazis had done to it. I couldn't think of Bonyhád as home any longer. I knew that somehow I would have to make a new home. But where?

One day the rabbi came to find me. He had news. The Swiss government had offered to take hundreds of Jewish child survivors and give them shelter. Rabbi Schacter had been charged with organizing the transport.

"What do you think? Would you and your sisters like to go to Switzerland?"

A chance of leaving Germany? Of course I said yes.

But the world still knew so little of the death factories we had escaped. The Swiss didn't understand that nearly all the young children had been murdered in the camps.

"They are only taking children under sixteen," he explained, with a meaningful look.

I nodded. I understood. We had to be on that list. There was only one way to be sure of that.

"I have a document. Could I borrow a pen?"

The piece of paper stamped by the mayor of Schönberg. Luckily, the writing on this was quite faint. Blue ink. It was not so difficult to change a 3 to a 9. Suddenly I was six years younger. My birthday was still on December 29. But now I had been born in 1929 instead of 1923.

I explained to René and Piri what we had to do. I knew I could rely on them. They always did what I said.

"You're twins, now. Understand?" It was the only way all three of us could plausibly be under sixteen.

"Yes. But when were we born?"

I thought René could pretend more easily than Piri.

"November the 12th." That was Piri's birthday. "Nineteen thirty. Nineteen thirty. Yes?"

"Nineteen thirty," they agreed. "Nineteen thirty."

"I'm fifteen," I said. "You're fourteen."

"We're fourteen." In fact, Piri was still only sixteen.

We were agreed.

Survivors from the camps and death marches were lucky to have their lives. Not one of us had papers from before the war to prove who we were or where we came from. In mid-June, a nurse from the Swiss Red Cross arrived at Buchenwald to oversee who would be allowed on this transport, and who would have to stay behind. Her name was Sister Elsbeth Kasser, and she was very strict. She set up an office in the camp buildings and all the girls and boys lined up outside to be sent into her room, one by one, for interviews. If she accepted you, she stamped a card and you took it away and that was the ticket that would get you onto the train to Switzerland. Maybe because we three were so small, she believed our story. We got our stamps. We were on our way. But there was lots of confusion and upset, for days, about who was going and who wasn't allowed to go.

And I think that must have been when the rabbi's assistant came to say goodbye to us. He was a young man from New York, who was about my age. He had a strong face, very kind eyes, and he was direct and straightforward. He spoke some Yiddish, like the rabbi, and thanks to that we could understand each other, more or less, because Yiddish isn't so very different from German. He liked me, because I wasn't shy, and I always enjoyed talking to new people.

He wanted to wish us well for the journey ahead. He was going to be coming on the train with us, but he'd have lots of children to take care of and didn't want to miss the chance to have one last talk. The soldiers had already given us prayer books, and a mezuzah—a tiny silver case containing a piece of special parchment inscribed with a prayer: the *Shema Yisrael*. We used to have them on every doorframe in our house in Bonyhád. We were still a long way from having a home, or doorways, but it made us feel that perhaps that day was a little closer. Was it then, or a little later, that I attached the little mezuzah to my pendant chain, and wore it with my angel?

"Well, this is it," said the young man, smiling. "You're nearly on your way now. Soon you can start again. A whole new life."

"Thank you so much for everything you've done for us." The American soldiers had been so kind to us. We had been with them for only a short time, but what a difference they had made.

"You're welcome. You're welcome. Now, just a minute."

He took out a pen and started to feel in his pockets. "I'm sure I've got some paper somewhere." First one pocket. Then another. No luck.

"Ah! Here we are!" he said at last, and then he laughed.

Instead of the scrap of paper he was hoping for, he'd pulled out a banknote. It was special military currency: an Alliierte Militärbehörde ten-mark note. I'd never seen one before.

He wrote ten words on it.

"A start to a new life. Good luck and happiness."

And then he signed it: "Assistant to Chaplain Schacter."

And he tried to write his name in funny Hebrew letters. Neither of us knew Hebrew very well, but it was a symbol of our shared faith and understanding.

His gift was so heartfelt and personal. It was the first spontaneous human kindness we'd experienced for a long, long time. I thanked him in the funny language we were making up—a mixture of German, Yiddish and hand signs, and I put the banknote away carefully. This was something I knew I'd keep forever. A reminder, after all the cruelty we'd endured, that people could be compassionate too. There was some hope and humanity left in the world.

Crowds of people were milling around the station yard at Weimar, all talking in different languages. A stout woman with spectacles did her best to take charge. She stood on a military tank so everyone could see and hear her. There were other people from different organizations calling out names, checking off lists—always so many lists!—handing out cards, sorting us into the right groups, shouting for quiet, blowing whistles, guiding us into place. It was quite chaotic. There were tall American soldiers in uniform and forage caps, women with berets, grown-up survivors—plenty of the men still in their striped camp shirts and trousers—as well as a few small children, bigger children, teenagers, boys and girls. Orphans from Hungary, Poland, Czechoslovakia, Romania and some who were now stateless. Everyone was chattering away and so excited. I made sure that we girls from Altenburg all stuck together.

The three of us lined up with the others, wearing, yet again, our green-and-white checked dresses. Margot too, of course. It was June by then, and so hot I had to carry my coat over my arm. Some children had suitcases or bags or little knapsacks. But some of us were travelling with almost nothing at all.

We were to get on board a German train, marked "Allied Forces," a passenger train, not a goods one. But there were more of us with tickets than could possibly fit on the wooden benches. So they started taking out the seats, piling them up outside to make room for all the orphans. There was no platform here. Shepherded by friendly soldiers, we walked along beside the rails until we got to the right carriage. We needed help to climb up onto the very high steps to get on board.

Remember, we were all very small! And the steps were a long way up.

At last we were getting on a train to somewhere we could be safe. There were windows and doors. We knew our destination. We knew they'd give us food on our journey. And water. We weren't afraid. The rabbi was with us, and also his kind assistant.

Almost exactly a year earlier we had been crushed into goods wagons at Pécs with over a hundred members of our extended family. Now we were only three. Where was Imi? What had happened to Hilda? Had anyone else survived?

The train moved very slowly through the German countryside. Children waved flags from the windows, and we sang Hebrew songs, all the songs we could remember. I couldn't wait to arrive. The journey took several days. On Friday June 22, we finally drew into the station at Saint-Louis, a French town just a few kilometres from Basel, right on the border with Germany and Switzerland. And the train stopped. And we waited. And waited.

There was a problem.

June 22–late July 1945

The Swiss nurse who had questioned us one by one was here to
check us again. Sister Kasser was furious. She didn't believe for
a moment that everybody on the train was on the original list
she had made in Buchenwald: close to twice as many had now
arrived, nearly 260 in all, and most of the stowaways looked
older than sixteen. She was convinced that Rabbi Schacter had
tricked her.

Still we waited. People leaned out of the train window to try to
find out what was going on. I did my best to reassure my group.
Rabbi Schacter didn't look any happier than Sister Kasser.

"Are they going to send us back?" some of the girls started
to ask. "They can't send us back now, can they?"

"No," I said firmly. "The rabbi won't let them. I'm sure he
won't."

Eventually, everybody got off the train. Rabbi Schacter organized a Friday night service, and I believe we slept in a rented
hall in Saint-Louis for one night. The next day, some boys went
on to France. The rest of us changed trains. And finally, finally,
we were safely in Switzerland, through Basel, and our train was
pulling into Neuchâtel, a lakeside town at the foot of the Jura
Mountains. When we got off the train, on June 23, we found
the platform caged in with chicken-wire fencing. Nurses in Red
Cross outfits and men in uniforms with notebooks stood at

the gate, writing things down as we filed through. We sat on benches while they told us what to do next.

All the worry and confusion at the border reinforced the feeling we had that they didn't really want us in Switzerland.

They didn't expect so many of us to be Jewish. They expected us to be frail and wasted away, like the skeletal victims pictured in news reports. Of course, by then we had had plenty to eat for several months. Our hair had grown. We looked just like any other girls and boys of our age. Even if we didn't feel like that inside.

Because we'd come straight from Buchenwald, they immediately put us into quarantine. They thought we might harbor diseases, and a number of the group were indeed suffering from tuberculosis, or the after-effects of typhoid or frostbite, or urgently in need of dental care. First we went to the Camp du Mail, where they made sure we were healthy enough to be released. Near Neuchâtel the Swiss Red Cross had a beautiful house called La Rochelle. About fifty of the girls were then sent there. And then at last the Jewish organizations came to find us so that they could look after us. They didn't care that we weren't small children. They understood the scale of the catastrophe.

Representatives arrived from three of these organizations: Poalei Agudat Yisrael, Hashomer Hatzair/Hechalutz and Bachad. All the groups wanted to help as many people as they could. Any hope for the future now lay with the next generation. It was important that youngsters like us, we who no longer had parents to guide us, didn't lose our connection with our faith, that we didn't forget how to be Jews. So the organizations came to La Rochelle and introduced themselves.

Really, it was up to each individual to decide who to go with, as far as I could tell, but I suppose all the groups wanted

to win followers, and all were Zionist. Hashomer Hatzair—
The Young Guard—was a secular and socialist Jewish youth
movement. The Bachad—short for Brit Chalutzim Dati'im, or
the Alliance of Religious Pioneers—was an Orthodox Zionist
organization which gave young people the practical farming
skills they needed to make Aliyah—to immigrate to the Holy
Land. The most religious of the three organizations was Agudat Yisrael, or the Agudah. I didn't know this then, but Agudat
Yisrael was founded in Poland by ultra-Orthodox Jews who
were against political Zionism because they didn't want secular
nationalism to replace the Jewish faith in any future state of
Israel. Eventually it became a political party.

By then, a lot of girls looked to me for guidance, especially
the younger ones.

"Where should we go, Lily?"

"What do you think we should do?"

"That's up to you. You have to make your own decision."

But they waited for me to decide. What did I know? There
was little interest in Zionism in the Bonyhád community. But I
did know that our faith was the most important thing for our
parents, and they would have wanted us to be in the care of the
most religious organization there.

In fact, most of the girls in our group were from very religious families—*frum*, like us. Or more so. Not everyone. As I
said, Margot was not brought up to be very observant at all. So
she was the odd one out of our little group.

"Margot," I said to her then. "You know you don't need us
any more. You'll be all right alone now if you prefer one of the
other organizations. You should go with the one that feels right
to you."

But we had stuck together all year, through so much. She
didn't want to be parted from us now, nor we from her. So we

all chose to go with the Agudat Yisrael together. In fact, just three girls went with the Hashomer Hatzair to the home they ran in Bex, in the Rhône Valley, and another eighteen girls, all either Polish, Romanian or officially stateless, were transferred to the Bachad home in Krattigen, south of Bern.

And so finally, finally, in late July 1945, we were taken somewhere we could settle, at least for a while. A place where we didn't have to worry about what the next day or next hour would bring. Where we felt cherished and safe. The Agudat Yisrael had taken over two fine hotels in a charming mountain town called Engelberg, which is still a very popular holiday resort. One "*Alijah Heim*" was for girls—the Hotel Alpina—and one was for boys—the Central Hotel. They had beautiful beds and pillows and quilts. Plenty of food. Balconies. And only two or three girls to each room.

There they did their best, very seriously, carefully and kindly, to bring us back to life, both physically and mentally. To rehabilitate us. To teach us how to be normal girls again.

We were a very close group by this time. We had already been through so much together. Not just Margot Kovacs, and Henchi, our good friend from the sewing room at Auschwitz. And Rivka, Henchi's sister—who was soon engaged to a very *frum* Swiss boy, and was the first of us all to get married. There were also Olga and Lenke Lipschitz, always known as Suri and Libou, the daughters of an important Chassidic rabbi from Kisvárda, in the far north-east of Hungary, near the Ukrainian border, where Henchi and Rivka also came from. The Lipschitz sisters were very serious, so religious: at home they would never have dressed up in the pretty Swiss national costumes we were all given—short white dresses with short, puffed sleeves and colorful pinafores and starched headdresses! The Fischer sisters, Eva and Klara, had, like René and Piri, become twins overnight in Buchenwald. Edit Bledy was the only one of us from Czechoslovakia, not Hungary, but she spoke Hungarian. Ibi Retek was from Nagyhalász. Etou Seligman was another good friend we'd known since Auschwitz who had been all alone, with no brothers and sisters. And then there was Adèle Goldmann—who had been at the grand house in Schönberg with us. She had a sister in America. Also with us were two sisters called Aranka and Susannah Basch, from another big family who were in Altenburg with us, so many girls that we used to call them "The Twelve Sisters." Not that they were all real sisters. But they were all cousins, from Máramaros, in the Carpathian Mountains.

When I think of our group now, the thing I remember most clearly is who had surviving family and who didn't. Who had a sister somewhere. Who had managed to trace a brother or a cousin still living, as Ibi had. Who was entirely alone in the world. That's what was most important to us. Brothers and sisters and first cousins. Our generation had to take care of the future. None of us had parents or grandparents any more.

We had Hebrew classes and English lessons. We went on long walks in the Alpine countryside. They arranged dances for us. We were taken on excursions. Those outings were the highlights of our week. When winter came, we went sledding.

But however good their intentions, somehow, none of this seemed to work. Inside, we felt worse and worse.

Because we had stopped. At last. All those months since our liberation, we had still been busy simply surviving, wondering what each day might bring. We had spent so long thinking only about how and where and why we might be killed, or what we would get to eat, how we could sleep, or where we might be taken the next day.

In Switzerland, we had space and time. We seemed to have everything we needed in life, and we were surrounded by extraordinary beauty and a great sense of freedom. It was a dream place. I had a room in the attic at the Hotel Alpina and each day, I could stand at our open windows or on the balcony and look out across snow-capped mountains. We breathed the purest air in the world. We were truly liberated, truly safe.

Yet it was a complicated reawakening. While our physical recovery was progressing well, and our bodies, though scarred, looked strong and healthy, our minds were not. Because only then could we begin to understand the full reality of our predicament.

When you're in the middle of a terrible situation, fortunately your brain cannot really take it in. But later, when you start to see things more clearly, when you have a little distance, you need to understand properly what it all means. You begin to ask questions. Impossible questions. Whether you're awake or whether you're asleep, they won't leave your head.

Why did they kill my mother?

I used to have a family. I had a home. I had another sister and two brothers. Cousins. Aunts. Uncles. Friends. Neighbors. Where are they all now?

Why are we here alone, in a strange country, with a strange language, with nobody we knew before?

No parents. No family. No home. No language. No belongings. No future. No past, it sometimes felt. We were nobodies and we belonged nowhere.

We had lost what was most important to us and nobody could give it back.

In Switzerland, it was like waking up to the truth. The full enormity of what had happened hit us hard and it was brutal. I remember looking around, and seeing everywhere Swiss people who really knew nothing about the war. All that time, through all those horrors, they had everything they wanted. It made us feel as though there was a wall between us and other people. We felt they could never, ever understand—how could they, when, as a neutral country, Switzerland had not even been through the war? When they had turned their backs on so many European Jews? By then we had learned a great deal more about world events. It was common knowledge that the Swiss government had sealed its borders to refugees in 1942. And too often it seemed that others didn't want to understand. If you began to say something, they turned away. They didn't want to hear.

To have suffered what we had, to have been so determined to tell the world about the inhumanity we had experienced . . . and then to discover that the world did not want to know. This was very, very hard to bear. Of course, we shouldn't forget that it was just after the war, and people had many other things to think about, even in neutral Switzerland. How could we expect strangers to understand what we had been through, or want to hear about it?

And so I felt I had to keep quiet. The promise I had made myself in Auschwitz was slowly crushed. How could I tell the truth to a world that wasn't listening? I realized I just had to try to carry on with my life as best I could, and do everything in my power to support my sisters and our little group. That was difficult enough.

This was the hardest time of all. For some of us, it was too much. A few broke down. Sister could not speak to sister about what had happened. Cousin could not speak to cousin. It was just too difficult.

Fortunately for me, there was one person in Engelberg I could talk to. A very kind Swiss woman called Berta Hertz was in charge of the girls' hotel, and looked after us all. She was

Jewish like us, and had a niece called Rosalin who was about our age. Rosalin was the first stranger in my life who really listened, who really wanted to know what had happened to us so that she could help in the best way possible. She became my best and most private friend there. We were very close. I told her everything. And somehow she knew how to respond. Just having one person who cared so much and was so concerned, who never turned away, made all the difference.

Little by little, we all began the difficult search for news of our lost families. René and Piri and I were quite desperate to know what had become of Imi. So much had happened to us three since we were separated. But what of our brother? We knew absolutely nothing about Imi's fate since the day he was taken away for forced labor, to join the *Munkaszolgálat*, before we had even left the ghetto in Bonyhád. Was there any chance that he could still be alive somewhere? If he was looking for us, how would he ever find us in Switzerland, so far away from our old home?

When we were being taken care of by the Swiss Red Cross, they explained that the International Red Cross could help people trace their relatives. They'd been doing this after wars for decades and were very experienced and had developed effective systems.

So we registered our names with the IRC. They sent letters to Hungary for us. We waited. We were not hopeful.

July 1945–June 1946

The Red Cross also broadcast the names of all the orphans from Buchenwald on the radio. Our story was on newsreels. And as a result, to our joy and astonishment, we discovered two relatives who not only had survived but were actually in Switzerland. Bella Brick was one of my father's many first cousins, younger than him, but a lot older than me, so we called her Auntie Bella. Her husband, Max, or Uncle Miksha as we knew him, was a teacher. They didn't have children themselves, but they had travelled with a niece, Dita Engelman, and were now taking care of her in their new home in Geneva.

As soon as they could, they came to visit us in the mountains. An incredible day. To see a relative from Bonyhád, people who had known us all our lives . . . We could hardly believe our eyes. And we were amazed to hear their story of survival, although it's now a famous one, and also very controversial.

Late on that Friday night at the end of June the previous year, after our mother had washed our hair and lit the Shabbat candles for us for the very last time on the sports field on the edge of Bonyhád, Bella, Miksha and Dita had boarded a train in Budapest. Half an hour after midnight, thirty-five goods wagons left Budapest, filled with nearly 1,700 passengers chosen for rescue by the Budapest Aid and Rescue Committee: Zionists, Orthodox and ultra-Orthodox Jews; rabbis, scholars, artists, farmers, industrialists, nurses. Rudolf Kasztner, the Committee's founder, who made the bargain with Adolf Eichmann, described it as a "Noah's Ark." The plan was to save Hungary's Jews from the Final Solution through ransom, and at first the Committee hoped to "buy" 10,000 Jews. "Blood for Goods." Some saw this as a form of collusion. It seems the Bricks had enough money to pay for three places on Kasztner's train. They had no idea where they were going—neither did Kasztner when the train left the station—but they knew that almost anywhere was safer than Hungary by then. It's possible they had already sent money for safekeeping in a Swiss bank. Their transport stopped at the Austrian border, and then Eichmann diverted the train to Bergen-Belsen. It finally arrived there on July 9, the same day that our own transport reached Auschwitz.

The passengers were taken to a special part of the concentration camp, called the *Ungarnlager*, the Hungarian camp, where they had little to eat, and lived crammed into a few rooms. But they could organize themselves. They even had concerts and lectures and put on sketch shows. My cousins were particularly lucky: after about six weeks, they were allowed to leave, in a group of just 300, though most of the rest of the group were trapped at Bergen-Belsen until December. Bella, Miksha and Dita arrived in Switzerland on August 18, 1944. They were saved. And they were wealthy enough to build new lives for themselves.

"Do you need any money, Lily? Here, take this," said my uncle quietly, passing me some notes.

We talked and talked. It was hard to take everything in. Auntie Bella mentioned a visit she had made to Palestine before the war, but I didn't think much about this at the time. We were just so pleased to see her. At that moment, for all we knew, they were the only living family we had left in the entire world.

I wore my necklace openly by then. When people admired it,

and asked me how I came to have such a thing, I told them the story of my clever, loyal brother Imi, who was so resourceful, who had hidden my treasure away for me so carefully. This was my last connection with my beloved brother, the best friend of my childhood. I also still had our mother's jewelry, no longer hidden. I gave each of my sisters one of the rings, and at last they felt safe to wear them.

I have worn the pendant ever since. I believe it is the only gold to enter and leave Auschwitz with its original owner.

I suppose when I told the story of my brother people guessed from the way I spoke how little expectation I had of ever seeing him again. I wasn't completely alone, I consoled myself. I had René and Piri. We three at least were all alive, and getting stronger. We would make new lives together. It could have been so much worse. But how I missed my old henchman. Unless I actually heard news of Imi's death, I was determined to keep alive a little bit of hope. It is always better to hope.

As time passed, different girls began to hear news of distant friends and families. Some good news. Some terrible.

I learned the dreadful fate of my dear cousin Hilda. After our last glimpse of each other through the fence, in September 1944, she was selected with a group of other girls from Bonyhád and they were transported to Stutthof concentration camp, built on an isolated marsh some miles from Danzig. From there 200 women had to march an hour and a half to a smaller subcamp at a place called Thorn (Torun). They lived in freezing barracks, which they never saw in daylight, as they had to march to and from their work in the pitch blackness of early morning and night. One girl, another good friend from my class at school, Sari Kuttner, could not bear to leave untended the girls who died from cold and hunger and exhaustion. Each night she went out again after work with a shovel and a prayer book. She buried my cousin Hilda one night, very late, but Hilda was so completely frozen they couldn't bend her arm to bury it. "I'm so afraid," she told her friends, "that the *Oberscharführer*'s dog will come and eat her." And then she turned back into the freezing darkness, and started again, to dig a grave that would hide Hilda's whole body.

Not one sibling was left alive from Hilda's family. Magda had killed herself in Auschwitz. Her other sisters, Borishka and Lola, died there too. Their only brother lived the longest. But having survived the camps, he died in the very last days of the war.

In April, when it was time for Passover, Berta and Rosalin and the others in charge of the two homes organized a beautiful Seder night in Engelberg for all the girls and boys from Buchenwald. They set out four or five tables, beautifully laid out with the best Passover china, and we all dressed up as nicely as we could, determined to enjoy the festival. We truly appreciated all the efforts the leaders had put in to make it special and memorable for us. Passover is a family festival which celebrates the ancient Israelites' freedom from slavery. We remember their exodus from Egypt, and gather each year to eat symbolic foods, and parents traditionally play games with their children to help them remember and retell the story. All focus is on the little ones.

But that night, in 1946, how could we help but remember our own recent persecution, enslavement and liberation? How could we not think of the homes from which we had been exiled? Every one of us saw in our minds our childhood Seders and our lost parents, and we all started crying at once.

It was a terribly sad night, but our leaders did their best to comfort us, and in the end they succeeded. They encouraged us to look forward and celebrate the fact that the worst of times was over, and now we had a future. Life could only get better, they reminded us.

Though so hard to bear at first, coming to Switzerland turned out to be the best decision I ever made in my life. Every day we felt a little bit stronger. And quite a lot safer. I even began to stop worrying so much about René and Piri. I dared to let them out of my sight. They started to make little trips on their own, visiting Auntie Bella one by one, sending postcards back to Engelberg to let me know they'd arrived safely.

And then a truly extraordinary thing happened.

One of the girls we'd been with in Germany was from Arad, a large town with a complex history: now Romanian, Arad was Hungarian until 1920, and became a major refugee center at the end of the Second World War. When we resolved to come to Switzerland, this friend had decided to go back home, to try to find her family. One day she was walking down the street when she noticed a young man who looked unbelievably familiar, though she knew they'd never met before. She was so very struck by his resemblance to me, and particularly to Piri, that she stopped to talk to him.

"Excuse me, but I think I know your sisters," she said. "I was with them in a camp in Germany. At Auschwitz to begin with, and then at a place called Altenburg."

"I've never heard of Altenburg," confessed the young man.

"Are your sisters called Lily, René and Piri? The Engelman sisters?" our friend persisted.

"Yes!" replied our astonished brother. "I'm Imre Engelman."

"I knew it!"

"When were you with them? Where are my sisters now?"

The girl shook her head. She couldn't tell him.

Still, it seemed a miracle. If either one of them had set off five minutes later or five minutes earlier, they would have missed each other. Imi had made his way to Arad because it was not far from where he'd been liberated from his Labor Service and he'd heard that from this town it was possible to get a train that would take you somewhere else, and from there you could get to Eretz Israel—the Land of Israel—or Mandatory Palestine, as it still was then. But he also knew the journey ahead would be very complicated. It wasn't easy to get into Palestine, legally or illegally. You needed help.

He was convinced that we were all dead. He couldn't face life completely alone in Hungary. He wanted to make Aliyah and by the time he reached Arad, he was on his way. Or so he thought.

As soon as Imi realized that we were alive, he changed his plans. He decided the best thing to do would be to return to Hungary and wait for us. He quickly began to make his way back to Bonyhád. But first he also asked the Red Cross to help him trace us. Happily, they were able to find our details, and eventually tell him where we now were.

And so a telegram arrived for us in Engelberg. Imi was alive and looking for us. So we had found each other again at last.

Our happiness then was overwhelming. Of course, we didn't know any of these details at first. Only later could we write to each other, and exchange our stories. But surely it meant we would see him soon, somehow?

Meanwhile, we had to start making decisions. The Swiss authorities wouldn't let refugees stay forever, not even the young Buchenwald survivors. Even though we had been invited, and there were only 370 of us in total. Six months at first. A year was the limit. So as a group we started to disperse. Adèle had heard from her sister in America. She went to join her there. A couple of girls got married to Swiss boys they had met through Agudat Yisrael, and they stayed in Switzerland. I think a few of the Buchenwald boys in Engelberg even married Swiss girls, but that didn't mean they were allowed to stay, because a woman's nationality didn't count. One couple immigrated to Australia. Just two or three made almost the most difficult choice of all, and left to return to their hometowns or villages, to see whatever remained there.

I was more convinced than ever that my new life couldn't begin in Hungary. I didn't even want to stay in Europe. No way. Not after all that had happened to my family. By then I wanted to get away from this continent completely. We had been made to feel that we didn't belong here. Was it possible that we could belong in Israel?

As I said, Zionism was not a big thing at all in Bonyhád. Although everybody talked about Israel, it was more as a distant dream or fantasy than as a real country. I certainly had no picture in my mind of Palestine. I knew almost nothing about the place at all, and had no idea what it was really like. But I knew it wasn't Europe. And that was the most important thing at that moment.

Auntie Bella was very unusual in having visited Palestine before the war. I think perhaps Miksha was more interested in Zionism than we had realized when we were children. I talked to Bella, and I also talked to Rosalin, and to her aunt Berta, they told me how the Agudat Yisrael could help us. The British, who had administered Mandatory Palestine since the Ottoman Empire lost its Middle Eastern territories after defeat in the First World War, kept a very tight control on the number of Jewish immigrants they allowed to enter legally, but the Agudat Yisrael controlled a small quota of these. The organization could help us through the whole process, filling in forms, making sure we had the right papers, arranging our travel.

It didn't feel like such a big step if we all took it together. We had encouragement from the organization that had taken care of us, as well as from our aunt and uncle. We knew by then that Imi had been on his way there when he heard the news in Arad that we three sisters were still alive. Our hope was that eventually the four of us might be reunited in Israel.

And because I wanted to go, the others wanted to come too: Margot, of course, and Etou, who also had no sisters, and the Lipschitz sisters, who were so very serious and religious, and Aranka and Sassi, the sisters from Máramaros. These girls were more like our family by then. I did my best to take care of them all.

In early June, Auntie Bella and Uncle Miksha invited us to Geneva to spend Shavuot with them and Dita, who was just a bit younger than me. It was the first Yom Tov since leaving Bonyhád that we could celebrate in shul with other members of our family. Bella cooked milky food that reminded me of home: a creamy soup with sour cherries, traditional for this festival. It was a very happy and special time.

And then, just a few weeks later, we packed our bags and said goodbye to Switzerland. I had all my paperwork. When I had my photograph taken for my Swiss Identity Certificate I was proudly wearing my little gold cherub pendant round my neck again. One day soon, I hoped, Imi would see me wearing it, and understand how important it had been to me. Next to the pendant hung the little mezuzah the Jewish American soldier had given me in Buchenwald.

I was twenty-two years old, but according to my official

documents, I was still just sixteen. Yet I felt I had led two lives already. My first life, my happy childhood in Bonyhád, had ended abruptly with the invasion of Hungary. My second life, after my mother and brother and sister were killed, was over now. It seemed miraculous to have survived the worst of times, and even more astonishing that René and Piri and Imi had done so too.

In Israel, I decided, I would begin my third life.

DOV

July 5, 2020

Ten words of hope.

At about half past eight on Sunday morning I post a tweet.

"Yesterday my great-grandma (Lily Ebert—an Auschwitz survivor) showed me this banknote—given to her as a gift by a soldier who liberated her. Inscribed, it says 'A start to a new life. Good luck and happiness.'"

I tag a few organizations that might be interested. Then I mute my phone and set off for shul with my dad. I don't usually go on a Sunday morning, but it's the first time synagogues have been open since the start of the pandemic.

A few hours later I look at my phone again. I've got 8,000 notifications on Twitter.

What?

I start scrolling through and realize that the Auschwitz Memorial Museum, which has over a million followers, has retweeted the banknote post. Messages are piling up, from complete strangers and from quite well-known celebrities too. Other European accounts involved in Holocaust education have also picked up on the tweet and they're spreading the word and sending encouragement too.

I can't believe what's happening. I want to call Lily and tell her but I can't even respond to the replies fast enough. They're so warm and supportive.

At around three in the afternoon UK time the USA wakes up. And then things really take off. As soon as the Americans start sharing, I'm really struggling to keep up. It's turning into an international hunt for the mystery soldier. This is going viral.

When I see the tweet's hit one million views, Mum and I go round to Lily's to show her all the replies. I'm getting lots of questions I can't answer, and I need her help. I also realize I should have taken photos of other things she's got—like the mezuzah she was given by an American soldier, and other pictures that nobody outside the family has seen before.

So we're sitting in her flat together, and I just keep reading out the nice messages to Safta as fast as they're coming in, and trying to reply to everyone. Lily's laughing and joking, and telling me what to say. We're all blown away by the scale of the response. It feels completely unreal.

Then someone replies with a photograph.

It's a photo of a photo: the face of a young man in a soldier's uniform. A couple of army dog tags lie over his picture. The sender's tweeted just five words, quoting the writing on the banknote: "The assistant to Rabbi Schacter."

It's 4.20 p.m. Not even eight hours have passed since I posted the original tweet.

"I think someone's found him, Safta!" I yelp. "Wait . . . hang on . . ."

HYMAN I SCHULMAN, read the dog tags. 32621927 743 44. EVA SCHULMAN (His mother? In case he died?) 225 DIVISION AV, BRKLYN, NY.

Not just a name, but his address too.

Wait a minute, I think. I'm trying to stay calm. Don't want to jump to conclusions.

"This Rabbi or Chaplain Schacter probably had loads of

assistants," I say. "How can we be sure this Hyman Schulman was actually Lily's soldier?"

And this is the weirdest part of the story. A direct message suddenly arrives from the same person on my Twitter feed, with a link to an article in the *New York Times*.

But I'm still not quite sure what to think. Because it looks like it's come from some bot account, one of those automated zombie ones that spread fake news: there's no profile picture and the name looks strange, a funny combo of letters and numbers. They've got pretty much zero followers. Also, it's a locked account, so I can't even reply. Why don't they want me to know who they are?

The newspaper story is an old one, from 2015, about Private Hyman Schulman's letters to his wife. He'd written to her forever, it seemed, and she'd written back. Loads of love letters when they were courting, aged just sixteen—my age! And then after their marriage, all through the war, when he was sent away to Europe, he'd continued writing to Sandy back in Brooklyn, almost every day. One letter begins with these chilling words: "Yesterday we visited something that you might have already read about in the newspaper or heard about over the radio. Not very far from here there is a concentration camp."

Nearly two weeks later he reveals its name: "Buchenwald, located near Weimar here in Germany."

How strange to think there was a time when hardly anybody had heard of Buchenwald. When the world had no idea what happened in Nazi extermination camps.

Rabbi Schacter was the first Jewish chaplain to enter Buchenwald, I discover. Schulman was his aide. Surely he's got to be the man we're looking for?

I begin to quiz Safta. I know about Auschwitz and Altenburg

and the death march, but I don't remember her talking much about Buchenwald before.

"That's because we were only there for a few weeks," she explains. And yes, of course she remembers Rabbi Schacter. He'd come on the train to Switzerland with them.

My anonymous correspondent has noticed something else. The Hebrew letters written on the banknote spell out something close to a transliteration of the soldier's name: "Hi Yom Shul Man." Hyman Schulman. My guess is that he didn't know that much Hebrew, but the language was an important connection between them. It probably made sense to Lily then, even if she later forgot he had done this.

"So you think this is the man who gave you the banknote, Safta?"

"Yes!"

Lily can't believe what's happening. None of us can.

I ring my grandparents. My grandma, Mum's mum, is Safta's second daughter, Bilha.

"What do you think?" I say. "How can we check it's definitely the right man?"

"Let's see if the handwriting matches up," suggests my grandfather, Julian. "Follow that link to the archive."

Hyman's correspondence with his wife lay in a box in their attic for decades. Over 6,000 pages. Hundreds and hundreds of letters, which nobody had looked through properly or sorted since they'd first arrived. The Schulmans had five children to bring up. They didn't exactly have time to read through old letters, about a past they'd both prefer to forget. It was only after Hyman died in 2013 that his wife Sandy began to re-read them. The *New York Times* article was about how an online arts hub called POBA, set up to preserve creative legacies, had recently scanned and digitized lots of the letters. POBA is how you pronounce *phowa*, a Tibetan term meaning the transformation of consciousness at death.

One of its founders, Jennifer Cohen, was a friend of Hyman's daughter-in-law, Arlene. At first Jennifer thought Hyman and Sandy's correspondence was just a great example of the lost art of letter writing, but she soon realized it was even more important as a record of historical events. And Hyman wasn't just a witness to history, but an accidental participant. So POBA decided to feature a selection of the letters on the website, along with transcriptions of key extracts.

It's strange to read something so private that's now so public. And he writes about the war with such immediacy. It makes me realize how little I know about the liberation of Germany. I'd never really thought before about what it must have been like to be a soldier suddenly discovering what remained of the abandoned camps. With no warning. No idea of the horrors they'd find. It makes me want to learn more about the liberation. But there's no time for that now. I need to be certain that we're on the right track.

Julian and I spend hours looking at Hyman Schulman's 1945 letters, comparing them with the message on the banknote from the same year.

No doubt about it. The handwriting is identical.

Lily is excited and amazed. I love seeing her so happy.

"You said twenty-four hours, Dov. We've found him in eight! Eight hours! Unbelievable."

She's sad to learn of Hyman Schulman's death.

"Shall we try and contact his family anyway, Safta?" I suggest. "See if they know anything about all this?"

And that's when our detective work really gets going.

We decide to start with Arlene. (Luckily, the *NYT* journalist mentioned that the next generation of Schulmans had dropped the "c" in their name.) It turns out she's an artist. We find a website with her name that refers to POBA so we're pretty sure it's hers.

I'm beginning to feel a bit like a stalker.

Together with Grandma Bilha, Julian and I compose a message on the contact form, explaining who we are and what's happened. And we hit send.

For Arlene and her husband, Jason, our news comes out of the blue. At first Jason isn't even convinced we're right. His father never mentioned any such encounter.

"I was deeply moved and must admit I was shaken by seeing my father's handwriting and his kind words on the banknote," Jason quickly writes back to us. He's looked at our Twitter feed and watched some of the video interviews with Lily that are on YouTube. He's certain now. "It brought back so many feelings."

Although Hyman had written faithfully to his wife, telling her as much as censorship allowed, when he came back after the war he was unwilling to talk about all the horrific things he'd witnessed.

In March 1945, Private Schulman told Sandy about a "lucky break": at the age of twenty-one, he'd managed to get the job as assistant to the Jewish chaplain of the US Third Army's VIII Corps. The chaplain's name was Rabbi Herschel Schacter, and he was also from Brooklyn. Hyman must have had some *chutzpah*: he told the rabbi he knew how to drive, and then learned on the job!

The previous December, in 1944, when Lily was working at the munitions factory in Altenburg, Hyman was engaged in savage hand-to-hand combat in the sub-zero conditions of the "Battle of the Bulge." Fought under General Patton's command, this was one of the bloodiest battles in America's history. A few months later Private Schulman and Rabbi Schacter were walking into Buchenwald together, unable to believe their eyes. Hyman had been too traumatized to share with his children any details of those difficult years. But he never forgot his work during that time, and the Jewish prisoners he and his fellow soldiers liberated.

"He carried what he saw and experienced deep inside him for the rest of his life. I can only imagine the fortitude your mother has had in order to carry her own terrible experiences and not only survive, but thrive." Jason gives us the sad news that, just a few months earlier, his mother Sandy passed away. It's his deepest regret not to be able to share this moment with her.

The following weekend, we meet on a family video call: Arlene and Jason Shulman are in New Jersey and Lily and her family in London—four generations of us in all.

"Nice to meet you!" Lily declares, beaming.

"So nice to meet you!"

"Wow! I can't believe it!"

"Neither can I!"

"How did these two little dots meet—out of millions of dots?" says Arlene. "It's such a miracle."

"Really, it's a miracle to meet you! It's the ultimate proof that the Nazis didn't win!" Lily's overwhelmed by the reunion. We all are.

"Your father showed me there was good in humanity and gave me hope for a better future," Lily tells Jason. I see Grandma Bilha wiping away a tear, and feel my own eyes pricking. "It was such a special occasion because I think really he was the first man who was kind to me. We weren't used to people being kind to us. I've looked after his note all this time because it was so special for me. Unbelievable. I wanted to keep it always."

Jason tells us more about his efforts to get his father to talk about the past, at family gatherings such as Passover.

"He was a very special man. He did a lot for people after the war. But it affected him. It affected how he was in the world, how he was with his family, and all of us."

Hyman had a tiny camera, and took photographs of what he saw. Prompted by our message, Jason had looked at these images again, and he tells us how disturbing they are. I remember his father's letter, telling his mother about the stench from the dead bodies they found, unburied corpses that were left lying around the camp.

I show Jason and Arlene the mezuzah, which Lily's also kept so carefully for so long.

We arrange to meet again, with other members of the family. Now it seems like we have an unbreakable connection. They'd seen a whole new glimpse of Hyman Schulman. So it wasn't just that *we'd* discovered more about *our* story. They had learned more about their father too.

At this point my plan is simply to use Safta's photos and clips from videos she's made in the past to make my great-grand-mother's experience more accessible. I thought social media would help people understand what she had to go through, just for being Jewish. Short clips might draw them in to longer interviews.

Everything snowballs so fast. Hyman's banknote has given me extraordinary opportunities. Our efforts to reach a wider audience with Lily's story through social media puts me in touch with leading museums and organizations devoted to Holocaust education around the world. Experts in lots of different fields come forward with advice and suggestions. We begin to get other messages on Twitter offering help. Somebody kindly explains the banknote to us. It's not Deutschmarks as I'd originally assumed, but a special currency used only in the Allied Territories after the war—AMC, or Allied Military Currency.

A journalist from *The Times* interviews Lily. The headline: "Scribbled note that gave Auschwitz survivor comfort." Suddenly she's a media sensation.

But even more life-changing is a tweet from another stranger.

After a few days, a message pops up from someone called Bashi Packer, saying that her own mother and her sisters had been on the same transport from Auschwitz to Altenburg.

"I have the transport lists," she tells us. "I've highlighted their names and other documentation for your grandmother. Let me know if she wants to see them."

Of course we want to see them!

We exchange direct messages and then emails. "I'm not so good at Twitter," Bashi tells us. It turns out she's seen a clip of Safta and me on Sky News online in America, and then found us through Twitter.

A different version of Lily's past quickly opens up. This is the official one. It's chilling, and it tells us so much.

At first Bashi shares only a few pages of two much longer documents. Lists. Five hundred women. Densely typed paperwork showing the Jewish Hungarian women transported from Auschwitz-Birkenau to the munitions factory in the state of Thuringia on October 12, 1944. One list is some kind of negative reproduction—blurry white typewriter letters on black. Name after name. Dates of birth. Number after number. Place after place. On the other list, which is slightly easier to read, there are little ticks and small corrections and scribbled notes here and there. I imagine an SS officer with a clipboard, checking the list at roll call. Five hundred young women standing, waiting to be counted. Not knowing what's going to happen to them. And nobody much older than thirty.

Bashi has marked Lily's name for us in luminous yellow. There she is on page two, eighty-eighth on the list. She's got a new number now, for this new camp. Now she's 37151. Her birthday is right, but not the year: 12.29.1924. The typist has stumbled, and misspelled Bonyhád, although for her sisters, on the next two lines, it's correct. Piri is listed under her full name, Piroska. And underneath her René. All three sisters are described as *Schneiderin*: seamstress.

Also highlighted in yellow are Bashi's mother and aunts: five Grossman sisters, all so close in age, Iren, Berta, Anna, Adel, and Ester, born in 1911, 1912, 1916, 1920, and 1921, respectively.

But actually I can't begin to take all this in because I want to show Lily. It's proof. It's evidence.

"Look, Safta! Here you are. Here's your name. And Piri's. And René's."

Now we know exactly where she was and when she arrived.

I start to read out the names on the list, and Lily lights up in recognition. Yes, she remembers the Grossman sisters. Of course. She can tell us where they slept, and how, like Lily and her sisters, they all managed to be together on one of the top layers of the wooden bunks. Other names are also familiar. We find her friend Margot, also spelled Margit. And Henchi. And other girls she'd forgotten who went to Switzerland with her. Here they all are, with their birthplaces, birthdates and camp numbers. Each one a separate life. This list is bringing back the past in a way our ignorant questions have never managed to do before. And that's when I realize just how important this kind of documentation is. All these years we've listened to Lily telling her story. Before I was even born, she recorded her testimony in interviews that are now held by the British Library and in the Imperial War Museum in London, and at the USC Shoah Foundation—the Institute for Visual History and Education in California, set up by Steven Spielberg soon after he finished making *Schindler's List*.

But despite her tattoo, and even though I've always been horrified by the way the Nazis turned Safta into a number, I'd simply never thought about the historical records which could tell us more about her life before any of us knew her. Here was a way to fit the whole jigsaw together, officially, undeniably. And in the process find out even more about Lily's history, and our own. The more we know, as a family, the less can be forgotten.

Bashi has volunteered for thirteen years at the United States Holocaust Memorial Museum in Washington. She knows how to access the documentation, where to look, what to order up. She'll guide us through the process. She's so generous with her time. So kind and helpful. We arrange to meet by Zoom to talk through her findings later in the month. But first, she sends a link to her own family's story, told by four surviving sisters from a different part of Hungary, who made different choices after liberation, but shared so much of my great-grandma's war-time history.

To me, this is another revelation. Safta's always made it clear that her story is hers alone. She can only tell what she witnessed, what she remembers. Every individual who went through Auschwitz will have a different story to tell. A different experience. A different perspective. It's important to remember this. Every number is a name. Every name a human being. Every one unique.

Reading the testimony of Bashi's mother and aunties is incredibly upsetting. I find myself shocked and tearful as I realize how utterly terrible it was in the camps. Far worse than I'd ever pictured. I can't help imagining my beloved Safta in the situations they describe.

The details the Grossman sisters gave are so much more horrific and gruesome and specific than anything Lily's ever chosen to tell us. The parallels between these two sets of sisters, always looking out for one another, keeping each other alive, really brings their histories home to me. They were there together. They all must have witnessed these appalling scenes.

Bashi's mother Esther and her sister Goldie (Iren) recall Mengele beating to death four newly arrived Polish girls after they hid under the Grossmans' bunk. Esther volunteered to carry the dead from one place to another in the hope of finding her parents in a different part of the camp. There were just so many dead people. They remember young women going mad. The constant smell of burning flesh and hair. A mother being shot as she tried to get a little soup for her child, and then her daughter being electrocuted. Esther, like Lily, had scarlet fever and nearly died, and then, when the fever broke, she and her sister Berta were selected for the gas chambers. They immediately tried to kill themselves on the electric fence—to touch the wire—but were saved by the *Blockältester*. They talk of their dreams and nightmares. Dreams of their parents. Of carrying their dying grandmother.

Safta remembers no dreams at all.

I don't think Lily deliberately hides anything. Grandma Bilha, who's a psychologist, tells me about an idea that people who've experienced profound trauma often have what you might call a "cover story"—a version of events that's truthful, but bearable to tell, and less painful for a listener to hear. I wonder if years of trying to protect her family from such traumatic knowledge have buried Lily's worst memories too deeply to retrieve. Perhaps part of her knows they're too hard to hear. She is used to talking to children. Her story has so much impact precisely because she doesn't tell you so much that you are forced to turn away from it. In a public situation, surrounded by other people, a listener can only take so much horror. And you can't help but listen to Lily.

The *Times* article sparks a global frenzy of press interest. Suddenly I'm organizing interviews with news stations around the world.

"Let's do something, Dov," Lily said to me. It was less than a week ago. We never imagined this. Sky News, CNN, the *Jerusalem Post*, Euronews, BBC World News. People are listening to the story of Lily and Hyman Schulman's ten words of hope in Australia, in Brazil, Israel—all across the world. Our Twitter followers are steadily mounting.

Toward the end of July we have another incredibly emotional meeting on Zoom: from the other side of the world, Bashi talks us through all the new documentation relating to Lily she's helped us retrieve through the United States Holocaust Memorial Museum and the Arolsen Archives, formerly the International Tracing Service. Paper monuments, as the archive describes such material. For the vast majority of those murdered, these files are their only memorials.

For Bashi, it's moving simply to hear Lily speak. Her Hungarian accent, still so strong, reminds her so much of Esther, her mother, who died in 2012.

"Yes, I remember the Grossman sisters," Lily says. "They slept not far from us. They always looked after each other. That's what made the difference. Not being alone. That's what kept us alive."

Of course, Lily's never seen the paperwork associated with her imprisonment before. She never knew what records her captors kept, or that it might be possible to find such things decades later. And there are other lists too, from after the war, of the children sent to Switzerland, records from the Swiss Red Cross and UNRRA (the United Nations Relief and Rehabilitation Administration) and USFET (United States Forces, European Theater), and also "tracing and documentation" files from the International Tracing Service. (Lily's got a T/D number too: 362779.) All the paperwork and correspondence certifying one young girl's incarceration and liberation. Where she was registered and when.

Thanks to Bashi, so much evidence comes to light and comes to life.

Between them, Bashi and Lily explain to me and Mum what it all means. We can match up Safta's memories to the historical records.

It's eye-opening for me. I hadn't realized before that the munitions factory where she was enslaved at Altenburg was part of Buchenwald. But here's a card with KL at the top—*Konzentrationslager*, or concentration camp—and "Weimar-Buchenwald" pencilled in.

"So they must have filled this in when we arrived," says Lily. "Always so efficient. So much paperwork."

"Everybody classified," says Mum.

"It's how they dehumanized us. *Häftlings-Personal-Karte*. Inmate's Personal Record. Look, it even has my address in Bonyhád." Lily points to an inverted triangle in the corner marked U. "That means I'm Hungarian."

How strange this must be for her, I think. As she talks, I can almost see her moving back and forth in time.

"'Religion: mos.'?" I'm confused.

"Short for *mosaisch*. It's what the Germans called us. Of Moses, it means."

"And 'Grund'?"

"That's the reason. The ground. For me they've written 'Polit. Ungarin-Jüden.'"

"Political Hungarian Jew?" I translate.

"I knew nothing about politics," says Lily. "They could take you because you were a Jew. They could take you because you were a communist, or socialist, or anarchist, or trade unionist. There were so many different reasons. You could be a Jehovah's Witness. Or a Gypsy—Roma or Sinti. Or homosexual. Or disabled. Or a convict. They took you if they thought you were different. Lower. But I think they hated the Jews most of all."

I'm astonished at the level of detail on this record. Lily's height—157cm. Her shape: middle. Her round face, brown eyes, full set of teeth, black hair, the languages she speaks. Her nose is "normal." Does that mean her nose doesn't look Jewish? The obsession with cataloging these physical features sickens me. This is how antisemitism works. Always marking out difference. Never seeing our common humanity.

Although Twitter has brought us all this extraordinary information, it's also bringing hate into our home. Lily's story has now touched millions of people. We've drawn attention to ourselves. Some people will always resent that. Almost every day now I wake up to antisemitic abuse and tasteless jokes about the Holocaust on my Twitter feed. As soon as I block one sender, they create a new account to send me the same material again. It's nearly always in direct messages, so that other Twitter users can't see. Why do they go to so much trouble to be hateful?

It's not as if I've never encountered antisemitism before. It's been on the rise all through my lifetime. Some people might imagine that having strangers shout "Dirty Jew" at you in the street is the kind of thing that only happened in Nazi Germany. Unfortunately it also happens right now, in London. In the area where I live, there's security outside the Jewish primary and secondary schools, synagogues and community centers, kosher shops and even just on the streets. Children in Jewish schools practice hiding under their desks in case of terror attacks. I don't know of any Jewish friends who haven't had antisemitic abuse, simply because they're Jewish. My earliest memory of antisemitism comes from when I was seven, and walking home from school with my older brother. Suddenly a blue pick-up van stopped beside us. The people inside rolled down the window and shouted abuse at us. We didn't understand why they'd picked on us but we ran home in shock.

Safta always says, "the Holocaust didn't start with actions—it started with words," and I have seen how dangerous such words can be.

I still wear my kippah without worrying about who knows my religion, on principle, but plenty of my friends are more cautious. I'm proud of my heritage, proud to be Jewish, and the important thing is for everyone to learn how education can deal with ignorance and prejudice. I like to talk about Lily's testimony whenever I can. I'm determined not to let my attackers win, in the street or online.

But I wish I could protect my great-grandma from people who use hashtags like #Holohoax. Strangers who accuse her of lying. Those who question survivors' testimonies and claim exaggeration. The cruel comments. Of course, I don't tell her. But she's seen far too much of this kind of thing in her lifetime to be naive about it.

So I take my strength from Safta.

"We have to be very strong and say it again and again: it happened," she says in one interview. "It is very important that the world should know what happened. We are only a few of us . . . Most of us are not here any longer. What will happen in a few years' time?"

My research is taking off now, and it's exciting. All this stuff nobody in the family knew before—partly because they didn't know where to look, partly because they didn't have the time. I'm finding myself almost addicted to the detective work. The more I discover, the more details I want to know. It's actually not quite like a jigsaw puzzle, because when you fill in one hole, another opens up.

I didn't know that much before about the death marches, or just how many there were, or how many thousands of prisoners forced to leave camps toward the end of the war have never been accounted for. To be honest, I didn't know that such a huge number of camps for forced labor existed right across the Third Reich. On Wikipedia, Altenburg is just one on a great long list of Buchenwald subcamps, but there's not much information about any of them.

The biggest gap in my knowledge is definitely the history of the liberation. If those US soldiers hadn't found Lily on the road and taken care of her in 1945, I wouldn't exist. Before finding the banknote, I'd never even heard of the man who was so important in Lily's story: Rabbi Herschel Schacter.

What I discover makes me want to tell everyone about him too.

On April 11, 1945, as soon as they heard that American troops had liberated Buchenwald, this Brooklyn-born rabbi and his assistant, Hyman Schulman, commandeered a jeep and drove to the camp from their HQ in Weimar to help any Jews who might still be alive.

Rabbi Schacter later said that he was "overwhelmed, stunned, terrified." Neither he nor Hyman would ever forget what they saw. As I read Schacter's description of the floor-to-ceiling lines of shelves that served for bunks, strewn with stinking straw sacks and skeletal bodies, my mind can't help but return to the shocking photographs taken by his father that Jason Shulman shared with us after our meeting. He thought that most were too horrific to send, so I've seen only a few. But I can't get those out of my head. Even now, even when I think I "know" so much more than I did, so many aspects of the Holocaust, so many specific details of what happened, remain almost impossible to confront. It's always easier to turn away.

Rabbi Schacter had no warning of what he would find at Buchenwald. And so he just stood there, overwhelmed, face-to-face with "the stark, bitter, sordid reality of Jewish tragedy."

"I looked up at those people and there I saw eyes," he said later. "They were nothing but skin and bones; they were starved, emaciated, they looked down at me out of those eyes that were haunted, crippled, paralysed with fear, with confusion. They just didn't know where they were, what was happening."

Not knowing what to say or do, he impulsively shouted out in Yiddish: "*Shalom aleichem Yidden, ihr zeit frei!*" Greetings, Jews, you are free!

He told them he was a rabbi, and they couldn't believe it. He went from barracks to barracks, repeating the words.

"I realized that these are flesh of my flesh." His father had immigrated to New York from Poland before he was born. "If my father had not caught the boat on time way back in 1903, I would have been there."

Rabbi Schacter made it his mission to find Jews like my great-grandmother in the whole region around the camp. He held religious services in the German officers' recreation hall at Buchenwald. He even officiated at marriages. He helped to resettle thousands. He organized Lily's future.

But how, exactly, and when? I know the rabbi died in 2013, the same year as Hyman, because his obituaries are one of the few sources of information I find at first about this extraordinary and passionate man. The Shulman family told us he had a son, who was also a rabbi, so I decide to get in touch with him.

Rabbi Jacob Schacter is easy to find, as he's a professor of Jewish History and Thought at Yeshiva University in New York as well as being an Orthodox rabbi. He's as pleased to hear from us as we are to find him. But there's someone else he wants us to meet. Another American scholar, Rafael Medoff, is writing Herschel Schacter's biography. He'll be able to help explain exactly how Lily ended up in Switzerland, and why she had to change her age.

My grandparents join in the Zoom call and the two professors tell us the whole story. Jacob Schacter explains that his father's big thing was trying to bring Jews back to their Jewishness. Young people especially, who no longer had parents to remind them of traditional laws and practices, people who'd been cut off from their religion, and unable to practice throughout the war.

That was why he went out in the jeep looking for Jews who'd been imprisoned in the different slave labor camps round Buchenwald, serving factories that made chemicals, explosives, aircraft, engines, bullets, bombs, grenades and railway parts.

He tried to find survivors from the different death marches. The rabbi and his colleagues searched everywhere, giving out mezuzahs and prayer books.

The Allied HQ had put Rabbi Schacter in charge of the transport to Switzerland and he was furious when Sister Kasser rejected the youngsters he'd chosen because she said they were too old, or not sick enough. He refused to leave any behind. He could see how damaged these young survivors were and wanted as many of them as possible to have a new start in life, with proper care and thoughtful rehabilitation. He didn't think it was immoral to make the fake stamps, or change their ages, or smuggle more young people onto the train. What Lily didn't know when she was waiting with her sisters and friends at the border at Saint-Louis was that the Swiss authorities wanted to send the "illegals" back to Germany. Rabbi Schacter responded by threatening to call an international press conference. He understood that the offer to take in refugee children was a political maneuver more than a humanitarian one, designed to put Switzerland in a good light. There had been a great deal of outrage about the fact that so many Jews who were fleeing Nazi persecution and sought refuge in Switzerland had died after the country sealed its borders in 1942. So the best way to get these young people into Switzerland was to make their rejection of these refugees public now.

My admiration for Herschel Schacter only grows. I'm writing down dates, figuring out exactly when Lily and her sisters moved from place to place: from Pfaffroda to Schönberg, from Schönberg to Buchenwald, from Buchenwald to Switzerland. Lily has her identity documents beside her.

But this meeting's not all about fact-checking. Again, we're feeling very emotional about this encounter, which stretches across continents and time zones and generations and decades.

Again, it's hard to hold back tears. For Rabbi Herschel Schacter's son as well as for us.

Then, out of the blue, he says: "For me to get a *brachah* from you would mean a great deal. Could you please give me a *brachah*?"

Lily's completely shocked. Actually silenced for a moment. We all are. It feels quite mystical. For a lot of people it's important to get a blessing from a Holocaust survivor. Lots of my friends have been to Safta for a *brachah*. Big rabbis give blessings in a similar way.

But for a rabbi to ask Lily . . . !

Lily smiles shyly. After an astonished pause, while Rabbi Schacter lowers his head, she replies: "You are asking for a *brachah* from me? I wish that you should be healthy and happy and carry on how you are your whole life, with good health. And *mazel*."

"Amen."

My grandpa and I decide to start searching for news coverage and pictures of Safta's journey to Switzerland. It's all a bit confusing and hard to know exactly where to look at first as it seems there were two trainloads of Buchenwald orphans. And there was actually a second Jewish army chaplain working with Rabbi Schacter to take care of them: Rabbi Robert Marcus, from New Jersey, who was with the US Air Force 9th Tactical Air Command. Rabbi Marcus looked after a different group of young refugees, who were destined for France. They'd set off from Weimar a few weeks before Lily had, travelling in a train marked with the words "*Hitler kaputt*"—Hitler is finished—in multiple languages. Very, very few Jewish children who were really young had survived Buchenwald, so this group, like Lily's, was also mostly made up of older teenagers and young men in their twenties with forged paperwork, many dressed in outfits made from German uniforms, the only material available. At one point on their journey they were mistaken for Hitler Youth. There were only about thirty boys under the age of thirteen in the group on this train that was taken to a children's home in Écouis, in Normandy, run by the OSE—the Oeuvre de Secours aux Enfants. One of the teenagers at Écouis was Romanian-born Elie Wiesel, who wrote of his experiences in a book called *And the World Remained Silent*, published in 1954. Originally in Yiddish, it was translated into English in 1960 as *Night*.

"Each time a representative of the outside world tried to approach us, we withdrew further," he wrote. "We totally refused you. We did not want your help, your understanding, your psychological tests, your charity. You entered our lives too soon; we were still in mourning."

Another seventeen-year-old said afterward, "In order to feel the liberation, it was necessary to feel, but we did not feel anything. We were not people . . . at that point we were sick. Sick in body and spirit. Everything hurt—our whole bodies hurt, and our souls hurt too."

Luckily, the documentation Bashi sent gives us precise dates. Lily and her sisters are on the UNRRA list of "Hungarian girls approved by Sister Kasser." June 19, 1945. That's when the second train loaded with orphans left Germany. So my grandpa and I start by searching this date on the website of the US Holocaust Memorial Museum. Almost immediately we come across a short clip called "Orphans of Buchenwald." It's taken from a three-hour silent film made by the US Army Signal Corps, whose soldiers documented combat operations and took images of the war that were never accessible to civilian journalists.

The first shot shows a great crowd of people standing around. And then the camera cuts to a stout bespectacled woman in uniform handing out papers. She must be calling out names. We see the backs of people's heads. A young man wearing a cap made from a striped concentration camp uniform. US soldiers are getting people into line, and moving them forward. And then I glimpse the back of a familiar checked dress, and someone walks in front of the camera, and that girl vanishes, and the camera pans on along the line, and soon we're back on the face of the woman in charge.

And then it moves back along the line of waiting children—some clearly young, others not so young. Hundreds of orphans.

And there, to our astonishment, less than a minute in, is Lily!

"Look!" I say urgently. "There! Go back!"

"Are you sure?" says Grandpa.

"I'm sure."

She's got a bandage on her face. She's talking. And the camera moves away again.

We rewind, repeatedly.

We scour the rest of the film—young women being helped down from a truck. The kind of truck that must have brought Lily from Schönberg to Buchenwald. People walking down by the railway track, because the platforms had been destroyed in the war. They're carrying suitcases, sacks and kitbags. Young boys being given a hand up onto the train. And it's over.

We look at the photographs we have of Lily and her sisters wearing the identical checked dresses they made. It's unmistakable. It has to be Lily.

"Look, Safta. You won't believe this. We've found footage of you."

She doesn't believe it.

She watches the film on my laptop. Mum and I watch her. Doubt and confusion are written all over her face. We freeze the film on her image. But still she's not convinced.

"It can't be me!" she says. "Where's René? Where's Piri? I never let them out of my sight. They were always by my side."

"But look at your dress, Safta. Look at your face!"

"How can this be possible?" she says. The truth is sinking in.

"Do you remember the cameraman?" I ask.

"No, all I could think about was getting on that train. I knew nothing was more important than being on that train with my sisters. Let me see it again."

We stare and stare at the images. And eventually she relents.

"You must be right. Incredible."

On August 4, 2020, I post a tweet showing the footage. It's such a rare thing to be able to identify Lily in the video, to see her at that point in time. To have found it so quickly is mind-blowing, as the names of individuals in the videos are almost never included in the catalog descriptions of archival footage. For the next few days, weeks, months, both Lily and I share our amazement.

"I just didn't think such a thing could be possible. It's another miracle."

In late December I contact Rabbi Jacob Schacter again. Can he point us toward any recordings of his father speaking in detail about the train to Switzerland? Being found by Rabbi Schacter, and given that opportunity, made such a difference to Lily's future life. He sends me a couple of links and wishes me lots of luck—*hatzlachah*—in my research. Yet again, my respect and admiration are strengthened. In one recording, Rabbi Herschel

Schacter holds up a photograph. I email his son again, asking about any pictures, and he sends back a brief reply, suggesting I check out another YouTube link I've not seen before.

A burst of German greets me. A train is pulling into a station. Children hang out of the window.

Überlebende aus dem KZ Buchenwald bei ihrer Ankunft in der Schweiz.

Survivors from the Buchenwald concentration camp on their arrival in Switzerland.

It's the other end of Lily's journey. This is footage from the *Swiss Weekly Film Show*, a regular news program that's now in the Swiss national archive, the Bundesarchiv. In June 1945 it was screened in cinemas all over Switzerland.

Young people are pouring off the train onto a platform. They're coming through a gate in a fence that looks almost like a cage, and they're counted and checked off as they pass through. There's a glimpse of a woman in white with glasses and a headdress—perhaps a nun or a nurse. Maybe it's Sister Kasser? Just twenty seconds in, the film camera cuts to four young women waiting behind a pile of suitcases and bags. They've changed their clothes on the journey. Now Lily's wearing a short-sleeved white-collared shirt and a dark waistcoat. But there she is again, instantly recognizable. The three sisters are in matching clothes as usual, more or less. Margot's round face appears between Lily and René. The older girls look a little worried, but Piri, who's sitting on the luggage, is leaning forward and smiling at the camera. They've arrived in Switzerland. Their new lives are beginning.

Every miraculous discovery brings me closer to Lily. Each glimpse of her in the archives brings to life another element of history: slave labor, death marches, liberation, the "displaced persons" camps. Above all, the extraordinary challenges faced by young survivors trying to start new lives, survivors who had their freedom but nothing else.

Lily's story is becoming part of me. It's hard to explain. I don't just know it; I feel it, deep inside.

I watch a recording by Rabbi Herschel Schacter made in 1992. He describes his first moments in Buchenwald, and speaks of the need to remember the life of European Jewry before the Holocaust, and to perpetuate the ideals for which they gave their lives. He insists that it's up to survivors to keep alive the truths.

"The one thing we must remember is that we must remember. We must tell the world . . . we must not let the world forget. We must continue to tell our children, and our children's children."

That was also Lily's promise to herself. But it was so much harder to fulfill than she ever imagined.

LILY

June 1946

We were the lucky ones. We arrived in Haifa with official certificates, as legal immigrants to Mandatory Palestine. Thousands
of other Holocaust survivors were meanwhile secretly making
their way from Europe to start new lives in the only country
they thought would welcome them. They came however they
could, in ramshackle ships disguised as banana boats or claiming to carry some other cargo. The very strict limits on the
numbers of Jews legally allowed into Palestine that the British
had set in the late 1930s, when persecution in Europe was intensifying every year, became ever stricter. After the Holocaust,
it became so hard to get in that the Jewish community of Palestine, the Yishuv, launched a mass illegal immigration campaign,
using an escape network called the Bricha.

One of our friends from Engelberg, a boy called Shayou Ber-
nard, accompanied us to Marseilles to see us off. After coming
all the way to the ship to say goodbye, he suddenly changed his
mind about staying in Europe and jumped on board. With no
belongings, nothing! A completely last-minute decision! I've no
idea how he got away with it, or how he managed to get into
Israel with no papers or certificate.

His timing was perfect, though. Just a few weeks after our arrival the British began a naval blockade to stop the clandestine

ships from Mediterranean ports docking in Palestine. And after that anyone caught without papers was taken to the internment camps in Cyprus. There they could wait for years in limbo, never knowing if they would finally be allowed to live in Israel or not.

Our own small vessel, the *Cairo*, was so rough and ready you'd hardly transport wood in it these days. We'd no experience of open water like this before—the only boats we'd ever been on were little pleasure craft on the Danube during day trips to Budapest. The voyage across the Mediterranean from Marseilles was a difficult journey, and we were so happy it was nearly over. Although the sea was calm, we'd all been violently sick, throwing up constantly. We couldn't bear to eat and couldn't bear to be in the cabins, so we spent all our time on deck, even sleeping under the stars. That meant we had too much sun and too little rest.

But we were young and hopeful. We didn't care, because we believed we were on our way to rebuild our lives in peace. And we knew each other so well by then, the girls and boys from Engelberg. We were like brothers and sisters. We'd supported each other through thick and thin.

The last night, Friday, we didn't sleep a wink. The sun rose bright and strong over the water, and then we saw land. The Land of Israel—Eretz Israel. We could not have been more excited. I remember how intensely blue and beautiful the sky appeared that morning as we stood on the deck, gazing at the country we'd soon call our own. We suddenly all fell silent as we took in our first impressions of our new home. It was so different in every way from everything we'd left behind. And then we burst into song—even though I really can't sing at all—singing "Hatikvah"—"The Hope"—with all our hearts:

O then our Hope—it is not dead,
Our ancient Hope and true,
To be a nation free forevermore
Zion and Jerusalem at our core.

Of course, it wasn't a national anthem then. Israel wasn't yet a nation.

The buildings took shape, growing bigger and bigger. We got ever closer to a quay that was like a bridge, and finally anchored. It was a sunny Shabbat morning. Hearing that youngsters were coming from Switzerland, people had come to the port to meet us. So we were greeted by lots of well-wishers as soon as we landed. A great welcome. So kind and warm. We felt as though we had come home.

"That's it," said René, as soon as her feet touched dry land. She'd been the sickest of us all. "I'm never ever going on a boat again."

Some people threw themselves down and kissed the ground. We all danced.

But we did have a bit of a problem. As it was Shabbat, we couldn't carry our belongings, but the boat was going on to Egypt. So they put everything from the ship in a place in the port to keep it safe for us until we could collect it the next day. Amazingly, among the people who'd come to meet us was a Hungarian family originally from Bonyhád. They invited us to spend Shabbat with them, just the three of us, and urged us to be their guests anytime we came back to Haifa.

On the Sunday, we went back to the port offices to collect our bags and sort out the paperwork. In the Quarantine section, we all lined up for smallpox vaccinations. I came away with a certificate, stamped in English, marking me out as

"IMMIGRANT," under "SPECIAL OBSERVATION." The date of my arrival was June 22, 1946. I had a new number: 5109. Now I see that I was supposed to report to a Health Office within twenty-four hours of arrival, and again on the third and fifth days, but there's nothing marked in the chart to show this ever happened.

It seemed at first that everywhere we went people were waiting for us, ready to help. We didn't have to organize anything. Somebody else had sorted it out. So on Sunday we travelled in a bus down the coast to Tel Aviv. Here we were welcomed by relatives of one of the boys we'd come from Switzerland with: the Schechters, a big leather-manufacturing family. They took quite a few girls and boys into their home in Rechov Aliyah, and they let us stay for a few days while we decided where to go next. There weren't enough beds, of course, so we slept on the floor. They made us comfortable with pillows and blankets, fed us and altogether took great care of us. We were exhausted but full of anticipation. A new beginning at last.

What now? Once again, we had arrived in a strange country, without money, without family and without a language. It was not just a strange country; it was also a very young and very poor country. We had not the faintest idea what life in Israel would be like.

Still, like so many of our generation, we arrived full of ideals and optimism. We wanted to help build the country in any way we could. The obvious way to do this was to join a kibbutz: a community and home you can choose for yourself. The whole idea is that everything is fair and equal, and everyone works together to help each other: it's a way of life based on co-operation and shared resources. For the last two years we'd survived thanks to an instinctive kind of mutual aid. Now we thought we should join a settlement based on that principle.

But which kibbutz to choose? The earliest kibbutzim were socialist and Zionist utopias, and many were secular. The Agudat Yisrael, the Orthodox organization that had looked after us in Switzerland, and helped us get to Palestine, had recently been involved in setting up a new kibbutz in the Judean foothills called Hafetz Haim. The community there was more religious than most, so we thought it would suit us well. Most of the people who'd been there from the beginning were German Jews, young pioneers who were very committed. The kibbutz sent a bus to pick us up, twelve boys and girls altogether, including Margot, Aranka and Sassi and quite a number of others in the group from Máramaros we used to call the Twelve Sisters.

It was a lovely feeling, that sense of belonging. It was the first time we'd truly experienced it since leaving Bonyhád. But we found life on the kibbutz far from easy. It was hard to get used to the heat. Of course, we couldn't speak Hebrew yet. And when they showed us where we were to live, we were astonished.

This was a very poor kibbutz, in its very first year in a new location. There were hardly any buildings finished at this point, so we slept in tents—big white canvas bell tents, with nothing inside except for rows of beds. The bathrooms were far away in a wooden shed. The whole area was fenced, and there was a big dining hall which also served as our shul, but everything was very basic: no tablecloths, crude cutlery and plates, no comforts at all, really.

Half the day we worked for the kibbutz and half the day we worked on our Jewish studies and practiced our Hebrew.

In the mornings we girls usually worked in the kitchen: washing up, chopping vegetables, peeling potatoes. But sometimes they put me in charge of the little children, for on a kibbutz even parenting was then a collective responsibility. It was very funny trying to take care of a kindergarten of three- or four-year-olds when they couldn't understand a word I said and I couldn't understand them. Somehow we managed.

A wonderful rabbi was there at the time—a very special, very spiritual man called Rabbi Yosef Shlomo Kahaneman, who had come to Palestine from the Baltics on a visit and then been trapped by the war. His yeshivas, his school and his orphanage in Lithuania were all destroyed by the Nazis, and many of his students and family murdered. But he'd started again in a small town outside Tel Aviv called Bnei Brak, founding a new yeshiva and several new orphanages for Holocaust orphans. We found his teaching very inspiring. He made us feel good about being Jewish.

But the truth is, although everyone at the kibbutz was nice and kind to us, we couldn't feel comfortable there. I knew very quickly that it wasn't going to be the right place for us. It just wasn't what we needed then. We seemed to be going from one extreme to another. Switzerland had been very luxurious. And now we were back to living in poverty, with barely enough to eat. It felt very primitive. We'd had quite enough of communal living—always sharing bathrooms and sleeping arrangements with lots of others, never being able to make a decision alone, always sitting down to meals with so many people, always the big pots of food—though not really big enough. Maybe it reminded us too much of the other camps that were still always in our minds, though we never spoke of them. Maybe it just seemed to us that we were going backward in life, instead of forward.

It wasn't easy to work out what to do next, but I tried to make contact, through word of mouth, with various people. After a few weeks, I had found a solution. So we quickly said goodbye to kibbutz life and went to try our luck in Tel Aviv.

1946–1948

Tel Aviv was such an exciting place to live—one of those cities that never sleeps, a garden city that had grown out of sand dunes. I'd never seen anywhere so modern, so bright and light and new. I'd never been anywhere so cosmopolitan before. Such a contrast with the darkness we had left behind.

Everybody worked so hard during the day and then at night . . . the nightlife never stopped. The white concrete buildings were bright but very hot, so the evenings were extremely sociable: people poured out of their apartments onto the streets, strolling in the small parks between buildings and sitting outside at cafes and restaurants. It was always unbelievably busy, day and night. And so many people came together from so many different parts of the world—not just Europe but also Africa and the Middle East—all bringing their own culture, food, music and ways of doing things.

But in fact, we decided we'd be happiest and safest living not in Tel Aviv itself, but in Bnei Brak, the much smaller town nearby that Rabbi Kahaneman had told us about. There were so many young women like us, newly arrived in Eretz Israel, without families, without protection, without jobs, that the Agudah had set up an organization to support them, the Sarah Schenirer Institute for Girls, at number 27 Rabbi Akiva Street. The Institute was named after the Polish pioneer of education for Orthodox Jewish girls, who died in 1935. The boarding house was already full, so we found a shared room to rent in an apartment nearby, but we could go to the Institute for food and company. An old lady cooked a simple hot meal for us in the evenings. Still short of Hebrew, we muddled through with all the languages we had, signing with hands and feet or whatever we could think of to communicate!

Once again, our sewing skills saved us. Piri got a job at an underwear shop called Newmans, where she made nighties and camisoles and knickers in a workshop at the back. René and Margot and I were all employed at a mattress factory, stitching the outer layer of the fabric casings. Every morning we'd set off on the bus from Bnei Brak to the factory in Tel Aviv, where work started at 9 a.m. and ended at 6 p.m., six days a week. It was very tiring, but we felt it was a good start, and were happy with our lot. We realized just how spoiled we'd been living in the hotel in Engelberg, with everything taken care of. But at last, we were independent! And I knew my sisters were safe.

And Imi? We knew only that he had returned to Bonyhád to look for us, and to rescue what remnants he could of our former lives together. At around the time we were leaving Switzerland, he tried to send a brief message to let us know that, although he too wanted to leave Hungary for Israel, he had been detained for the moment. He didn't, or couldn't, say why. "Go," he told us. "I shall come after you." The message went through several different agencies in different countries, and must have been translated into one language after another. It took more than half a year for that telegram to reach us in Bnei Brak. All we could do was hope and pray that he was finally on his way to join us. Who could have predicted what that delay would cost us all?

We had a favorite cafe where we met our old friends after work. Many of us were doing different things during the day now, and some were still looking for jobs, but we often found each other there around sunset. One evening, I was sitting in the cafe with Shayou, the Hungarian boy who'd come with us to Switzerland from Buchenwald and jumped aboard the *Cairo* at Marseille at the last minute. He really was more like a brother than a friend by then. Our shared history had turned us into a makeshift family. Our bond was so strong.

It was busy inside, and we ordered our coffees. I always paid for my own drinks. Never let a boy buy me anything. We were chatting away—never about our past, always about the present—who was doing what, who had work, who didn't, maybe laughing about things that had happened that day— when a confident young man walked in and looked around. There was something about the way he behaved that made me assume he'd been born in Eretz Israel.

But to my surprise he came right up to our table and addressed me in Hungarian.

"Hello! You must be one of the new girls from Switzerland." His voice was loud and commanding. "I just heard you talking in Hungarian. I had to come and introduce myself."

"And you're . . . ?"

"My name's Shmuel. I'm a friend of someone you work with at the mattress factory. He told me about you and your sisters and friends."

"Did he?"

At first I was a bit suspicious. I wasn't sure exactly what he wanted. One of the things we'd had to come to terms with during that year in Switzerland was that our faith in humanity had been completely destroyed by the Nazis. We had been deceived so dreadfully. We had seen human beings do things to one another that we could never have imagined possible. That eats away at the heart of you forever. It had become very hard to trust anyone, particularly strangers. Especially men.

"Yes," he said. "I'm sure you could do with some help. Since you're new here. And it's not easy, I can tell you. I've been here quite a while . . . eight years now. I know the ropes. So if there's anything you need—finding jobs . . . finding somewhere to live . . . Any help you need at all . . . I'm your man."

He was quite full of himself, I thought. But I had to admit, I could do with some help. We still had a lot to sort out. Those were hard times for everyone then: it was a struggle to get by for all the newcomers like us, but also for the Zionists who'd come to Eretz Israel before the war, and who suddenly found more and more people competing for work.

"Thank you," I said. "I'll think about it."

He pulled out a pen and paper and scribbled something down.

"Just ask for me here," he ordered, handing it to me.

Shmuel Ebert. Export/Import. And an address.

I was sorted for work myself, for the time being. René and Piri were happy enough in their jobs, and we liked where we were living well enough, so we were OK. We were definitely surviving. But I still felt a responsibility for the others. Some didn't have work yet, and we had so little money between us. We were so alone in the world. We had to make decisions about everything by ourselves—where to go, what to do, where to live—and we always had one problem or another to solve. The important thing was to help each other whenever we could. All for one, one for all.

I was a fighter. A real fighter. Not just for myself, but for this whole group of girls who looked up to me and listened to me. I didn't want to take help from anyone. But in a way I knew that, however strong I was, I could do with a bit of guidance. It didn't seem fair on the others to turn down the chance of some good advice from someone who really knew their way around.

And there was something unforgettable about this young man.

So I called on him at his workplace. He had a business importing Borsalino hats, those stylish fedoras made in Italy and worn by all the Orthodox men.

We agreed to meet later that evening. At a different cafe this time. I suppose he didn't want us to be interrupted.

"There you are," he said when he spotted me. He pulled out a chair for me, and made sure I was comfortable before calling the waiter over for the menu. "I'm so glad you came by."

"Why?"

"Because to tell the truth, I really wanted to see you again."

What was this?

"Oh, don't get me wrong—"

I must have looked annoyed.

"I was being quite straight with you. I *can* help your friends. I can get them all jobs. No problem."

I relaxed a bit.

"But you're the one I'm really interested in."

"I'm fine," I said. "I've got a job. You know that."

"Yes, but there are so many different things to sort out when you first arrive. I know that too. Believe me. And things are changing here, fast. So many new people arriving every day. You need to keep on your toes. I can help."

I got straight to the point. We spent some time discussing who needed what, who could do what, a few other problems that had come up with my friends. We had a coffee. He did seem to have all the answers: the best places to eat, shop, drink, where to find this, that and the other. How to manage.

And soon we were meeting again. He explained what he'd sorted out, who he could introduce us to, what the next step was. And then we had another coffee. And then he took me out for a meal.

And I found I liked it. I liked him.

He was so persuasive. The kind of man who could sell ice to Eskimos, as we used to say. Completely charming. And it looks like he charmed me!

Speaking Hungarian with a new person in my life was a wonderful thing. Our common language made a strong connection between us. Funnily enough, although he'd been in the country so long already, he didn't yet speak Hebrew properly. Before the war there weren't very many Hungarians in Israel. That meant being able to talk together in our shared mother tongue was very important for him too.

Shmuel had come to Mandatory Palestine from Budapest in 1938, when he was just seventeen. He had a sense that something terrible was going to happen. That Hungary would soon be no place for Jews. Especially in Budapest, antisemitism was becoming stronger every day. He was never the type to hide his head in the sand. His older brother, Tzvi, had left not long before Shmuel, arriving a few months earlier, but, despite their urging, the rest of the family was reluctant to abandon everything they knew and take such a huge step into the unknown. It wasn't easy, as I've said, and I don't know exactly how they got official immigration certificates. Perhaps through Zionist connections in Budapest? You knew someone here . . . they knew someone else . . . that was how it seemed to work. It was a big advantage to have a certificate, to be legal. Or maybe Shmuel wasn't legal? To be honest, I think I didn't like to ask.

But I do know that when his boat was coming into dock, and he jumped ashore, he was shot at by a British soldier.

One day we were walking down Rothschild Boulevard, one of Tel Aviv's oldest and most beautiful streets. Wide and shady, it has a park running down the middle, a long lawn lined with sycamore figs and banyans—a lovely place to take a stroll or meet your friends, with plenty of places to stop and chat.

"See that bench," he said, pointing. "That was my first bed here. That's where I slept my very first night in Tel Aviv."

So that was his story. I discovered it, little by little. He really had built himself up from nothing. I didn't tell him much of my own story. And he didn't press me.

My mind was not at all on marriage in those days. We were still so young, and our new lives just beginning. The important thing for me was that my sisters and I settled down and established ourselves in Israel. We needed to find security for ourselves. I had no desire to find a husband. I didn't feel any of us were ready for such a big step.

But he was such a larger-than-life character. And handsome too—not so tall, but taller than me by just the right amount. He had a sense of power about him, with his irresistible smile and fine white teeth, thick wavy hair and bushy eyebrows, and his big, clever forehead. Even his voice was loud and powerful. You could always hear him coming. The better I got to know him, the more secure I felt. He took great care of me, and it felt surprisingly good.

The truth is, I was a little tired of being responsible for everything, always thinking ahead, always making sure everyone else was all right. Well, I liked it in one way, of course. But after so long . . . it had become exhausting. So to have someone who knew exactly what he was doing come along and take charge felt like a blessing.

"Don't worry. I'll sort it out," he always said. And he always did.

The constant burden of anxiety was lifted when we were together.

Shmuel and I had so much in common. We were both very gregarious, and we always loved meeting new people. Both of us found it easy to talk to anyone, anytime, anywhere we went. Like me, he was a born organizer. He was tough, yes, but he had a very big heart. He had strong values and opinions, and was never afraid to express them. In lots of ways, we were a perfect match.

But then again, maybe we were a bit too similar. Both a little too independent. He was certainly commanding, even controlling. Like all men, maybe. Somehow they think they know best. Do this. Do that. But I was used to being in charge myself. I'd been leading the whole group of us for years. So that wasn't easy.

Nobody tells me what to do, I thought to myself.

Sometimes we even broke up over it. For example, he hated to be kept waiting. And I couldn't always be on time.

One day, after I'd hurried to meet him at a park after work, I found him tapping his toes and looking at his watch, in a terrible mood.

"This is the last time," he told me, impatiently. "If you're late one more time, you'll see. I won't be there. I'm not having it."

Really? I thought to myself. I didn't say anything, but I was not happy to be given an ultimatum like that. What gave him the right?

So the next time we'd agreed to meet, I decided to set a little test for him.

Family photos from when Esti, Bilha and Roni were young children. (*Top right*) Lily and Shmuel with a baby Esti; Piri is on the left and René the right.

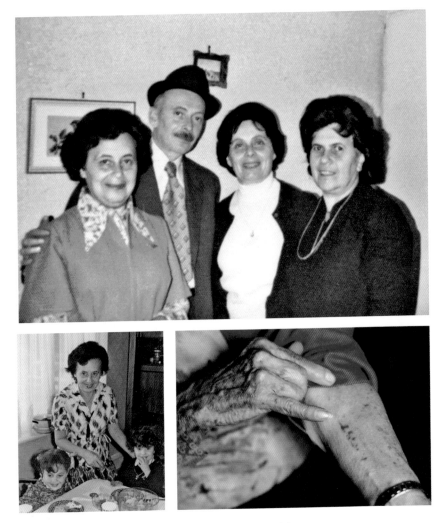

(*Top*) The siblings later in life—
(*left to right*) Lily, Imi, Piri and René.

(*Above left*) Lily with Nina (*left*) and Daphna (*right*);
although Lily's tattoo was openly on display, no one asked about it.

(*Above right*) Lily's tattoo: her number is A-10572.

Lily's first trip back to Auschwitz in 1988.

(*Below*) Lily's second trip back to Auschwitz in 1996, in the watchtower where she talked to the group about her experiences.

(*Above*) Lily with her granddaughter Sharon (*left*) and daughter Esti (*middle*) in one of the barracks at Auschwitz where the prisoners used to sleep.

(*Left*) Lily with pictures of her sister Berta and her mother on the train tracks at Auschwitz; neither has a grave to visit.

Dov Forman @DovForman · Jul 5, 2020

Yesterday my great Grandma (Lily Ebert - an Auschwitz survivor) showed me this bank note- given to her as a gift by a soldier who liberated her. Inscribed, it says "a start to a new life. Good luck and happiness". Later on, she met up with those who freed her (third photo).

H.E.T. and 3 others

💬 250   🔁 2.2K   ♡ 15.3K

Dov Forman @DovForman · Jul 5, 2020

@yadvashem @yadvashemUK @HolocaustUK @HMD_UK @HolocaustCentUK @HolocaustMuseum @AuschwitzMuseum @wienerlibrary @Gen2GenUK

💬 5   🔁 15   ♡ 104

The tweet that started the search to reconnect Lily with the soldier who gave her the banknote.

(*Below*) The viral tweet announcing Lily's recovery from Covid-19.

⚑ Pinned Tweet

Dov Forman @DovForman · Jan 21

My 97-Year-old Great Grandma, Lily Ebert BEM - Auschwitz Survivor, has just recovered from Covid- 19.

Today she went on her first walk in a month after making a miraculous recovery.

🖤 🕊️ A fighter and survivor 🕊️ 🖤

Auschwitz Memorial and 9 others

💬 5.8K   🔁 19.3K   ♡ 264.7K

Anyuka's earrings and the pouch that Lily made from her old dress after being sent from Auschwitz to the Buchenwald sub-camp at Altenburg.

The family Shabbat candlesticks that Imi retrieved from Bonyhád.

(*Below*) Lily's angel necklace—believed to be the only gold taken into Auschwitz to leave with its original owner.

Lily and Dov.

(*Next page*) Lily and all her grandchildren and great-grandchildren.

עטרת זקנים בני בנים
ותפארת בנים אבותם

I left work deliberately late. I sauntered to the cafe. I gave him every chance to give up on me.

But there he was. And every time it was the same, whenever he tried to chip away at my independence. I just wouldn't have it. And he always came back to me.

So when he asked me to marry him, I agreed.

It was April 1948, just before Passover. Being such a determined character, and also well connected, Shmuel had finally managed to get his parents out of Hungary and they came to Tel Aviv around that time. They had spent the war in hiding in Budapest, and hadn't seen their two oldest sons for ten years. Shmuel was still trying to get his other brother and his sister out, and, astonishingly, he eventually succeeded, but not in time for our wedding. The changing political situations in both countries in those years meant that it was getting increasingly difficult not just to enter Mandatory Palestine, with or without papers, but also to leave Hungary. It was certainly an advantage to be in Budapest, rather than a small town in the provinces. I continued to worry about Imi. If he hadn't turned back at Arad on our account, he might have made it to Mandatory Palestine before us. And now the Iron Curtain was falling, faster than we realized.

Shmuel's mother was a lovely, larger-than-life character, just like her son, who welcomed me into the family with great warmth and treated me like her own daughter from the moment we met. Being also physically quite large herself, she was shocked, I think, to find me so very tiny. She never said anything, of course, but I always had the impression that, having heard that I'd been in the camps, she worried that her son was marrying someone very weak and frail. And I was indeed still very thin. So she cooked and baked for me, and made me freshly squeezed orange juice to try to build me up. She was always extremely kind to me.

I sometimes wonder what my own parents would have thought if they'd known I met my future husband in a cafe. There was something so strange and sad about the idea that they would never meet Shmuel, that they could never know who any of us would marry. It wasn't easy, making such a big decision and preparing all alone for our simple ceremony. But I tried not to think about this too much. What choice did any of us have? Luckily, being so busy made it easier to push such thoughts from my mind. And, of course, I had my sisters to help.

I can't pretend René and Piri were happy to lose the person who'd looked after them so devotedly. But they were happy for me, and I knew they now had the strength to be fine on their own. A friend took my place in the small flat they continued to share. I wouldn't be far away, and the Sarah Schenirer Institute would look after them. This new change would be good for all of us, I thought—it was a big step forward in our lives.

May 1948

I needed a white dress for the wedding. That it was white was all that mattered. The dress I wore had been worn already by perhaps a hundred other Holocaust survivors before me. It would be worn by a hundred more after me. One bride passed it to another. For some, it was too short. For others, too wide. But we didn't care.

It was quite a simple gown, with a high neckline, decorated only with a small spray of artificial flowers. Long sleeves, puffed at the shoulders. I had a veil too—also borrowed—held to my head with another band of flowers, and puffed up high over my dark hair. I wore high-heeled white strappy shoes and white stockings, and carried a bunch of fresh flowers. We were given a lot of flowers—carnations and roses. Shmuel looked very handsome in a black suit and tie, and a white shirt with long lapels—and one of his own hats, of course. But by the end, he was dancing in rolled-up shirtsleeves.

Mrs. Benedict, my mother's second cousin, walked me down the aisle to my *chuppah*. I'd only met her a few times, when she invited us for Shabbat lunches. We really didn't know her well at all, but she was the closest person I had to a parent. It was terrible not to have my mother and father there. To be so alone, at such a time, when you come from such a big family . . . I felt the loss greatly. But we were all in the same boat. Very few people of our age in Israel had living parents.

The previous year had been tumultuous, not just in our personal lives but also for the whole country. In fact, for every remaining Jew in Europe. The Holocaust is called the Shoah in Israel. This is a biblical word—Hebrew for "calamity" or "complete destruction." In 1947, having already experienced the calamity of the Holocaust, over 4,500 Shoah survivors who were travelling to Eretz Israel in a ship called the *Exodus* went through a second catastrophe: they were attacked by the British. The refugees were forced back to live in atrocious conditions in a displaced persons' camp in Germany. These were people who had no homes. Nowhere to go. Their situation was already so terrible, not only because of the Nazi regime but also because, in the face of mass murder, the rest of the world had done nothing. To treat them like this now? To inflict new calamities on them? We simply could not believe it. Our shock and anger following the *Exodus* attack were overwhelming.

Yet then, only ten months later, such joy exploded in Tel Aviv. Israel's Declaration of Independence was announced on Friday, May 14, 1948, in the last hours of the British Mandate over Palestine. The news rushed around the city. Everyone poured out onto the streets. Literally anybody who could walk hurried to Rothschild Boulevard, and we were swept into the biggest party I've ever seen in my life. We'd waited 2,000 years for this moment. Suddenly, after all our trials, after everything our people had suffered for centuries, we had our own country. We had returned home, to a place that belonged to us. A place where we belonged. You cannot imagine what that meant.

Thousands of us celebrated together, young and old, new arrivals and early pioneers, all dancing and singing and cheering. Such smiles and laughter. Such ecstasy. Such rejoicing. A bit too much tooting and hooting for my liking—those blaring horns were far too loud. You couldn't hear anything else. But all in all, I couldn't have felt happier that day. Our country had been reborn. And I was in love. Our wedding invitations had been delivered and in twelve days' time I would be married.

But our hopes were soon threatened. By the evening of May 14, Egypt had launched the first air strike on the newborn state. A few hours after midnight Israel was invaded by all the neighboring Arab states—Syria, Lebanon, Iraq and Jordan as well as Egypt. A civil war between Jewish and Palestinian militias, begun in November 1947 after the UN vote to divide Palestine into separate Jewish and Arab states, turned into a full-scale conflict. Shmuel, who had fought in one of the militias, had already been called up for Israel's new army. He was given six weeks off to get married.

Bombs fell on the day of our wedding. At the very moment I joined Shmuel under the *chuppah* for the final part of the ceremony, sirens began to scream.

We all froze.

Our courageous guests were almost stranded, because we couldn't get a taxi to come to the hall in Bnei Brak—this hall was the only one we could find—and we had to ferry them home, in twos and threes, in our own car. We were lucky to have any pictures to remember it, because it was so hard to persuade a photographer to brave the blackout at the end of the evening.

So we began our married life in difficult times. Everything was in such short supply. But still I felt I was one of the lucky ones. Shmuel knew everybody. He was in a chess club with David Ben-Gurion, Israel's first prime minister, and had fought against the British with another future leader, Menachem Begin, though he never told me much about this. He had studied at a yeshiva, so also knew many great rabbis. Survivors who married other survivors had next to nothing in the beginning, but Shmuel found us a tiny one-room flat in Tel Aviv, and we even had some furniture. Number 3 Ge'ula Street was right on the sea front, with a white sandy beach just the other side of the road. We had a balcony looking over the Mediterranean. After growing up in landlocked Hungary, I loved to see the water every day, so blue and beautiful, stretching for miles and miles. We watched breathtaking sunsets together.

Shmuel was very good company, and I began to see more of his gentle and spiritual side. He always made me feel special and cherished, and I loved our new life together in the little home that belonged to us alone.

We bought a small sofa that turned into our bed at night, and people gave us very practical wedding presents to use in our new home. I was one of the first people I knew in Tel Aviv to have a fridge. Actually, this turned out to be something of a mixed blessing because all our neighbors came to use it too. It was difficult to keep milk and chicken and fish from going off in such heat, and I could hardly refuse. Nobody who had been through the war could ever bear to waste food.

In fact, I didn't cook much myself to begin with. For all my cake-making with my mother, I wasn't very experienced in making everyday food. At first, Shmuel and I usually went to restaurants to eat. Slowly, I began to teach myself to cook. And though I could never speak about my mother, she was in my heart as I chopped, stirred, tasted and seasoned. When I went shopping, I looked for the food of my childhood—tomatoes, red peppers, paprika—and, little by little, I learned to recreate the flavors of my mother's meals. My tiny kitchen began to fill with the smells I remembered from Bonyhád.

1948–1950

But where was that girl who was so determined to change the world if she survived? What had happened to the promise I made to myself?

I suppose I had started to bury it in Switzerland. In Israel I covered it up completely.

Nobody talked of the past at that time, for lots of reasons. After the Second World War, everyone had their own problems to deal with, and in Israel our biggest problem was a new war, and a different kind of fight to survive.

So there was that.

But, even more importantly, we found it all so difficult, so painful to talk about. There was no point in discussing it with each other, with our "family" from Buchenwald, from Altenburg, from Auschwitz-Birkenau—we all knew what we had been through together. And there was no point in discussing it with people we had met since, because however we tried to explain it, our story was so terrible it seemed unbelievable. How could it have really happened?

The Nazis' "Final Solution to the Jewish Question" was a form of mass murder that was unique and unprecedented. The genocide in Hitler's empire was so completely beyond comprehension that people who had not been through it themselves simply couldn't absorb information about it, even when it became available. Perhaps it is never possible. Even though there were so many of us in Israel, for survivors, the best way to protect ourselves once the war was over was simply to keep quiet. The silence was national as well as personal. It was both an individual trauma and a social one.

The Jews who had arrived in Mandatory Palestine before the war had mixed feelings. Some even believed Hungarian Jews· had themselves to blame, that we had let ourselves be taken, like innocent fools. It was somehow our fault. We should have seen what was coming.

There was little discussion, and even less understanding.

I didn't want René or Piri to think about what had happened to us. I managed to convince myself that if we never spoke of the past, it would be easier for them to forget. I thought I could continue to protect them in this way.

Even with Shmuel, I just couldn't talk about it. Not for a very long time. He knew, of course. My tattoo spoke for me. But he didn't want to upset me. He didn't want to intrude. He never asked questions. It was a very hard thing to speak about, for everybody. It's hard to ask the questions and it's hard to hear the answers. Some people, like my sisters, kept their silence for the rest of their lives.

Within six months came another big change. I realized I was pregnant. It seemed a miracle. I think many of us girls worried that our experiences in the camps may have made us infertile. The thought of a baby, new life . . . the prospect of being a mother myself. This meant an enormous amount to me. Our family could begin to grow again.

I was so innocent. We had nobody to tell us the things we needed to know, what was going to happen, what we had to do. Even though I got on very well with Shmuel's mother, it's not quite the same as having your own mother. But we were all in the same position, so I didn't feel sorry for myself.

When I began to get sharp pains in my tummy, I imagined that I'd eaten something bad. I had no idea that I was in labor. I had no idea what giving birth would be like.

I told Shmuel about my stomach ache and his face changed.

"Let's go," he said. "Right away."

"Where to?" I replied.

"To the hospital! The baby's coming."

There were no taxis to be had, so we walked to the hospital. It was a very quick birth, only two hours from when we arrived, and I didn't find it too difficult, but close to the end, when the doctor examined me, I could tell that he was beginning to panic. Of course, they didn't let husbands into the room then. The doctor vanished. He came back. He didn't tell me what was happening.

Instead of a head crowning, a little bottom appeared. My daughter was breech, and the doctor hadn't realized. Luckily, she slithered safely out, and all was well.

But afterward, my husband told me that the doctor had rushed out with a question for him: "Should I save the mother or the baby?"

It still makes me furious to remember this. We were the ones giving birth. Yet nobody told us anything. Nobody asked us what we thought.

We named her Esther Nechama, after Shmuel's mother and also mine, but we always called her Esti. She was my first *sabra*. That's what we used to call children actually born in Israel. It's the name in Hebrew for the fruit of the prickly pear: tough and spiky on the outside, soft and sweet when you get inside. But there was nothing spiky about Esther. Her birth was easy, and she was an easy baby. I spent only a week in hospital, which wasn't long in those days.

But it was when I came home with her that I really missed my mother. It was so frightening to be in charge of such a tiny thing, and have no idea how to hold her, or how to bath her. She seemed far too fragile and was so terribly precious to me that I imagined I could accidentally break her. I thought I might do something dreadful. Right from the beginning, I think I was overprotective. I worried about everything. I wanted to create a perfect world for my babies, so they would be perfectly safe. I couldn't bear the thought of any harm coming to Esti.

Shmuel's brother Tzvi and his wife Margot already had several children. Margot came round to our little flat and calmly showed me what to do: how to hold Esti in the bath, how to check the water temperature, how to keep her head and neck safe, how to change nappies. I was nervous about that too! I was so afraid of hurting Esti I didn't dare use safety pins. Luckily breastfeeding—and everybody breastfed in those days—seemed to come quite naturally, and she thrived. Every week I took her to the doctor to be weighed, and proudly watched the numbers go up. But going so often might have been a mistake. I think it was at the hospital that she picked up whooping cough, so that was another worry.

René and Piri were so happy to be aunts. Even today René's daughter remembers how joyful every newborn in the family used to make my sister. Babies were the best revenge against Hitler, René always said. Both she and Piri came as often as they could to help me look after Esti. In those days we washed nappies by hand, and had to boil them too, so there was a lot of work. And, René being René, she helped me with everything. She'd do absolutely anything to ease someone else's burden. My sisters also came to keep me company. We had enough money from Shmuel's various businesses for me not to work. But staying at home all alone with a small baby was hard for me. I love going out and meeting people.

Before long, one of my neighbors also had a new baby. I could see that she was having exactly the same problems I'd had, so I showed her how to bath her little one. And so our generation continued to look after each other.

One day I was on my balcony chatting to another neighbor who had come out to hers. We were just getting to know one another. She was Hungarian, and it was always good to find other Hungarians to talk to.

"So, where are you from?" she asked me. Nearly everyone in Israel was from somewhere else.

"Oh, you won't know the place. It's just a small town."

"What's it called?"

"Bonyhád," I said, expecting her to look blank and shake her head.

But her face shone.

"That's where *we* come from! My brother Lajos was the doctor there."

"Not Dr. Litzman? He delivered me! And all my brothers and sisters. Dr. Litzman was our family doctor! When we were little we always used to climb the walnut tree and hide when we knew he was coming so he wouldn't make us stick our tongues out and listen to our chests with his cold stethoscope."

And it was Dr. Litzman who had taken the last ever photograph of our family. The picture Bela didn't stay for.

His sister told me he was now living in Stockholm. Their other sister, Fani, his wife Aranka and their children, Bella, Gyuörgyi and Marianna, all perished in the Holocaust, but we didn't talk much about this. My neighbor and I quickly became good friends. And then I wrote to Dr. Litzman. And that was how I managed to retrieve a few of our precious family photographs.

When Imi returned to Bonyhád, he found more. Not many. It seems that in 1944, after all the Jews had been taken, somebody had found photos, papers and valued personal possessions in rubbish heaps thrown out from looted Jewish homes, and collected this together and put it in a basement for safekeeping. Imi was able to search through these piles and rescue a handful of our family pictures and documents. In my childhood, I remember, my grandparents had a great many large photographs of all members of their family. After the war, we were left with just one picture of my mother and one of my father. I still feel lucky to have even those.

But in a small town, cut off from the capital by the ravages of war, it was hard to comprehend how fast the world was changing. Imi didn't realize how urgently he needed to rescue himself until it was too late.

Russia's Red Army had marched into Bonyhád at the end of November 1944, barely a month after Churchill and Stalin's secret meeting in Moscow to discuss how to carve up post-war Europe. By October 1947 the Communists had maneuvered full control of Hungary's government, and in August 1949 our country became a one-party state: the Hungarian People's Republic. The first barbed-wire fences and minefields along Hungary's borders with the West were soon installed. Although some of Bonyhád's Jews tried to escape in these years to the new state of Israel, most were caught and jailed. Hungary had become a prison. Along with millions of others in the Soviet-controlled Eastern Bloc, Imi was trapped.

1951–1955

Less than three years after Esti's birth, I was in labor and walking to the hospital again. This time I knew perfectly well what was going on. But they sent me home!

It wasn't a convenient time for the doctor. I think he wanted to go to a party. An hour or two after I'd got back to our flat, I was convinced my baby would soon arrive and returned to the hospital. I was right. Like Esti, her sister Bilha was born very quickly. All that walking probably helped. And everything was so much easier. I wasn't afraid. I knew what I was doing. It didn't feel that much harder having two instead of one. And it was lovely to welcome into the world our second beautiful child, who brought so much joy to our family.

I dressed my babies only in white for almost a year, and was very careful always to follow the advice and do the right thing: so when they said pacifiers were bad, I refused to give them to my babies, even though it meant Esti sucked her finger, and of course, that's much harder to stop—you can't take a finger away.

It wasn't long before my daughters could play together. As they got older, I often took them to the beach, where the water was warm and calm. But still I worried. I was even anxious about the girls mixing with other children when we went to the nearby park.

The good thing about those early years is that in Bnei Brak

and Tel Aviv we were all more or less the same age—between about eighteen and thirty. With nobody to tell us where to go and when to be back, we could meet other people much more easily than at home in Hungary. We were free to choose our friends. We could mix with the people we liked, boys and girls. Our independence wasn't by choice, of course. But that's how it was.

Bnei Brak was a small, religious community. The language you now heard most often on the streets and in shops and cafes and at shul was Hungarian. The first thing we all did as soon as we arrived there was try to find members of our own families. Then we searched for neighbors and friends from our own towns and villages. And then friends of relatives or relatives of friends from places we knew further afield. Really, anyone we might have the remotest connection with. Whenever new survivors came from Hungary, word spread very quickly.

That's how René and Piri learned of the arrival of our new cousin. His name was Imi, like our brother, and he was the son of one of my mother's sisters. We'd never actually met before because he grew up in Czechoslovakia, in Bratislava—often called Pressburg then—where he'd spent the war hidden by Gentiles. My sisters and Imi became very close, and remained so all their lives.

When you don't have parents or aunts and uncles to offer guidance, you have to make your own decisions in life. It's up to you to work out what to do and how to do it. But naturally, René and Piri continued to look to me for advice, especially when it came to marriage.

I was very happy when friends introduced René to Osi because I felt we already essentially knew his family. He came from a town in Hungary called Makó, which is about the same distance from Budapest as Bonyhád, and it used to be a similar kind of place too, with a strong Orthodox Jewish community. We had even visited it, because we had cousins there.

I knew right away that Osi would be perfect for my sister. I knew he'd look after her properly. He was a very unassuming man, very easy-going and so kind to everyone. He worked as an administrator for a company, but in his spare time he was always visiting the sick, and going to the hospital to help other people. One of the most altruistic men I've ever known. He wasn't a pushover, but he was steady, generous and compassionate. The kind of person you could always rely on. After they married, they lived extremely modestly, always very satisfied with their lot in life, never straining after impossible dreams.

And René's wedding dress? It was the same one that I'd worn myself a few years earlier. The ceremony was in the same hall that Shmuel and I had used. I walked René down the aisle to the *chuppah*. And then a few years later Piri wore the same dress in the same hall too, and I also led my younger sister to her new husband, Volví. With each wedding there was a little more food, and a few more distant family members, but not a lot more luxury.

It had been Shmuel who first noticed Volví. They worked near each other, and Shmuel would often see Volví lifting very heavy rolls of fabric at a textile factory. He was struck by his strength, and how hard he worked. They soon got chatting. Don't forget that Shmuel could strike up a conversation with anyone. Volví was from a city called Eger, the other side of Budapest from Bonyhád, but not that far away. His parents were also both dead. Only one of his brothers had survived.

Thinking they'd be a good match, Shmuel introduced Volví to Piri. And I was just as happy for Piri to marry Volví as I had been for René to marry Osi. It was a great comfort to me that both my sisters had found such kind men, whose only ambition was to make a good home for their children. I was confident both husbands would take great care of their families, and keep them safe and secure, and I was right.

There wasn't a lot of time for socializing then. We were all so busy working and looking after our young families. Around that time Margot, our friend through such hard times, unfortunately became involved with a man I wasn't at all sure of. I worried he wasn't good enough for her. She then drifted apart from us, sadly, and eventually we lost touch completely. But we saw our other friends from Switzerland, as much as our hectic lives allowed, and some, like Henchi, I still see to this day whenever I can.

Volví and Piri also set up home together in Bnei Brak. First of all, they started a textile shop in Tel Aviv, selling fabrics as our father had done in Bonyhád. Then they gave that up and opened a shop in Bnei Brak itself, so that Volví wouldn't have to work too far away. The new enterprise was a Hungarian bakery, a simple place, with grey stone tiles on the floor and rows of metal shelving laden with cakes, buns and bread. They smelled wonderful, and reminded us all of home. The yeast cakes were so famous people even came from Tel Aviv to buy them. My children usually wanted the poppy-seed yeast cake, which was very good indeed, but their apple strudel was also excellent.

Besides working in the shop, Volví also had a special and difficult responsibility as a volunteer: if there was an accident or a bomb attack or a military incident, he would go to the crisis scene and collect the bodies and any body parts to make sure they were buried properly. (There's a humanitarian organization called ZAKA that does the same thing today.) According to Jewish law, a person should be buried as they came into the world, complete with all limbs and organs.

All six of us got on exceptionally well. Osi and Volví were good brothers-in-law as well as husbands, so we always stayed extremely close, enjoying each other's company very much. Shmuel travelled for work, and on the few occasions he had to be away during Shabbat, I'd take the children and stay with Piri in Bnei Brak so we could all be together. For all three sisters, it was terribly important to create the kind of secure and observant homes for our own children that we had enjoyed ourselves thanks to our parents. We wanted our own families to grow up always keeping *mitzvot*, following all the commandments, understanding our faith as we had done ourselves. Shmuel felt this strongly too.

As for work, my husband was an entrepreneur by nature, with lots of different business ventures on the go. Later he worked on the stock exchange, and in a bank. But when our daughters were little, he also opened a shop, a stone's throw from our flat. The windows displayed household linen, men's shirts and fine straw panamas as well as Borsalino hats. I'd often go and work there, and always enjoyed chatting to the customers. Esti and Bilha liked coming to join me there after school. They loved the sweet shop next door, and used to sit for hours watching the cobbler at work just along the street.

As the children grew up, neither Shmuel nor I ever mentioned the Shoah. Not even to each other. How could we? Shmuel had not been there, and I had. I couldn't help but feel he could never truly understand what it meant. I'm not sure I understood myself. And, of course, he wanted me to be happy. He didn't want to upset me. A warm-hearted and generous man, he imagined that talking and remembering would only cause me pain. That was what most people thought then.

I think, in a way, they were right. It was the wrong time for us to talk. It was too fresh, too raw. It still hurt too much. If we had tried to speak about such pain at that point, we'd have been unable to continue living.

And for some years, that was far and away the most important thing: to live and to build. We had to establish our new lives entirely from scratch: new homes, new families, new dreams. We had to look forward. You can't forget such a thing, however much you'd like to, but you also can't keep on reliving it, or you will never be able to rebuild. It seems to me that this is one of the most interesting things about human nature: you can go through hell, but nothing is so strong in life as life itself. Despite everything, we must have continued to believe this. If we hadn't had this faith, we would never have been able to bring children into this world.

All we wanted for Esti and Bilha was for them to have normal lives. I never wanted them to know anything about what had happened. We wanted them to be happy and carefree and completely ordinary, totally free of horror and fear. We believed the best way to protect the next generation was to keep them as innocent as possible for as long as possible.

Now I realize that, in a way, you can protect a child too much. And there is a price to that. Now I can see that they always understand more than you imagine.

1956

Everything changed in Hungary in 1956. First there was the huge demonstration on October 23 that turned into a nation-wide revolution. Then, within weeks, came the Soviet crack-down, when tanks rolled into Budapest and crushed the resistance. In Tel Aviv we listened to the radio and followed the news as best we could, but there was no way at all to discover what was happening to individual friends and family still in Hungary.

And another world event was dominating our lives in Israel at exactly that time: the Suez crisis, when Egypt nationalized the Suez Canal, and Israeli forces joined with the French and British to invade Egypt.

For ten years, my brother Imi and I had been exchanging letters. He was still trapped behind the Iron Curtain. I couldn't visit him—that would have been stupid. What if I had got trapped too? It's hard for people to understand today how lit-tle communication was possible. The post was very unreliable, and we had to endure long silences. We couldn't make phone calls. Imi sometimes used to send us newspapers from Hungary. We read them eagerly, desperate for every scrap of news from home, though of course it was history by the time it reached us.

When Imi had returned to Bonyhád, as well as the photo-graphs and a few other bits and pieces, he'd found and rescued our blackened Shabbat candlesticks. One he spotted lying in the street. The other was still hidden in our old cellar. In Bonyhád, he met and married another survivor, Edit. She'd had a terrible time during the war, and afterward too, in a Soviet labor camp in Siberia. For the rest of their lives they never spoke a word of their experiences to their children, Fruma, Nechama, Aaron, and Hillel, their youngest son, who was born after the revolution. Imi qualified as a dental surgeon in Bonyhád, but a few years later he and Edit left our home town to make a new start 250 kilometres away, in Sopron, near the border with Austria. I knew that the Soviet regime had meant he had to change his job. At this point he was making metal tools and bells, and could only work secretly at home as a dentist, from his children's bedroom.

But in 1956, when the revolution erupted, I didn't know what he'd do next. For months, I had no way of finding out.

Some Jews in Hungary had defended the Communist government, but others were imprisoned, even killed, for supporting the uprising. Jews were attacked all over Hungary, if not for being Communist, then simply for being Jews. About 200,000 Hungarians fled the country and became refugees, 20,000 Jews among them—a fifth of the country's remaining Jewish population.

It's not easy now to piece together precisely what happened to Imi. He never told me much. But it seems that when the revolution was savagely crushed by Moscow on November 4, Imi and his family took their chance to flee. Edit's brother managed to retrieve the candlesticks, some pictures from childhood, silver, linen and bedding from the house in Bonyhád and then came to meet Imi, Edit and the children in Sopron. And then they abandoned all their other possessions and joined the mass exodus.

The Soviets had cut off the main routes to Austria and

Yugoslavia. But thousands of refugees set off on foot, in carts, or on bicycles, once again taking with them only what they could carry. It was bitterly cold. They had to make their way through icy marshes, and, even with small children, had little choice but to attempt terrifying crossings over the border canal using makeshift bridges of planks and tree trunks.

Imi and his family headed for the Austrian border. Here refugee agencies waited to greet the escapees, and ferried them in trucks to refugee camps. Various countries offered homes to Hungarian exiles, but of course, Imi wanted to come to Israel. He was determined to be reunited with us after all these years of separation. In Vienna, the family was able to register for help to emigrate with the AJDC—The American Jewish Joint Distribution Committee—always known as the Joint. It had secretly helped thousands of Jews to emigrate safely from Nazi-occupied Europe. When the British started to intern Jews who arrived in Israel without legal immigration certificates, the AJDC helped the detainees in the camps in Cyprus.

Their names were recorded on their AJDC cards in a mixture of English and Hungarian: Imre and Edith, and their children Agnes, Sûsi and Peter—names I'd never known him use before. Fruma—or Agnes—the oldest, who had just turned seven, was the same age as Esti. Edit was twenty-eight, just a little older than Piri.

The family arrived in Israel destitute. They couldn't even come directly, and had to spend some time in a Cyprus camp, so we had no warning about their arrival. Somehow René got some news, and I think she was able to rush to meet the boat at Haifa. I imagine her waiting at the dock, anxiously scanning the passengers leaning over the rail. Everyone there seemed to be looking for someone. She recognized him instantly. We still looked so much alike.

René and Piri brought Imi and his family to our flat in Tel Aviv as soon as they could. Opening the door was an incredible moment. We were all so excited to see each other again. We had last seen a young boy, and here was a grown man, with three children. I only knew Edit through our letters, but from our very first meeting she seemed like another sister to me. We had endured similar experiences during the war, so we had that unspoken bond. Her character was very open and giving, and we soon became very close—she was a perfect sister-in-law, and a fantastic wife and mother.

When Imi suddenly appeared that day, I was wearing the necklace he had saved for me, as I always did. I had kept it safe and secret all through the camps, and now I never took it off. Our first reunion was full of happiness but also a kind of numbness—it was bewildering to think of those lost years, all that time we had spent apart, never meeting each other's spouse or children. Our emotions were so confused. We were all too busy introducing all the little cousins to each other, too full of wonder at all the new people who hadn't existed when we said goodbye to each other twelve years earlier in the Bonyhád ghetto. I didn't remember to show him. And Imi didn't notice it around my neck.

The next time we met, we were both a lot calmer.

"Lily!" he suddenly said, his eyes lighting up. "You've still got your beautiful necklace. I can't believe it."

"It's all because of you," I told him.

"I didn't dare hope that you'd survived yourself! How on earth did you keep your necklace safe too?"

And then René and Piri showed him their hands.

"The rings as well! That's incredible!" said Imi.

"Don't you remember the hiding place you made in Anyuka's heel?" I said.

"Of course I do! But I never imagined it would last forever. I can't believe that you were allowed to keep your shoes."

"We couldn't either. It was so unusual."

I told him how the heels had eventually gone through, and about using my bread ration as a hiding place instead, and how I secretly used to move the jewelry every day without fail. And I showed him the little bag, where I still kept our mother's earrings.

Imi glowed with pride at his own foresight. Edit nudged him.

"I've got something to show you too," he said. "You'll never guess what I managed to find when I went back to Bonyhád."

"Our Shabbat candlesticks!" said my sisters. They already knew. "He brought them!"

Imi put an arm around his wife, who was as delighted as he was by our response.

"Edit polished them for months. We have her to thank for bringing them back to their splendor. I was afraid that the chemical I used to make them black had nearly destroyed them."

"So, entirely thanks to you, Imi, we all have one treasure from home," I told him. "You don't know how much it meant to us all these years. To keep our memories of childhood, and our mother. To have a little piece of you too, when we thought we'd lost you forever. And all through these years apart when we didn't know if we'd ever see you again."

I wear that pendant every day still, without fail, in honor of the memory of my family. It's a constant reminder of what was lost and what survived.

We had a larger flat by then, so Imi and Edit and the children came to live with me and Shmuel for a while. It wasn't easy for them to start life all over again, with no money, and no connections besides us. Times were still hard for everyone in Israel. And there were so many more people in Tel Aviv now . . . the city had doubled in size since our arrival ten years earlier.

Imi was very independent. We helped him find work in Tel Aviv, but he wanted to be in Jerusalem. Our new-found cousin Imi helped him settle in there, and the two soon became very good friends. He found a small flat to rent, and worked everything out quite quickly. Soon our brother Imi had his own dental practice, and lots of patients as he was such an excellent dentist. How he made any money I don't know, as he was always so generous. Some of the people of the Old Yishuv, whose families had come to Jerusalem many decades or even centuries earlier, or whose ancestors had always lived in the southern Levant, were very poor indeed. Yet he would happily take care of their teeth and charge nothing at all. He really was one of the kindest people I've known in all my life.

To have the whole family together again at last, a whole new generation growing up together, cousins spending time with cousins: this made us all so happy. By the end of 1957, Shmuel and I had another baby in the family—our son Ahron, named after my father, like René's son. We called him Roni. While I was recovering, René looked after Esti and Bilha, who were both over the moon to have a little brother. Everyone had been hoping for a boy this time, and he was quite the prince in the family, as you can imagine. Another very easy baby, and completely spoiled by every one of us.

1960

When he organized our deportation to Auschwitz-Birkenau, Adolf Eichmann changed my life. He was the mastermind behind the murder of Hungary's Jews. Eichmann's trial in Jerusalem in 1961 changed everything for a second time.

This wasn't the first public trial in the years following the war. There had already been the Nuremberg trials, which proved that the Nazis were criminal, but nobody talked of the Holocaust then, not in the way they do now. The voices of its victims were hardly heard. In Israel, there had also been the kapo trials, when survivors suspected of collaboration were investigated and put in the dock. These were the Jewish functionaries in the ghettos and camps. But strangely, these trials were barely reported in the newspapers.

Then there was the Kasztner trial. That wasn't really a trial in the same way, but a libel case: the man who had organized the train that took my aunt and uncle out of Hungary, and who was now a civil servant in Israel, was also accused of collaborating with the Nazis. I thought they were mad, all of those involved, all fighting over what had happened, and really for political reasons.

Some people said Kasztner was a hero. Some said he was a traitor. And the truth is, I believe, this poor man was neither. He was an ordinary human being trying to do what he could in impossible times. The judge ruled against him and said he had "sold his soul to the devil," and less than two years later the unfortunate Kasztner was assassinated on the street outside his home in Tel Aviv, on Shabbat, in March 1957. The whole country was shocked. It was terrible, and made worse by the fact that, not long after his death, the Supreme Court overruled most of the original verdict.

So you see it was impossible to forget the Shoah. However hard we tried, something always happened to remind us.

By this time a quarter of Israel's population were survivors. Still we didn't talk. When we had tried, immediately after the war, it was clear nobody really believed us. They simply couldn't grasp what we had been through. As I've said, without ever discussing it with my sisters or my friends, we all did exactly the same thing. We just kept everything to ourselves, and locked away our memories. Somehow we imagined that, if we never mentioned it, it couldn't happen again. We thought—and we hoped—that everything could be forgotten.

It was for the children's sake, above all. I never wanted them to know anything about the Holocaust. What good would it do to know? That's what I thought then. How could it help them to hear what had happened to me? To their family. How could it help me to tell them? We had been through an experience designed to destroy our humanity. Perhaps, in a strange way, we felt a kind of shame about it. Even a sense of guilt. We had survived when so many had not. The trials had tried to portray everyone as either heroes or villains. They made the world think that only bad people survived. And that all good people resisted.

And then, in May 1960, Adolf Eichmann was captured in Buenos Aires by Mossad, the Israeli secret service. Eichmann, the chief murderer of the Jews in Europe. The man who arranged to have us killed so efficiently. The civil servant who would claim he was "only following orders." In April the following year—the same month that the astronaut Yuri Gagarin first circled the earth—Eichmann was brought to stand trial in Jerusalem.

This trial was a very different affair from those at Nuremberg. Survivor after survivor appeared as witnesses, and told their stories in public for the first time. In a way, they themselves were judged. I cannot imagine what that must have been like. One collapsed and fell into a coma under the strain. Their long and devastating testimonies were reported all round the world. This wasn't about documents, but about people. The prosecutors didn't just want to convict one man, but to change the entire world's view of the Holocaust, to expose the complete history of the genocide. They wanted the next generation in Israel to learn the full truth.

And that was exactly what happened. The gates were unlocked. The knowledge was out. Eyes were opened.

Week after week, night after night, it was on the radio and in all the newspapers. Suddenly all the people in Israel who had not lived through those times in Europe were confronted with the horrific details of the genocide.

We could hide nothing after that.

My children were still very young. By June 1, 1962, when Eichmann was hanged at a prison in Ramla, Esti was thirteen, Bilha was ten and Roni only four. Still I hadn't said one word to any of them. I couldn't find normal words to explain it, even if I'd wanted to. Even now, that's part of the problem.

To protect each other—or so we thought—within the family, we continued to keep our silence about the Holocaust, children and parents alike. They never asked me questions. I volunteered nothing. But, of course, we couldn't keep concealing the truth. Children go to school. They talk. They find out things, even if you don't tell them yourself. And I carried the evidence with me everywhere, and so did their aunties. Those blue numbers said so much, even if we didn't.

So it was that, despite all my efforts, my children grew up with the burden of loss I'd hoped they'd never have to shoulder. We tried to make up for their family history by giving our children more of everything, mentally and physically—more certainty, more love, more money and material things than we'd had ourselves. We also watched over them obsessively, and always wanted to know where they were. We couldn't bear it if they went out and were late back—in no time at all, one of us would go out looking for them.

I can't help but be very careful about everything. It's become my nature.

"You never know what might happen tomorrow," I'd warn the children if they ever wanted to throw anything out. "Keep it just in case . . ."

Esti and Bilha and Roni sometimes pretended not to be hungry, in case they were given more food than they could eat, as they knew that whatever happened they had to finish every last morsel on their plates. All the cousins grew up understanding that food was precious, above all bread. My sister René used to hoard sugar compulsively. You wouldn't believe how many bags she had. In case disaster struck at Passover, she even kept bags of kosher sugar for Pesach in one cupboard, for so long that it went solid.

"Shall I throw this away?" her son Aaron once suggested.

"No! Please don't!"

"But it's hard as rock! How could you ever even use it?" he protested.

"As long as we have sugar and water, we won't die," she told her children. "It's better to have and not need, than need and not have. You don't know what's round the corner. You never know."

If she ever saw food wasted, she'd cry.

After the trial, I felt no sense of relief. It was little comfort that at last everyone knew more about those terrible times, especially what had happened in Hungary in 1944. The shocking speed of the whole operation. The innocence and ignorance of its victims. If I felt anything when Eichmann was convicted, it was anger. Because it wasn't just one man who was responsible. It was so many. Eichmann could have been stopped, if the world had only cared just a bit more. If they had listened before it was too late. I felt rage at the whole world for letting the Holocaust happen. Everywhere—in Hungary, in Europe, in America—people had done so little to prevent the genocide. When people spoke up about what was happening while it was still going on, nobody listened. The world was silent.

1967

Shmuel was a strong family man who could also be very warm and thoughtful. But he was a strict father, and still quite controlling, which was sometimes a source of tension at home. Work pressures had a lot to do with it. He was involved in a number of different businesses, and always busy—never the type to have hobbies or take a break. Although he loved singing and music, the older he got, the harder he found it to relax. No more time to play chess. With a growing family to look after, Shmuel increasingly felt the weight of his responsibilities, and put even more of his energies into work. Meanwhile, repeated outbreaks of violence on Israel's borders were a constant worry.

Perhaps it wasn't surprising that, in his early forties, around the time the girls were starting secondary school, he began to have some problems with his health.

Nothing that serious, or so it seemed at first. I noticed that he was getting increasingly tense and irritable, and his moods became more unpredictable. The children started to tiptoe around him. He gradually became ever more breathless, and then began to get pains in his chest, and even his left arm. I made him see the doctor. We didn't tell the children what was wrong, of course. We didn't want to frighten them. But we knew it was his heart.

One day in late May he suffered a full-scale heart attack.

It was all so distressing that I can't even remember the exact sequence of events. Just the fear we all felt. It was such a huge shock. A man like Shmuel, such a tower of strength for me, always so commanding, suddenly in hospital with tubes coming out of him, unable to take a sip of water without help.

Meanwhile, relations with our Arab neighbors were worsening. The dynamics in the area had never really settled since the conflicts of 1947–9. The impact of the 1956 Suez Crisis reverberated for years, leading to frequent border clashes. In 1967 we were once again on the brink of war. Pressure kept mounting over access to water and shipping routes. After a military pact between neighboring Arab countries, Egypt's President Nasser expelled the UN Emergency Force from the Sinai Peninsula, our border with his country. Israel mobilized the reserve army in response. It was terrifying.

Of course, Shmuel was too old by then to be called up, and not well enough anyway, but we all felt the stress of the political situation. Israel seemed so isolated in the Middle East. Efforts to get diplomatic support internationally had come to nothing. Yet again, there seemed a real chance that we could be completely wiped out as a nation.

But my biggest worry was my husband's health. And that's when I thought again of Switzerland. I remembered the wonderful climate in the mountains—such a contrast to the heat of the desert. I knew how good the Swiss doctors were. I decided that the best thing for Shmuel would be to get him out of Israel, away from his concerns with work, and take him for treatment and recuperation in Switzerland.

We intended to be away for a short time. A rest. Fresh air. And Shmuel would return rejuvenated. That was our hope. We had a lovely home-help called Ilonka, who was such a part of the family that we called her Ilonkanéni—Auntie Ilonka. She lived in Bnei Brak and came every morning to help me look after the household. She agreed to stay in the flat and take care of the children while I took Shmuel to recuperate.

In my mind, all the unhappiness and shock we'd experienced over twenty years earlier, when we'd first come to Switzerland as vulnerable orphans, had been supplanted by the happy memories that followed. Switzerland was where I had become a human being again, and I was excited about seeing Berta and Rosalin after so long, and introducing them to my husband. They had made me whole when I was broken, and we had kept in touch ever since.

And for the first few days we enjoyed visiting all those places I remembered so well.

"Look! Can you see that?" I kept saying to Shmuel. "That balcony up there was my room."

"See this spot here . . . This is where we posed for that photograph . . . you know, the one where we're dressed up in costume."

"And this table here . . . this is where we used to meet up with the boys. Oh, look, their home is an ordinary hotel again."

When we went on walks and visited neighboring villages, the memories of the outings we'd enjoyed together came flooding back.

But very quickly, our peace was destroyed. On June 5, we woke up to dramatic news: Israel had launched surprise dawn air strikes on Egypt. There was a ground attack in the Gaza Strip and the Sinai Peninsula. Full-scale war had erupted in the Middle East. This was the conflict now remembered as the Six-Day War.

How I hated being separated from the children in such

dangerous and uncertain times. But I couldn't leave Shmuel, and he certainly wasn't fit to fly such a long distance home. In fact, it was becoming clear that his recovery was going to take a lot longer than we'd imagined, and he would need more medical attention.

It was such a dilemma for me. At such a difficult time, I naturally wanted my children close to me. We'd never been so far apart in our whole lives. Bilha and Roni were fifteen and nine by then, but Esti was eighteen and in her final year at school. She was right in the middle of important leavers' exams, the Bagrut. We were a family who really valued education and we felt that a lot depended on these results. We couldn't jeopardize that, but not knowing when Shmuel could safely return to Israel, and unwilling to be separated from our little ones any longer, we decided the best solution would be for Bilha and Roni to join us in Switzerland, while Esti stayed at home to finish school.

We had to make lots of decisions at once. I don't think I had ever made so many international phone calls in such a short time before.

I could hardly believe what I was doing. I had always coddled the children so much. Watched over their every step. I had hardly ever let them cross the road on their own. I never even asked Bilha to babysit for Roni. But here I was suddenly letting the two of them fly on their own, across continents! Shmuel's brother Tzvi helped by organizing the air tickets, and he saw them safely onto their flight. Bilha was always an independent kind of girl. She managed everything beautifully. It must have been hard for her to come without Esti, and difficult for Esti too, so far away from us, at such an important time in her life, but we had little choice. I knew she would be well looked after by Ilonkanéni and my sisters and all of Shmuel's family too. She was surrounded by cousins.

The Swiss doctors still had concerns about Shmuel's heart. What should we do?

Several years before the outbreak of the Second World War, the daughter of one of my father's first cousins, Klári Sternberg, had met and married a Hungarian who lived in London. She moved there too, but used to visit Bonyhád very regularly, to see her grandmother. She and her husband lived in Golders Green with their two sons. She was the kindest person we ever met.

"Come and spend Shavuot in London with us," she suggested. "I'll help you find a good heart doctor, so that Shmuel can have a second opinion."

In mid-June, the Sternbergs welcomed all four of us into their home with great warmth and generosity. Klári helped us find our way around, introduced us to her community, and took us to the ballet.

Only Bilha spoke a little English, which she'd learned at school. The rest of us were helpless. Bilha settled in quickly, and was so good at making friends that she was soon happy to join a youth group at the local synagogue. I was worried about how she'd find her way there, but it wasn't far. Klári explained the route and she eagerly set off alone. I was looking forward to hearing how she'd got on, but fretting a little, as was always my habit when the children were out of sight.

The hours went by, and there was no sign of her.

I kept looking out of the window. Nothing.

"What are we going to do?" I said. "It's nearly dark!"

"Maybe she's gone home with one of the other girls?" Klári suggested. "I'm sure she'll be back any moment."

After a while we started looking outside, walking the neighboring streets. Shmuel was resting upstairs. I didn't want to worry him.

"Do you think she's forgotten the address?"

I imagined her struggling to read the English street signs, panicking as the time went by, worrying herself about how much I would be worrying.

Walking back to the house, I pictured her waiting for me. I even felt a bit cross. How could she have frightened us like that?

But still she wasn't there.

I fretted and fretted. It got steadily darker. Should we call the police? Should we go out and search again? Anything could have happened. Klári tried to calm me down. We mustn't stress Shmuel, she reminded me. I didn't want him to be anxious, so we got ready for bed and hoped for the best.

At last, very late, there was a knock on the door. It was one of the neighbors.

"Have you heard? An Israeli girl has been knocked down in a road accident. I think it's your cousin."

Klári quickly translated.

"Bilha!" I cried. "What happened? Where is she?"

"The paramedics who rescued her didn't know who she was or where she's from. But they found a piece of paper in her pocket, and it had a Hebrew song on it. They've been going from house to house to try to find out if anyone knows who she could be," my cousin explained. "She's been taken to New End Hospital."

It was a terrible shock. I really did go weak at the knees.

"Quick! We must go right away!"

Leaving Shmuel and Roni asleep in bed, we rushed out of the house and into Klári's car. We raced to the hospital in Hampstead still wearing our nightclothes. We had no idea how bad Bilha's injuries might be. We didn't even know if she'd survive.

When we got there, we saw her whole head was bandaged, and she was still unconscious. There were dressings all over her face, which was terribly bruised. She looked so strange and pale, lying completely still in the hospital bed, with nurses and doctors checking on her all the time. It was obviously very serious.

I forced myself to act calmly, but panic was surging through me. We sat all night by her bed. Every time the doctors spoke to Klári, my sense of dread grew worse because I couldn't understand what they were saying.

What if she never woke up? What if I never saw her smile again? How could I bear it? I imagined having to tell Shmuel our daughter was dead, God forbid. After having protected her so carefully all my life, how could I have let this happen?

Bilha finally regained consciousness the following morning. Klári and I hadn't moved from her bedside. I'll never forget the moment she opened her eyes. I'll never forget the kindness and care we all received. We were complete strangers in the country, but they treated us simply as human beings who needed help. There was no mention of money. The priority was to save Bilha's life, no matter who we were or where we'd come from.

Klári called the doctor who had been looking after Shmuel so that he could give him a sedative. Then we broke the news of the accident to him.

Although she would have to spend several more weeks in hospital, and the damage to her face was so bad that she'd need facial surgery, the most important thing was that she was alive. But her beautiful face . . . I didn't want Bilha to see herself in a mirror.

So now we had two patients to look after. It was clear we wouldn't be going home to Israel anytime soon. We tried to make the best of things and Klári continued to look after us. After several operations and other kinds of treatment, Bilha finally came out of hospital and began her convalescence.

We couldn't bear to tell René and Piri the awful news. What was the point, when it would only upset them? I couldn't break my old habit of trying to shield them from pain. And I wanted to keep everything calm for Esti, still alone in Israel, finishing her exams. Everyone would have to know eventually, because at some point she'd need some dental treatment too and I refused to let anyone but my brother Imi repair my daughter's teeth. But that would have to wait until she was well enough to fly back to Israel.

Bilha had been home for only a short time when we were rushing for the phone to call the emergency services again. Despite all our efforts to keep him calm, the stress had brought on another heart attack for Shmuel.

In the middle of all this drama, as the paramedics were carrying my husband on a stretcher into the back of the ambulance, one of them caught sight of Bilha. He couldn't help commenting on the state of her face.

"She's been in the wars!" he said, kindly. "What happened?"

I still only had a few words of English, but Bilha could speak for herself by then. Her weeks in hospital had made her a lot more fluent.

"I was in a road accident," she told him. "I was crossing the North Circular and I think I must have automatically looked left instead of right, like we do in Israel. I was knocked down by an articulated lorry."

"Oh my goodness, you're a lucky girl!" he said. "I can't believe you're up and about now. I was the one who picked you up. That was a nasty scene. It's amazing you're here today talking to me."

What a miracle Bilha's survival had been. Another one.

We had more difficult decisions ahead. The doctors advised against flying for Shmuel, and we were also worried that the summer heat in Israel would be bad for his health.

"Don't worry . . . you can stay with me for as long as you need to," Klári said. "I can show you a bit more of London."

"But what about the children? What about their education?"

"We have schools in London! I'll help you. I know which the best ones are. Think how good their English will be after going to school here!"

It felt completely overwhelming. To start all over again, a whole new life in a whole new country, a whole new language and culture, at the age of forty-three? But this time without my sisters. And I'd be parted once more from my brother. The thought of another family separation was very hard. I'd never imagined for a moment we'd ever have to leave Israel after the difficulties we had in getting there.

So I was determined our new life would be only temporary. A year at most. As soon as Shmuel was well enough, we'd be on a plane back home. As soon as possible, we'd be back in our old flat in Tel Aviv. The last thing I wanted was to live in Europe again. It just didn't feel a safe place to be a Jew.

The whole situation made me feel like a refugee again. But I told myself not to worry. We weren't about to be rounded up and killed. It would be OK. It had to be OK. And I knew exactly where my sisters and brother were. We could keep in touch by letter, and even the occasional telephone call, although phoning abroad was still a big event in those days.

Klári helped us find good schools for Roni and Bilha, which was very important to Shmuel and me. We found a house to rent not far from hers in Golders Green. After the summer holidays, Bilha and Roni seemed to find it easy to make friends and settle down to their studies in their new schools. Shmuel and I were both amazed at how quickly they learned their new language—we found it much harder, of course, having already had to learn Hebrew, and being so much older.

"How do you say *this*? How do you say *that*?" Shmuel was always asking the children. They did their best to help him pick up English, enough to get by. Out of kindness, or self-preservation? I'm not entirely sure. The move and his health problems had made him no less strict a father. He wasn't an easy man to refuse. And he still wasn't well.

By the end of 1967 it was clear that Shmuel's health could not stand returning to Israel. So we turned our move into an opportunity for the children.

Volví helped Esti pack up our flat in Tel Aviv and she flew out to join us. Soon she was applying to English universities. One thing we had learned in life was that the most important thing you can give your children is an education. Nobody can take that away from them. Money, possessions . . . all that can vanish. But education, what's inside you—never.

The children worked hard and they did very well at school, and then at university. All three went on to have interesting and fulfilling careers: Esti trained to be a schoolteacher, and then she became a university lecturer, an expert in Jewish studies. Bilha qualified as a psychologist and family therapist. And, some years later, after gaining a degree in economics, Roni became a chartered accountant.

We went back to Israel on holidays when Shmuel was well enough, and managed to visit our families most years, but we never lived in Tel Aviv again.

We kept our connection with Israel in other ways. On Jewish holidays, Shmuel arranged services in a community center across the road for Israelis in London, and often led the prayers too. I found this extremely moving, especially on Yom Kippur, not just because he was my husband, and the father of my children, but because he was so emotional himself in his davening. He sang and rocked back and forth with all his heart and soul. Shmuel had a fantastic voice, powerful, tuneful and intense. He practiced carefully for weeks beforehand every year, rehearsing some of the melodies we had both grown up with in Hungary, and new ones he'd learned in Israel. Hearing his rendition of the final prayer for forgiveness on the Day of Atonement, the Ne'ila, which comes before the blowing of the ram's horn, always brought tears to my eyes. I know I was far from alone.

1973–1984

Suddenly our family began to expand again. Both girls met their future husbands and married soon after university. How strange and joyful it was to welcome Bilha's Julian into the family: he was a young man so perfectly English we couldn't believe it. His grandparents were originally from Romania and Poland, but his parents were born in England. Julian had started to attend Shmuel's favorite synagogue, Hager's Shul, in his teens. He'd walk there alone all the way from Edgware. He met Bilha at a youth event at the Sassover Shul on Finchley Road on the Festival of Simchat Torah, the day that celebrates the end and the beginning of the annual cycle of public Torah readings.

How different their wedding was from our own. How much calmer the early years of their marriage. Happily for us all, our first grandchild was soon on her way.

There had been a time when I couldn't imagine ever becoming a mother. Yet, in 1974, I became a grandmother. It felt like a sudden transformation, because Bilha kept her due date from me and I hadn't known that she was in the operating room having a caesarean. She didn't want me to worry, and wouldn't let Julian tell me until after the baby was safely born.

He drove Shmuel and me to Middlesex Hospital in central London, where I held Baby Nina for the first time. All grandparents are filled with joy and wonder at that moment. It always seems like a miracle. But when you know what it has taken to reach this point, when you think about what has been lost in the journey to get here, then the beginning of a new generation, a third generation, has a truly special significance. Her Hebrew name was my own mother's, Nechama. But Bilha hadn't even known that Anyuka was usually called Nina. Her choice of names was extraordinarily special.

It's traditional for Jews from central or eastern Europe to name a newborn after a family member who's recently died—maybe a grandparent or a great-grandparent. It keeps their memory alive in the child, and makes it more likely that the new arrival will grow up to be curious about their namesake, remembering and honoring them, and living up to their best characteristics. Names are kept for generations. Usually we don't name new babies after anyone who's died in tragic circumstances. The Holocaust is one exception. Many survivors preserved the names of family members who were killed. It seemed a double punishment for their names to vanish too. Imi, René and Piri all have daughters called Nechama, which in Hebrew means comfort.

Esti had meanwhile fallen in love with another child of survivors, a young man called Mordechai, who was born in Germany. His refugee parents had returned home after the war, but they didn't want their boys to grow up in Germany, so sent them instead to a very Orthodox yeshiva in Gateshead. Perhaps it's not surprising that the children of survivors were drawn to others with similar upbringings, people who understand the way that scars can be handed down. I'm sure my own past experiences influenced our offspring more than we knew, in ways that are hard to understand or explain. Mordechai must have been similarly affected.

The Holocaust not only killed the people who died during the war, more people than the mind can take in, but also killed something in everybody who lived through it. It meant that survivors could never lead normal lives and neither could their children, as I eventually came to realize. Maybe the next generation was even affected too.

My niece said recently that in their family they were brought up remembering the anniversaries of deaths, not birthdays. Her generation really felt the absence of grandparents, great-aunts and uncles, and the aunt and uncle who had never grown up. The children of survivors grew up full of unspoken anxieties, trying to take care of their parents even while we thought we were looking after them. My children were bright and clever, and always worked hard at school and university, determined to succeed in life, as if success might be a kind of safety net. And maybe we encouraged this. Certainly we were extremely proud of all their many achievements.

But I didn't always know how best to help them. Like most of my generation, I had survived so long by avoiding this subject. And so my promise still lay buried, along with my memories.

I loved helping to look after my grandchildren. For a while, it seemed a new one was born every year. A year after Nina came Esti's first child, Tali. Then Nina's sister Daphna, then Esti's Sharon, and soon Bilha's youngest, Shuli. Esti had Danny in 1981, and by that time Roni was married to Linda. They met at a London Jewish Youth group called Sinai, and their first daughter, Dalia, was born in 1983. So many children in the next generation. I felt so happy and proud.

In the family and also in the wider world, the Shoah remained in the background, the great unspoken fact of my life.

Nobody dared to ask me about it. I still couldn't imagine anyone wanting to hear about the Holocaust. I certainly wasn't yet able to describe the horrors I had been through. One evening, in the late 1970s, I was at Bilha's house visiting the children. It was bath time, and I was helping out as usual, with my sleeves rolled up to my elbows, when little Nina suddenly pointed to my Auschwitz tattoo.

"Safta, what's that? Why have you got blue numbers on your arm?"

Bilha gasped. She confessed to Nina years later how stunned and upset she was by the question. Bilha, Esti and Roni had always been terrified of upsetting me. Mentioning my tattoo was completely taboo. Nobody in the family ever spoke of it, though of course they knew about it. How can you hide such a thing, especially in a hot country? But everyone still acted as if it was invisible.

I'm not sure what I said. I must have brushed the question aside . . . How could I possibly have explained Auschwitz to a five-year-old?

1984–1985

Shmuel had long ago returned to work. I tried to make sure that he didn't overdo it, and that he had plenty of time off, though it wasn't always easy to persuade him to take a holiday. The trouble was, he had been a chain-smoker, like many men of his generation, and when he gave up smoking, he put on weight. We got into the habit of going away to health farms—all the rage then—to try to lose a few pounds.

Yet despite this, in 1984 he had yet another massive heart attack, and was back in hospital. At first the doctor didn't want to operate, but then, in the middle of the ward round, Shmuel's heart began to fail again. Now open-heart surgery was the only way to keep him alive. Even so, Shmuel refused to abandon work, and could barely be parted from his bedside telephone. I had to remove the receiver from his hand so they could wheel him into the operating room.

I worried terribly. I felt so dependent on him in England—much more than when we had lived in Israel together. I still wasn't fluent in English. I still felt like a foreigner. Now that my children had left home and were settled with new spouses and children, I was all the more focused on my husband. And always at the back of my mind was the worry that Europe was a dangerous place for a Jew.

I was determined to keep Shmuel as fit and healthy as possible.

After Chanukah I booked the two of us into an alternative medicine center in Buckinghamshire. It was a residential place called Tyringham Hall. We would be there for my birthday, and for New Year too.

We'd been before, and liked it a lot. It was very reasonable, and most egalitarian. You never knew who you might meet there, rich or poor, because they weren't trying to make a profit and never turned anyone away.

Tyringham was a beautiful place—an eighteenth-century country mansion, with grand staircases and mirrors and a panelled library and lovely reception rooms looking out over elegant gardens. It was set in acres of woodland and farmland. The regime was austere, but it seemed to work for us. The idea of holistic treatment was quite new then. It was all about self-healing, and nutrition was a very important part: we had to eat only cleansing whole foods, raw and vegetarian, and not very much of those.

We stuck to our program seriously and did all the right things. If a doctor told Shmuel to run two miles, he was the kind of man who'd run six. So we spent a couple of weeks nibbling at our tiny portions of alfalfa sprouts, and swallowing down revolting hot drinks containing mysterious herbal ingredients that were supposed to make us slimmer and healthier. Women in white coats weighed us and gave us exercise plans. We had massages and osteopathy treatments. Shmuel swam every day in the special hydrotherapy pool, where you could swim against a current. We were determined not to leave without meeting our targets. Shmuel was well on the way to recovery, I believed.

The evening before we were due to go home, it began to snow very heavily, thick flakes catching the light through the window. Shmuel kept looking outside.

"Look at that," he said. "The roads will be awful tomorrow."

"Maybe it won't settle," I suggested hopefully. I knew how anxious it made him to drive in snow. "Or maybe it'll melt by the time we go home. We've got the whole day ahead of us."

"I suppose we could always stay an extra night if it's really bad tomorrow," he said.

"That's a good idea. As long as we set off early on Friday, we can be home for Shabbat."

The snow glowed in the darkness. We looked at our schedules for the next day.

"Don't forget that I'm planning to have a quick swim first thing tomorrow," he reminded me as we turned out the light. "You sleep in till your exercise class. I'll see you at breakfast."

"Breakfast!" I laughed.

When I woke up the next morning I had a strange sensation that there was somebody in the room with me. It was such a strong presence that I sat up in bed and turned on the light. But there was nobody there. Shmuel's side of the bed was empty. He'd stuck to his plan. So I got dressed in T-shirt and leggings and went to the gym.

The music was blaring, and I was concentrating hard on following the instructor and sticking to the beat when the manager came in. He was looking for me. He called me over. Took me to a private office. Made sure I was sitting down. And then he broke the awful news.

"Mrs. Ebert, I'm afraid your husband has collapsed. In the pool."

I understood what he was trying to say immediately. It had finally happened. I had dreaded this moment for so long. Done everything I could to ward it off. Yet now I couldn't take it in. I felt completely numb. My lips wouldn't move.

"We're quite sure he didn't feel any pain. He must have died instantly."

I couldn't speak. How could Shmuel be gone? We had been married for thirty-six years. How could I suddenly be a widow?

I thought I was so tough. I thought I could survive anything. But now, without warning, my last reserves of strength vanished. I felt completely forsaken.

I called my son Roni, and a few hours later he and Bilha were with me, organizing everything. There was so much to do, and also so much waiting—for doctors, police, the coroner, I don't know what. It took so long, and I was in no state to do any of it. I couldn't even bear to pack our bags.

He had been such a strong and forceful man and he'd protected me for so long. And now all the safety and security he provided was gone, in an instant. It felt too soon. I wasn't ready. Shmuel was sixty-three when he died, and I had just celebrated my sixty-first birthday, although officially I was still only fifty-five. Ever since I had to change my documents in order to get away from Buchenwald, I'd not found a suitable moment to put things right.

His death hit me much harder than I could have imagined possible. It was as if a barrier had finally been broken. All the tears I'd kept at bay for so many years came flooding out. All the grief I had kept inside since Auschwitz-Birkenau finally escaped, heaped on top of my agony at losing Shmuel.

I felt so terribly vulnerable. So terribly alone. Loss piled on loss, as if all the separations that had happened long ago had only just taken place. I felt like a young woman whose mother had only just been murdered. Brutally. Incomprehensibly. A girl whose little sister and brother had only just been killed. Who had hardly had time to recover from the death of her father. I still thought about the promise I'd made to him, to take care of my siblings when he was gone. I was forced instantly back into the past, and it was unbearable. I remembered my cousins Hilda and Magda, and all our other cousins, all my aunts, my uncles, my friends from Bonyhád.

All the loss I had already experienced returned in full force. I had been unable to mourn at the time. Nobody could afford to let grief in. Any weakness led straight to death. You had to be strong. You couldn't give in.

We had imagined, my sisters and I, that after having survived, our lives would be "normal." We could carry on, and put the past behind us. But despite our best efforts to occupy our minds with the day-to-day business of ordinary living, even the smallest thing could take us back. The truth is, it always will. Sometimes it's like being two people at once.

Now I realize that when Shmuel died I was able to grieve at last in a more natural way than had ever been possible before.

But at the time it made me feel—as grief does—that I was falling apart. The world seemed to collapse around me. It was very frightening. There was so much unexpressed pain, so deeply buried. I didn't know what was happening to me. Everything felt beyond comprehension, just as it had in the camps.

The family took care of everything. I couldn't be alone. I stayed with Bilha and the children—Nina, Daphna and Shuli—and I wept and wept. I didn't know I had so many tears inside me. I had never felt this way before.

One morning, about three months later, I decided that enough was enough. The longer I stayed away from home, the harder it would be to return, to live on my own. I packed my suitcase and went down to tell my daughter.

"I'm fine now," I said.

"What do you mean?" Bilha was amazed.

"I want to go home. Could you drive me home, please?"

I returned to the flat Shmuel and I had shared in London, where I still live today. I missed my own bed, and I like to have all my own things around me. But I have never liked to be alone on Shabbat, so I began to spend a weekend in turn with each of my children. One Friday night I'd go to Esti to stay, the next to Bilha and the next to Roni and his family. That way I was able to spend time with all my grandchildren too, and eventually my great-grandchildren.

1985–1988

I wasn't the only one in my circle of friends with a bit more time on their hands than before. Our growing families no longer needed us in quite the way they used to. It's different being a grandmother—Safta, as everyone now calls me. We certainly didn't think of ourselves as old. But many of us were beginning to remember the past in a way we'd never let ourselves before.

When someone dies, you can't help looking back, going through old memories in your mind, turning things over and over. Shmuel had been so strong for me when I was rebuilding my life, first in Israel and then again, for a second time, in England. Now I was having to rebuild for the third time, but without him. It was very hard. Far away from my sisters and brother, long separated now from the community we'd formed in those early days in Bnei Brak, I missed the companionship of people who had been through the same experiences as I had.

I couldn't talk to my children. They were busy being parents. Why traumatize them with my past now? Roni and Linda were having another baby—little Yudit. Four years later Naomi was born. And after Naomi came Shmuel, the first baby in our family named after my late husband. They all needed to get on with their lives. They needed to be looking forwards, not back. In the wider world, things were slowly changing. There were the first programs on television about the Holocaust, dramas and documentaries. Little by little, the world was beginning to show an interest in the experience of survivors. Still I worried that, for my family, my own story would be as difficult for them to hear as for me to tell.

A friend called Marsha realized that quite a few of us were struggling with the past, as she was, and invited me to her house to meet some other survivors. Marsha was from Lithuania, where some say the systematic killings of the Holocaust really began. The Jewish population there was large and long established, but in the course of three years it was almost completely destroyed, annihilated by massacres, forced labor and death camps. As in Hungary, many Lithuanians supported Nazi policies and took part in the genocide. That's a very hard thing to come to terms with. And in England, most people knew nothing about it.

Soon I was the treasurer of a little group who met each week. This suited me very well. I've always liked helping people. It gives me a sense of purpose in life and I've been doing it from an early age.

Word spread, and more people asked to join. Soon there were more of us than could comfortably fit in one person's living room. We needed to spread our wings. But how?

Marsha had an idea. She'd heard from a friend in Israel about a woman at Jewish Care in London who was an expert in Holocaust trauma. Her name was Judith Hassan, and her own grandparents had been in a camp in France. Her mother escaped to Britain just before the war, but many of her more distant family had been killed in Auschwitz. Judith was developing new ways to help survivors who were suffering later in life from the return of terrible memories. Very few people understood anything about this at that time, and so she really was a pioneer. She had already worked with refugees from Nazi persecution for over a decade, and also some Holocaust survivors. Marsha asked Judith for help.

We wanted to make our group more official, but to keep it informal. She told her that we needed a place to meet. Somewhere neutral, not part of an organization or institution. A place where we could be sociable and help each other and where everyone would be comfortable. Marsha was quite clear that we weren't looking for therapy or psychiatric help. There was nothing wrong with us! We just wanted to find somewhere we could get together to discuss life, and help each other, as we always had before. That was how we'd all survived during the war—through mutual support.

Judith seemed to understand perfectly. She found funding for a space where we could meet every Sunday morning, behind a big department store in Swiss Cottage, north London. She always made sure there was plenty to eat at the meetings, and that we could help ourselves to food and make tea and coffee whenever we liked. It's important for many people who have endured starvation to know they have control over what they eat and drink. We called the group SOS—Survivors of Shoah— and began to advertise the meetings.

I can't pretend it was always easy. People came from so many different backgrounds, nationalities and experiences, both in terms of what they'd been through during the Holocaust and after liberation. We spoke different languages. We had suffered in different ways and had different kinds of problems. For the first few sessions we spoke about the past, and got to know each other. Then it settled down into a pattern of bridge-playing, games, eating, outings, gossip and plenty of laughter too.

There were ongoing tensions, undeniably and understandably.

The interesting thing was how quickly people set a pecking order—who had been through what, how bad each survivor's experiences had been—and that urge has never quite gone away.

"What do you know, Hungarian?" someone might say to me. "How long were you in Auschwitz? A few months? We were there for three years!"

Another woman once said this to me: "When you were still at home in Hungary with your mother, you didn't even know the war was happening. I was already in the camp. What do you know about having no food? What do you know about suffering? Two years I had to suffer. What do you know?"

And do you know what? I never said anything in reply. I saw that, in a way, they were right. But I also knew it wasn't my fault. It shouldn't have happened to them. It shouldn't have happened to any of us. But I said not one word, because I knew I couldn't make them suffer even more. The important thing is to listen, and the problem is that most people cannot listen.

We were learning how to help each other. And one of the things we learned was that it's not good to compare suffering. When I understood that, I tried to help others see that it's not helpful. And, of course, different people react differently to the same bad thing.

Judith had a difficult time trying to support our self-help group. She had lots of professional experience and qualifications, but this was something new. People were suspicious, even hostile. Many survivors resented how little Anglo-Jewry had done to support Jews in Europe during the war, or help them when they first came to Britain. Since Judith wasn't a survivor herself, she was seen as "one of them."

"What does she know?" they said. "She wasn't there. How can she understand? We mustn't let her take over. She can't tell us what to do."

I came to know Judith very well during this time, and often took the role of mediator between her and the rest of the group. I thought she was exceptionally tactful in her approach. She never said "I know best." She always said "You teach me." It's true she was "on the other side," as some people thought, but she recognized that fact. She knew she could help but never completely understand.

And thanks to her great sensitivity about these things, slowly, slowly the whole group came to accept her.

I think it was Judith who first suggested that I write my memories down. But she says it was my idea. I don't remember now exactly how we started. Although I still found it too hard to talk to my family face-to-face about my past, I realized that I wanted to record what had happened to me in Auschwitz-Birkenau. I wanted my children to know eventually, and their children, and their children's children.

But how could I tell them in a way that was bearable both for me and for them? I didn't know where to start. I thought my English was too bad, and nobody would understand me. And remembering was so hard and painful.

I trusted Judith, and she offered to help me. It took a very long time. We talked and talked, and she listened, and after each session she wrote down what I said, as if I were writing it myself. Then the next week I would read it, and make sure it was right. Later, when she was writing a book that I helped her with, Judith said she became my scribe and I became her teacher. Sometimes I wrote down things I remembered on scraps of paper, notes that were half in English, half in Hungarian. These were memories—scraps of memories—that I had kept hidden for a very long time. It wasn't easy to get them back. It was the first time I had ever tried to put them in some kind of order, to make a story of my life. It was the first time I found the strength to bear witness.

I told Judith about my childhood, my happy home with my parents, and how important that had been for me in Auschwitz. I told her how the need to look after my sisters, and take care of them when my parents and brother and sister were dead, had kept me alive. I told her how my faith had helped me to survive. I told her about the miracle of finding my brother Imi again, and how I had slowly recovered in Switzerland, and rebuilt my life in Israel with my husband and new family, and then again in London. I told her everything I could remember. It wasn't a historical document. At that point, I couldn't check dates or place names or other details. I couldn't talk with my sisters because they were far away and didn't want to talk. But little by little, from somewhere deep inside, I retrieved the memories I had spent so many decades trying my hardest never to think about.

Eventually, we had a typescript I was happy with. Twelve pages. It took a very long time—over a year in all. It seemed I had to tell the story to myself to make sense of it. Writing it down allowed me to acknowledge the huge importance of the experience and how it has defined my entire life. And during that process, I found the strength to make an important decision.

I would return to Auschwitz-Birkenau. And I would go back with my daughter, Esti.

1988

We flew to Warsaw, arriving on May 5, 1988. Our coach took us straight to Lublin, once such a thriving center of Jewish culture that the city was known as the Jerusalem of the Polish Kingdom. After the Nazis' Wannsee Conference in 1942, Lublin became the headquarters of Operation Reinhard, the plan to exterminate Poland's Jews. Here men designed death camps so efficient that few people now even know their names, because there were so few survivors. At Belzec nearly half a million Jews were murdered. At Sobibor, a quarter of a million.

Our tour was organized by the Mizrachi, the center for religious Zionism in the UK. Most of the group came from London and its outskirts, and there were also people from Leeds, Manchester, Salford and even Israel. Few of them knew much about the Holocaust. People didn't, in those days. Some had read a few books, watched some films. The others were all closer to Esti's age than mine. She was in her late thirties, and her youngest child, Danny, was at school, so she felt she could leave him for a week. I was the only survivor.

Why did I want to return to Auschwitz? That's a very difficult question to answer. Most survivors—including my own sisters—never wanted to go back. Every time you think about what happened, every time you talk about it, you relive it in a way. But I felt I had to make this journey, partly just to prove to myself that I could. I also wanted to show my daughter, and to be with her at the place where even to dream of having a daughter had seemed impossible. I wanted to give her a sense, not just of what happened in the Holocaust, but of what has been lost as a consequence: the rich culture of Jews all over Europe, our beautiful heritage. I feel very strongly that one of the difficulties for the children of survivors is that they have no roots.

Something else was weighing on me heavily.

Usually, when your parents die, you know exactly where they are. You can visit the cemetery. You know they were buried according to their wishes and to the laws of Judaism. My mother has no grave. Her ashes are somewhere, I suppose, mixed with those of millions of others, including my brother and sister. There's nowhere in the world I can point to and say, "That is where my mother lies." But I could return to the place where I last saw her, and I could take my daughter there.

That first evening in Lublin, I took one mouthful of bread and I could not swallow. The taste was so strong and so sour, so full of terrible memories. I knew I could never eat Polish bread again. Luckily, when you keep kosher, you have to be prepared to face things you cannot eat. You never travel without some food. I was prepared for this. But not for the feelings that the taste of that bread brought back.

One of the most famous yeshivas in the world once stood in Lublin. From the synagogue, it's just five or six kilometres to Majdanek, the death camp where so many thousands of Lublin's Jews were killed. On one day alone, 18,000 people were shot there. It's so close to the city, you can walk there.

Yet people say they didn't know what was happening. At

Majdanek, a camp that had otherwise hardly been changed since it was liberated by the Red Army, we saw the mausoleum built after the war, a gigantic domed circular memorial that appears to hover above a great mound created out of the compacted, mixed-up ashes of the dead. They had been gathered from the heaps of cremated remains found all around the camp. The frieze around the dome is inscribed with a message: "Let our fate be a warning to you."

We climbed the steps and stood in front of a whole hill of human ashes, maybe twenty metres across. You could even see a few fragments of bone. This was very hard for my companions to grasp. So many people. So much ash. How could that be? How was it possible?

When you think about it, Poland is one big cemetery.

From Majdanek we went to Cracow. They had desecrated and destroyed most of the old Jewish cemeteries in the country. They had made walls, roads and pavements from people's tombstones. A few were left partially standing. Some have been unearthed and re-erected. In what's left of the Old Cemetery, I found the grave of a very famous sixteenth-century rabbi and Talmudic scholar from Prague called Yom-Tov Lipmann Heller. I'm directly descended from him on my mother's side, through his daughter Nissel. I can trace it back through so many generations I lose count. My mother was always proud of this fact, and all the other distinguished rabbonim in her line.

"He is your great-great-great-great . . . I don't know how many greats . . . great-grandfather," I told Esti. "You come from a very famous Jewish family."

We were due to go to Auschwitz-Birkenau on the third day of our journey. As the moment approached, I almost regretted my decision. On the evening before we were due to visit, my daughter came to me with a question.

"Ima, the others have asked me to ask you something. You don't have to say yes."

"What is it?"

"Tomorrow, at the camp . . . could you say a few words to the group? About what happened to you? Only if you want to."

Did I hesitate?

A little, perhaps.

Esti had come with me because she wanted to know more. Tentatively at first, and then with more confidence, for the first time in our lives, we were finally talking about the past. I knew how important it was to try to explain to her what had happened. To show her. I wanted her to hear my story, from me. But I was beginning to realize that my responsibilities were not just to my own family. Everyone on the trip had come to find out more, and I had seen how attentively they listened at the lectures and talks we'd already had. If there were people who wanted to listen, how could I refuse to speak?

The Auschwitz-Birkenau Museum was created very soon after the end of the war, and in 1979 the whole complex became a UNESCO World Heritage site. It's hard to take in the scale of the place. It's enormous. When we first got off the coach the next morning, you might have thought we were arriving at a holiday camp. There are beds filled with beautiful flowers. There's a shop where you can buy things: food, postcards, little souvenirs. Again, it was a lovely summer's day. The sun was shining. The sky was blue.

But every barracks contains a museum display to show visitors what happened. You walk in and see thousands of pairs of little shoes. And you think of those Jewish children, babies, who walked in these little shoes and are no more. They should be alive and they are not here. You see human hair, in glass cases. Perhaps some of it was mine. You see thousands of pairs of glasses. Yet although indescribably awful to see, these terrible exhibits cannot begin to convey what it was actually like here.

And finally, we reached Birkenau. It was very difficult walking into the part of the camp I knew so well. I felt a choking sensation. Everywhere, that smell . . . Perhaps it was just me, but I really didn't think I was imagining it. I could still taste the smell I remembered so well.

One of the watchtowers had been turned into an exhibit. I climbed the steps with our group and looked out through the glass. I was standing on the very spot where German guards used to stand watching us, night and day, machine guns in their hands. A place I never imagined I would ever stand.

It was so strange to look out over such emptiness. How powerfully I felt that emptiness. I vividly remembered thousands and thousands of people standing there on the *Appellplatz*. For hours and hours and hours. Morning and night. We couldn't move. We were numb with terror. And now there was nothing. Nobody at all. It was so quiet. Peaceful, even. Still not a single bird singing. But how much fear and how much suffering were endured here? How many people were killed for no reason? I thought the ground would be red from blood. It should be red. But it's not. It's grey. Even the air still seems grey from the ashes.

Time appeared both frozen and endless, as if it didn't exist at all. From this changed perspective, I tried to work out my own feelings about returning to the place where I could so easily have been killed. And I realized that, despite the pain, I also felt a sense of satisfaction.

You haven't succeeded, I thought to myself. In my mind, I was addressing not just Hitler, or Eichmann, but every single person who helped the Nazi regime. *You wanted me dead, yet I* am here, and my daughter is with me. *We came of our own free will, and when we choose, we will leave of our own free will. So you didn't succeed in destroying us all. You didn't win. You will never win. Not as long as we are here, and we remember.*

I wasn't their victim. I was a survivor. In 1944, when they brought me here choking for air, crammed into a goods wagon with my entire community, they planned to destroy every single one of us. Perhaps a few Jews might accidentally remain in the world, here and there, but they wanted to destroy us as a people completely. And after the Holocaust, we did indeed wonder how we would ever regain our strength. Yet luckily, thank God, today we are far from finished. We are here, and, most importantly, we have a voice. We can speak, and we can speak out.

I can't remember precisely what I said to the group, or what they asked me. A few had questions, but for the most part they simply looked and listened. For the first time they grasped the difficult fact that, even with all the books in the world, this is a place that's impossible to understand in its entirety. It's impossible to explain.

But it is possible to bear witness.

Learning what happened from somebody who had lived through the camp herself seemed to have the effect of transforming history into memory for my group. Confronted with all the numbers on the explanation panels in the museum, numbers so huge they seemed unfathomable, they could turn to me: one person. One life.

On that first trip with Esti, we went from Auschwitz to Warsaw. There we visited the cemeteries for hours, looking for our grandparents and great-grandparents, and the graves of famous rabbis. We went to the ghetto and to the place where they rounded up the Jews to take them to Treblinka, and then to the remote site of the death camp at Treblinka itself, where over a million Jews and Roma and Sinti were murdered.

It's a long road through a deep forest, nearly to Poland's border. The road was once black with human ashes.

I found this journey a very shocking experience. In a way, Treblinka was even worse than Auschwitz, because it was designed only to be an extermination camp, and people were killed even more quickly and efficiently, and in greater numbers at a time. There were no selections to speak of, and almost no survivors. None living now. The Germans demolished everything when they abandoned it, as the Russians were advancing. So now there is no gas chamber to see. No crematorium. No evidence.

But instead you see stones. Memorial stones. Stone after stone. Hundreds and hundreds of them, big and small.

Yet each stone is not for one single human being, or even for a family.

On some stones you see the name of a town. Cracow, perhaps. A single stone for 10,000 Jews. On another, another town. Perhaps that's 5,000 Jews. Or 2,000. Or 4,433. Or 42. There are also countries represented. At Treblinka, there is stone after stone after stone. Nothing but stones. And every stone stands in place of a community that can never come back to life.

Esti was quiet and reflective after we returned to London. Very serious. I felt something between us had shifted, in a good way. Our journey together had been exactly the right thing to do, for both of us. It opened the way for more conversations, and it meant that Bilha and Roni knew they could also talk to me if they wanted to. Not that this was easy. But sharing my written testimony with my children made it easier.

Some years later, in July 1996, I returned with a much

younger group: teenagers and people in their twenties. Three of them were my granddaughters: Nina, Tali and Daphna. They sang and danced and brought life and hope to a shul that had been a place of worship for hundreds, and now stood bereft and empty. Again, we visited Majdanek and Treblinka.

When we reached Auschwitz, on July 9, it was especially difficult for me to talk. This was the precise day, exactly fifty-two years earlier, that I had first arrived here with my family. How different it had been. We didn't know we had arrived in hell.

I decided to take these young people back up the watchtower.

"I will tell you what I went through in this place," I told them. "I chose this tower because this was the place where Germans with machine guns looked down on us. They could see the whole camp. Every movement. Everything we did."

I told them what had happened to our family, and in the watchtower we said Kaddish for my mother, my brother and my sister. There are certain religious obligations for Orthodox Jews which require a *minyan*, the presence of ten Jewish men aged thirteen and older. The Kaddish is a very important mourning ritual in which we give merit to the souls of those no longer in this world by proclaiming the sovereignty of God. That day we had a *minyan*, and this meant that at last I could hear Kaddish recited for my murdered family, for those I loved so much, who had been humiliated, hated and killed by the Nazis with no ceremony, no resting place. In this way I felt I could fulfill a *chesed shel emes*—literally, a selfless true kindness—for Anyuka, for Bela and for Berta, paying them the utmost reverence, respect and honor in this terrible place.

Many tears were shed. The young people were completely silenced by the experience. For some time they simply could not speak. There were no words.

I showed them everything I could, and shared my memories

of each part of the camp. Together we looked at the railway line and the Ramp where we had arrived. We stood at the place where I had last seen my mother and Bela and Berta, and I told my granddaughters how we had lined up in front of Mengele and he had sent us right and left with no warning. I find it hard to think about, and hard to speak about in any detail. But when I was there with my own family, I could see how they could feel and imagine the horror and panic of that separation in a way that was far more powerful and meaningful than if I had told them the story in the same words, sitting in my flat in London. Being there together on that spot connected us all in a very important way.

Together we looked at the barracks. They were just like the ones where I'd once slept. I showed them the kind of boards we had slept on, with only a bit of straw and no blanket, nine or ten of us sometimes stuck together like sardines, one layer on top of another. They saw everything through my eyes, and this made it real for them.

Daphna had felt quite numbed and unsure of her emotions when she arrived. But she left with the sense that every one of the six million who were killed had a name, a face, a smile, a soul, like me. All the young people seemed to leave the memorial museum not with feelings of despair or hatred, but with a determination to bring light back into the darkest parts of our shared history, and a sense of their own responsibility for passing on what they had seen.

The satisfaction of walking freely into Auschwitz with my granddaughters, and walking freely out again, through those gates of hell, made me stronger. It was one of the most significant days of my life. Who would have believed it would ever be possible? When I was brought to Auschwitz in 1944, they told me there was no way out—only through the chimney.

This was not your plan, I kept thinking. *Look at me . . . I'm back. You wanted to kill me and yet I am here again. You murderers aren't here any more, but I am. And this time with my daughters' daughters. There are even more of us now and we can all come and go as we wish. You wanted to destroy us. You couldn't. You can't.*

It was one of my proudest moments.

But it was terrible to return. There is no question about that. And I am certain that my faith made the difficult journey a little easier, just as it had when I was young, and actually living through the horrors. With faith, it was easier to believe that you could come through. With faith, you have a better chance of holding on to hope. It's so important to believe in something. If you can't believe in human beings, then how can you bring children into this world?

So where does belief like that come from? Not everyone has it, certainly. I saw this in the camps. I thank my parents for my faith. All through my loving childhood, they brought me up with the kind of certainties that even Auschwitz couldn't shake: a belief not only in our faith, but in family and in the human spirit. I see it now in my children, in my grandchildren and in my great-grandchildren too, still unshakeable.

1992–1993

Not long after we'd finished writing my testimony together, Judith asked me to speak in public for the first time. I agreed willingly.

This was at a conference she was running about Holocaust education called "Survivors as Our Teachers." I didn't know quite what I could teach—and my son-in-law teased me about what language I would speak in, as my English was still quite broken and my Hungarian accent very strong—but I was happy to help. It was important to me, and I knew it was important to Judith. The idea that there might be different ways to learn about the Holocaust was still new. The Holocaust Educational Trust was only founded in 1988.

Luckily, it was no problem for me to stand up in front of all those professionals. I don't know why, but I am never nervous about talking to anyone. I don't like to use notes. With notes, I'm lost. When people listen so carefully, so attentively, it makes me feel I have something to say that is worth hearing. I knew what a difference it had made to the people I had accompanied to Auschwitz to hear my experiences at first hand because so many of them had written afterward to tell me. So that gave me confidence too.

My decision to unearth my buried pain had made me stronger. I had hidden a great deal for a very long time. The despair that followed Shmuel's death had been intense, but now I was ready to face both the past and the future. I told my audience how my efforts to bear witness had changed things for me, and for my family too. I explained that it is never too late. For survivors, self-help groups like ours offered a "second opportunity" to face traumas that many of us had never before been able to address. Giving testimony and bearing witness was part of that second chance. Educators and survivors could work together to ensure that young people would learn about the Holocaust in ways that brought its lessons home.

Judith said afterward: "You could hear a pin drop."

Long ago, on Yom Kippur 1944, I had made that promise to myself. If I survived, against all the odds—and I never believed I would—but *if* I survived, I'd tell the world what really happened. I was so determined then to change the world, single-handedly if need be. I hadn't forgotten that promise, but for nearly half a century I had struggled to honor it. There was always some obstacle that made it feel impossible. So many years of silence. So many years of feeling that nobody wanted to listen. Why would you talk if nobody listens?

But at last, that had changed. I was ready, and the world seemed more willing to listen.

I would talk for my own sake, and I would also speak for those I loved who hadn't survived. And for all the millions of people I never knew who died with them, all over Europe. I want the world never to forget this terrible crime against humanity. I had once hoped, naively, that after this, such genocides could never happen again. I was wrong.

But that only makes my task more urgent. The way we can learn from what happened is by speaking about it.

It's so important to tell the world what can happen when we are not tolerant of each other. That is the main thing to understand. When somebody is different from you, it doesn't mean they are worse or better. They are only different. If we can understand that, we can live in peace with one another.

This was the beginning of a whole new life for me. I can't tell you how many people I've spoken to since. I've even talked at the Houses of Parliament. But it all started with the sense that I really needed to communicate with the generations that came after me, young people in particular, and it was nourished by the feeling that they actually wanted to listen to me.

Meanwhile, our Survivors of Shoah group was growing fast. We needed a new home, and a new kind of organization. The important thing was to have a place where people could go. In the early 1990s I worked with Judith to put our case for funding and premises to Jewish Care. Two centers were born. They're both still thriving side by side, in Hendon, with the help of staff who speak many languages: Hungarian and Yiddish, Hebrew, French, German and Serbo-Croat.

There's the Holocaust Survivors' Center, where people can meet socially, share meals at the drop-in cafe and enjoy games, music and all kinds of cultural activities together. We have a Shabbat supper once a month, lots of guest speakers and regular celebration meals and concerts. Survivors can enjoy the company of other survivors, in whatever way suits them best. The soup here is thick and nourishing and we're served properly, at tables, not from communal containers. There are no queues. There's plenty of bread. Everywhere is clean and bright, nothing is painted yellow, and you won't see any striped material anywhere. No reminders.

Next door to the social center there's Shalvata, which Judith founded in 1990. This takes its name from the Hebrew word meaning "Peace of Mind." Deliberately kept separate, but easily accessible, Shalvata offers counselling, therapy and support for survivors of Nazi persecution and their families. Memories of traumatic events can sometimes re-emerge later in life. You don't know what will prompt them. Anyone can phone or drop in and make a private appointment. That's important, because in the Holocaust mental and physical ill health or disability meant death, so it can remain a difficult thing to admit publicly.

I never found I needed counselling or therapy myself. I prefer to manage things on my own. I just want to give. I never seek support, and gain strength instead from independence. For me, the best therapy is helping other people, and feeling I can make a difference to someone else's life. I was happy to be elected to the Users and Volunteers Advisory Committee, and have remained involved with the Center ever since.

You can probably guess that there were some big personality clashes in the early days of the HSC, and sometimes difficulties between different groups who used the Center. Who really counted as a "survivor'? What about the hidden children? Those who had fled persecution before the round-ups? It was hard for camp survivors struggling with traumatic memories and experiences of their own, still so vivid, to relate to the sufferings of others who had "only" been babies during the war.

"What do they know?"

The rows could be awful. And I could see both points of view.

But eventually we got through all that, disputes of this kind were put aside and the Center flourished. Differences were more easily overcome when we learned to focus together on other things, such as bridge or art.

About sixty of us used to play bridge very seriously every Monday afternoon, steadily improving our skills with the help of our teacher, Shirley. Such focus. Such concentration. Concentrating your mind on numbers (which I've always enjoyed), giving the game all your attention, spending time with other people, sharing a common language: all that was fun, of course. But many of us also found that bridge took our minds off darker thoughts and intrusive memories.

When I was young, I always thought of Imi and Piri as the ones who were "good at art" in our family. My role was to take responsibility and organize everyone. Now, I had fewer responsibilities, less to organize, and after decades of building and rebuilding my family, at last I had time to explore. So I joined the art class and discovered painting.

Our teacher, Barbara, always gave us free rein. She set up still lifes and taught us how to use watercolors, building up color layer by layer. We painted bowls of fruit and replicas of the Lewis chess pieces—which, of course, reminded me of Shmuel playing chess in Tel Aviv, one of our daughters on his lap. But if we wanted to paint from our imagination, that was fine. If we wanted to paint a tree or flowers or some other beautiful memory, that was good too. One man, who at first preferred to sit apart, alone at his table, painted mostly images of himself, at Auschwitz. So art became a way survivors could express traumatic memories that were too hard to put into words.

I found myself drawn to the pictures of Marc Chagall, a Jewish artist who once said that painting seemed to him "like a window" through which he "could have taken flight toward another world." I loved his fantastical images of his own youth in a small Chasidic town in the Russian Empire. Perhaps the snowy streets of nearby Vitebsk reminded me of my own childhood in Bonyhád. Both Jewish communities have now vanished forever. I lost myself in my efforts to reproduce the simple shapes and colors of Chagall's painting, the vivid blue domed rooftops, the sweeping sled tracks and the floating figure of the pedlar with his staff and sack, flying over the rooftops. A rootless, wandering Jew, everything he owns in a small sack on his back.

The Center was there for us when we needed it most. It became a lifeline for me and my friends, at a very important time in our lives. It allowed us to rebuild a new community. We proudly held exhibitions of our paintings, and invited our friends and families to see our work. Another group put on plays. Others met to chat and share jokes in Yiddish, the language of their childhoods. Others discussed current affairs. All this still goes on. We don't spend all our time thinking about the Holocaust. Quite the reverse.

I gradually became less involved in the running of the Center as my other work in Holocaust education took me away from it. But, until the pandemic, I continued to go there at least once a week, without fail, and usually more often. We all missed it terribly during the lockdowns, and each other too.

The Holocaust Survivors' Center began to record spoken testimonies, with the help of Shalvata. In August 1993 I recorded my own for the first time. I sat with a young South African man and he interviewed me for over two and a half hours. Now that recording is also in the British Library, and anyone can listen to it online at any time. It was exhausting to do, exhausting to remember and think about, but I was determined to see it through.

What happened to me could happen anywhere, I told my interviewer. We thought we were more Hungarian than the Hungarians. Our family had been established in Bonyhád for centuries. Our complacency was a terrible mistake. That's why

I give testimony, I said. So everyone should be prepared for the fact that anything can happen, at any time. We mustn't live under any illusions. We must always be vigilant about intolerance. It starts with words and thoughts. But that's just the beginning. You don't know where it might end.

We wanted to link survivors to schools, to share these important messages as widely as possible, but particularly with younger generations. Once others, like me, took that first step of recording their testimony, they also found they wanted to share their experiences through educational programs in schools, universities and museums and at public events. Shalvata offered training in the skills needed for this.

The Holocaust Educational Trust campaigned to make sure that the Holocaust became part of the National Curriculum in the UK. Since Holocaust Memorial Day was launched on January 27, 2001, on the anniversary of the liberation of Auschwitz-Birkenau, many of us have taken part in this international day of remembrance. This has become one of the busiest and most rewarding weeks of my year. I am always strengthened by the hundreds of appreciative letters I receive after visits and talks, particularly from children: warm and positive words written by Jews, Muslims and Christians, people of all other religions and none, from all over the world.

Yet when I started to tell my story in public, in primary schools, I wasn't sure how such a thing could even be possible. Primary schools! How would I talk to small children about the Holocaust, when it had taken me so long to tell my own children, and they were adults before we spoke? Judith and I thought hard about the words to use, and how I could frame my story in a way that made its message clear, but not so frightening that the children would have nightmares.

It wasn't easy. Every time I spoke, it brought back memories a part of me preferred to forget. Each time was a step into the unknown. I couldn't predict what might come into my head. One of my earliest visits was to my grandchildren's school, a Jewish primary in north London. The teachers were very welcoming. The children sat on the floor and looked up at me, waiting quietly and expectantly. Here was a group of nine- to eleven-year-olds, really very young, and a few of my own grandchildren were among them. I stood at the front of the room for a moment, trying to find the right words for such a young audience. And as I gazed back at their innocent faces, I found myself suddenly frozen.

A horrible thought had numbed me. A thought I had to push away. I couldn't let it out.

If you had been there, not one of you would have survived.

2010s

The truth is, I've always found it easier to answer the questions of strangers, to talk to large groups in public, than to discuss my past with my own family, at home. I can't help wanting to protect them, as my own parents had protected me. That's changing now. Partly because they listen to me speak. The first time my daughter Bilha came to one of my talks, she heard me tell the audience that I had kept my Auschwitz experience a secret for many years from my own family. Afterward, she said to me: "Ima, you thought we didn't know! All that time, you imagined we had no idea you had been in Auschwitz? Of course we knew. We saw your tattoo."

That blue inked number. A-10572. I don't know how I had deceived myself for so long. I had never tried to hide it. And, of course, they would have seen my sisters' numbers too: A-10571. A-10573. Of course they had guessed. While all the time I continued to hope they never would.

"But you never said anything . . ." I replied, astonished.

"We didn't want to upset you. We just knew we shouldn't talk about it."

Why had I tried to fool myself? I could not bear to think of them growing up with that knowledge. Yet Bilha had been tormented by that scar on my arm from an early age. It was visible. It was tangible. It was something mysterious yet meaningful.

Did it hurt? she used to wonder. When did I get it? How? Why? She couldn't stop thinking about the pain she imagined I felt when it was done. And I had no idea those thoughts were in her head. I imagined I had protected her from them by not talking about it. After all, I felt completely differently about that tattoo. When they went to the trouble of marking me with my number, it was a sign that I had a chance to live, not die. Perhaps that's why I never felt the need to be careful to wear long sleeves to hide it.

You never know how a child will take these things, even when they are grown up. Esti, as I've said, was the first to confront her family's past in the hardest way possible: by coming to Auschwitz with me. I don't know if I could have returned if she hadn't been there at my side.

Bilha found this idea more difficult. She has never wanted to go. For a long time she was haunted by thoughts of the Holocaust, as if she had inherited some part of my experiences and memories, although I had told her nothing. She had mostly learned the history of those terrible times from books and films. She didn't tell me for years how frightening her thoughts became for her. In a hot, rush-hour train, where perhaps a child is crying for water, she would often feel overwhelmed by thoughts of babies gasping for breath in the cattle trucks. On an icy day, she'd suddenly find herself imagining victims standing naked in the freezing cold waiting in fear and agony for the gas chamber because there were so many in the line ahead of them. She knew that an average of 3,000 Jews died every day over five and a half years. In a crowded concert hall or at some other busy event with lots of people in one place, she would often look around and think, *All these people with their families, and that's not even near the number of Jews who were destroyed every day during the Holocaust.*

And then instead of enjoying the occasion, she'd find herself preoccupied and bothered by these thoughts, her mind repeatedly returning to traumatic events that happened before she was born. Her own imagination could torment her, making her feel fearful and upset, besieged by her emotions. Now, through her therapeutic work with others, she has learned how to notice the thoughts and feelings as they arise in her, and let them pass, like waves in the sea.

My son Roni has been to Auschwitz—not with me, but on a separate group visit to the Holocaust sites in Poland—and once was enough for him. He believes in thinking about the here and now. He likes to focus on the future, not the past. I'm not sure that he completely understands why I feel such a strong need to talk about my experiences. But it is natural that our family history should affect us all in different ways, some obvious, some less obvious. People are different. Not better. Not worse. There isn't a right way to react. There isn't a wrong way. It took a long time, but I eventually came to realize you can't grow up as the child of a Holocaust survivor and not be marked in some way.

Almost seventy years after I was sent to Auschwitz, I was faced with a personal trauma even greater for me than my suffering there. My beloved older daughter, Esti, became seriously ill. While she was in her thirties, she had quietly endured treatment for cancer. At the time, she said little to anyone, for fear of worrying and upsetting us. This was a family habit. Why make people unhappy if you can avoid it?

For several decades she was in remission, but then the cancer returned and spread. Esti continued to keep her illness to herself as much as possible, telling only her closest family. She didn't want pity. She didn't want to burden anyone. As a person used to taking care of others, she preferred to protect as many people as possible, even me, from the pain and worry she knew her illness would cause. She was such a devoted daughter and mother.

Esti was very gregarious, and so well loved. Whenever she went out—even just shopping at Tesco—you could never tell how long it would take. She'd always meet someone she knew, and then someone else, and then another person, and every encounter would turn into a long heart-to-heart. It was impossible for her to hear of a difficulty someone was having and not be interested and want to help them.

You can imagine this made her a wonderful teacher, and pupils kept in touch with her for years after they'd studied with her. She had hundreds of letters of appreciation. She was very intelligent and passionate about Jewish studies, continuing to learn even when she was too ill to leave the house.

There can be nothing worse for a mother than to lose her child. When Esti died, in 2012, I became completely numb. I suppose I went into shock. Her absence felt so unbearable. I simply have no words for the pain I felt at the time and will always feel about Esti's death.

How do you cope with such a devastating loss? You have no choice. Either you move on, or you go under. There is no in between.

These were not easy years for me. My sister René had died only two years earlier. My brother Imi died in 2014. A phone call from Israel brought the news in the middle of our celebrations for the festival of Purim. With each death, I experienced a terrible numbness. I felt frozen. I simply couldn't talk about it.

But it is amazing how the human spirit can return, even when you think it impossible. I am a survivor.

2020

It makes no difference what the color of your skin is or what nationality you are, because for all human beings one thing is for sure: our blood is red, and when you cut us, it hurts.

That's what I want children to remember when they hear my story. I thought there would be an end to genocide after the Holocaust. Yet still these murderous campaigns keep happening—in the former Yugoslavia, Rwanda, Cambodia, Sudan, Myanmar and China. We need to remember and speak out about them all. If we don't keep remembering, we can't change the future.

This has been a year of miracles for me. It started with something that seemed unbelievable to me: my great-grandson, only sixteen years old, asking me questions. So many questions. He really wanted to know everything about my life. That Dov should show so much interest in my story and take it so far has made me very happy. It was hard to talk about the past with my children. It became easier with my grandchildren. Now I feel prepared to cast my mind back and try to recover anything my great-grandchildren want to know about my life.

"Ask me anything!" I tell him.

I'm so proud of everything Dov's done to discover so much new information, to show me documentation I've never seen before, and to find new ways to share it, especially with his own generation. In a few years' time, it could be too late. It helps me so much for us to work together and to witness his own commitment to my promise, here and now. It gives me a special kind of strength. He is so determined. I believe he will never give up.

When I was young, only a few years older than Dov, two men helped me to see a better future: Rabbi Herschel Schacter and Hyman Schulman. This was a time when most of the world didn't want to know. The war had created thousands and thousands of orphans, but few countries wanted us. So many doors were closed. When Rabbi Schacter went to so much trouble to look after us, and keep us safe, it was because he recognized that the future depended on young people.

It still does. I know—I don't kid myself—I won't be here forever. To be certain that Dov will take over my story, even when I'm gone, gives me peace of mind. I've kept the promise I made myself in the camp. I've told the world what happened. And the extra special thing is that now I have help. Dov will go on telling the world. He will keep my promise too.

DOV

December 29, 2020

Lily's turning ninety-seven today and Mum's making her a chocolate cake. But we don't have ninety-seven candles.

I think about what I've heard Safta say so many times, and yet never enough times.

"Nobody should think I am better than somebody else. That was the problem. The Nazis thought they were superhuman, and they wanted to dehumanize us. And they succeeded in that. In the end, at times, I didn't feel I was a human."

I think about how a lucky encounter with a Jewish soldier from Brooklyn restored my great-grandma's faith in humanity, when she thought it had been destroyed. And how an anonymous stranger brought our families together again. I still don't know who the person was who sent me that Twitter message about Hyman Schulman, and I really wish I could thank them properly. They changed everything. I hope they're reading this.

I think about how much better I know my great-grandmother than I did a year ago, when we were happily celebrating her birthday in Bournemouth with four generations of family. About all the conversations we've been having and how much they've strengthened our bond. What a gift this time together has been. It's made me realize how much we have in common. I think it's why we work so well as a team. She likes to tease me that I'm doing her out of a job.

Since last summer, I've spoken to a lot of people who are third- or fourth-generation survivors. For most of them it's too late to do what I've been doing with Lily. Many tell me how frustrated they feel, how annoyed with themselves they are for never having asked enough. I feel so lucky.

Lily and I keep on making plans together. "Let's do something, Dov," she still says to me.

There are lots of things I want to do. Nearly thirty years ago a German artist called Gunter Demnig began to make, by hand, small, square stone cubes with brass plates bearing the names and life dates of victims of Nazi persecution. He calls them *Stolpersteine*—"stumbling blocks"—and installs them in pavements to mark the very last place an individual chose freely to live or work before their freedom was taken away. According to the Talmud, Demnig reminds us, a person is forgotten only when his or her name is forgotten. Lily's old family home in Bonyhád has been demolished. Her old synagogue is a warehouse. Very few Jews now live in the town. But thanks to the *Stolpersteine* project, we can be sure that the names of Nina, Berta and Bela Engelman are not forgotten.

This feels very important to me. But Lily herself has mixed feelings about her own family's *Stolpersteine*. She hasn't been able to trust Hungary since every single person in her family was thrown out of their homes and nearly all of them were murdered. There can be no guarantees in a country where all the old prejudices against Jews have been revived, antisemitism keeps intensifying and Holocaust denial is entrenched. It's institutional. Hungary has never addressed its own collaboration in the Holocaust. Lily isn't interested in memorial stones that could be dug up and cast aside as her ancestors' gravestones were. She simply wants an end to hatred.

So we have different perspectives on the *Stolpersteine*.

But when it comes to sharing her story, we are united.

Forced by the pandemic to give testimony online instead of in person, Safta has actually been able to speak to millions more people than ever before. She's the first Holocaust survivor to appear on Twitch—the leading platform for gaming and streaming. I've set up a TikTok account for us—Lily Ebert and Dov Forman—and we post videos there too. We're getting thousands of new followers every week, and Germans often send messages to Safta to apologize for what Germany did, or for the actions of ancestors who were Nazis.

You've got to be creative to engage new audiences. It's easier for young people to find new ways to speak to our own generation. It's becoming our responsibility. And not just to remember the Holocaust, but to expose every form of genocide. We need to make connections.

I phone Lily to find out what she'd like me to tweet for her birthday.

"I never expected to survive Auschwitz and start a family," she tells me. "Now I celebrate with ten grandchildren and thirty-four great-grandchildren."

I write this in a post, and add a beautiful picture of Lily, and photos of her many descendants.

Almost immediately, my timeline begins to fill with messages of love and congratulations. I can't wait to share them with Safta.

She's not feeling too good today, though, and we're back in serious lockdown after Christmas. So today only my mum, my uncle Roni and my auntie Linda are with me when we visit Lily later in the day, taking flowers and the cake and a present. We find her surrounded by birthday balloons and cards, and very pleased to see us.

Those photos I posted earlier on Twitter, of all her grand-children and great-grandchildren? We'd been collecting them to make a big framed picture—a sort of birthday card from all the family. My aunt Daphna, who's now the guardian of *her* great-grandmother Nina's earrings, still kept in the tiny bag Lily sewed in Altenburg using the rags of her camp dress, chose a quotation from Proverbs (17:6) to go in the center:

Ateret zekenim Bnei banim utiferet banim avotam.
[Grandchildren are] the crown of their elders;
the glory of children are their parents.

We are all links in a long and unbreakable chain.

I read out some of the birthday wishes sent on Twitter. There's not time even to scroll through every single one right now. Complete strangers and long-term supporters have re-sponded with heart-warming joy. There are more than 2,000 messages. Three million views. Not one antisemitic comment. Twitter can be a good place. It can spread light in darkness.

Even online, Lily sparks something in just about everybody she meets. Thousands and thousands of people are celebrating not just her life, but her attitude to life.

For the next two weeks we are all on a knife edge. Lily's not eating. She's exhausted and seems weaker and more tired each day. The doctor, who visits daily, is certain she has Covid-19. Luckily, she's had one vaccination and that seems to help. Of course, we're terrified she'll end up in hospital and we'll never see her again.

But Lily's a true fighter, a true survivor. It feels like another miracle when she pulls through.

"As long as you have hope, anything can happen," she says, when we take our first walk outside together again. "The only thing you can do is never, ever give up because there is always hope."

I'm more proud of her than I can say.

ACKNOWLEDGMENTS

This book has been seventy-five years in the making—never in Lily's dreams, back then, did she envisage she would survive Auschwitz, let alone live a happy and fulfilled life with her three children, ten grandchildren and thirty-four great-grandchildren (to date). After the joy of having her wonderful, loving family, the writing of this memoir at the age of ninety-seven is another of her life's dreams come true.

Lily and I would like to thank all those involved in the development of this official testimony.

Our first and greatest appreciation goes to Dr. Lydia Syson for all her help and for her invaluable contribution to this book—she went above and beyond. *Lily's Promise* could not have come together without her input and detailed research. Lydia—we are forever grateful for the amount of time and unparalleled effort you have put into this memoir. We must also extend our thanks to Jennifer Christie, who connected us.

We would like to thank Andrew Roach for reaching out on Twitter and taking the first step in the development of this book—introducing us to Diana Beaumont of Marjacq Scripts. We are entirely beholden to Diana, our literary agent, and her colleague Guy Herbert, for their insight and support, without which none of this could have been possible.

Acknowledgments

Of course, we are also indebted to the incredible teams at Pan Macmillan and HarperOne, who have worked tirelessly to bring Lily's dream to fruition. In particular, Ingrid Connell, Matthew Cole, Judith Curr and Rosie Black must be thanked for their judicious and expert attention to the book at every stage of publication. Our thanks are extended to all those at Pan Macmillan and HarperOne who contributed to this inspiring project.

We are honored, humbled and exceptionally grateful to His Royal Highness The Prince of Wales, Prince Charles, for his moving tribute to the UK edition of *Lily's Promise* and support for our work.

We must express our immense gratitude at having met our now close friend Bashi Packer, as well as the considerable number of resources provided for us by the United States Holocaust Memorial Museum and the Arolsen Archives. Without these resources, the chronology of Lily's testimony could never have converged. We are infinitely thankful for Bashi's extensive research and for sharing her own family's story with us, and granting us the privilege of disseminating their testimony on her behalf.

Those at the Auschwitz-Birkenau State Museum, in particular Pawel Sawicki, are also deserving of the utmost thanks for all the aid and positive incitement they have presented us with on social media by spreading and sharing Lily's message. We could never have reached thirty million social media viewers or discovered so much about Lily's testimony without all their encouragement.

We are eternally grateful for having found and made contact with both family Shulman and Schacter. The emotional impact that they have had not only on Lily herself, but on our entire family, is inconceivable.

Acknowledgments

A personal thanks from Lily to Judith Hassan, OBE, who encouraged Lily to share the evocation of her experience and for giving her confidence to inspire others. You can find out more about Judith's work in her book *A House Next Door to Trauma: Learning from Holocaust Survivors How to Respond to Atrocity* (2009).

Karen Pollock, CBE, and the team at the Holocaust Educational Trust also ought to be recognized for the remarkable work they have done to support Lily and me with this project. You do an astounding job spreading awareness and information about the horrors of the Holocaust.

We would also like to thank the following people for the amount of time, effort, and research they have contributed toward this book: Dr. Mona Becker, Dr. Madeleine Lerf, Rafael Medoff and Kurt Wyss, as well as Jane Rosen and Sophie Fisher at the Imperial War Museum, and archivists and librarians at the USC Shoah Foundation, the British Library, the Archives of Contemporary History (Das Archiv fürZeitgeschichte) at the ETH Zurich, the Family Research Department of the Central Zionist Archives, the National Library of Israel and the London Library. We owe a great deal to the work of Leslie Blau, whose book *Bonyhád: A Destroyed Community* was published in 1994.

We are overwhelmed by the amount of support we have received on Twitter and social media over the past year. Jack Mendel from the *Jewish News* especially, thank you for inspiring me to write about Lily's abhorrent experience, and for the motivation to continue our work on social media. We have received so much exposure online thanks to your original publications.

Mark Bridge was our tipping point. His first article in *The Times* spurred this entire enterprise. We are indebted to Mark for his efforts in publicizing Lily's testimony.

Acknowledgments

The contributions of my friends Leo Weiniger and Carmelle Miller must also be acknowledged. Their fine-tuning and support along each step of this journey have been exceptionally thoughtful.

The support and cooperation I have received from my peers and faculty at Immanuel College has been so appreciated. Lily and I would, in particular, like to thank my history teacher Mr. Geordie Raine for enabling Lily's first Zoom appearance and for all of his encouragement and inspiration.

A profound thanks must also be extended toward Imi Weiss, and toward the children of Lily's siblings (Imi, René and Piri). Also to Daphna Peters and Shuli Elituv for their contributions.

Lily's daughter and son-in-law, Bilha and Julian Weider, my grandparents, are deserving of the utmost thanks and gratitude. This entire undertaking could not have been fathomable without their unending contributions and unparalleled understanding. Saba and Safta, we love you and are forever thankful for everything you do for us.

To Lily's eldest granddaughter, Nina, my mother, and her husband, Saul, my father, you are the most loving and devoted parents. Your involvement throughout this entire process is unmatched, and Lily and I are forever appreciative of you. Orli and Jake, my siblings and Lily's great-grandchildren, thank you for putting up with me and for all your love, help and support.